Y0-BJY-583

Language, Discourse, Society

Series Editors: **Stephen Heath, Colin MacCabe** and **Denise Riley**

Selected published titles:

Matthew Taunton
FICTIONS OF THE CITY
Class, Culture and Mass Housing in London and Paris

Laura Mulvey
VISUAL AND OTHER PLEASURES
Second edition

Peter de Bolla and Stefan H. Uhlig (*editors*)
AESTHETICS AND THE WORK OF ART
Adorno, Kafka, Richter

Misha Kavka
REALITY TELEVISION, AFFECT AND INTIMACY
Reality Matters

Rob White
FREUD'S MEMORY
Psychoanalysis, Mourning and the Foreign Body

Teresa de Lauretis
FREUD'S DRIVE
Psychoanalysis, Literature and Film

Mark Nash
SCREEN THEORY CULTURE

Richard Robinson
NARRATIVES OF THE EUROPEAN BORDER
A History of Nowhere

Lyndsey Stonebridge
THE WRITING OF ANXIETY
Imaging Wartime in Mid-Century British Culture

Ashley Tauchert
ROMANCING JANE AUSTEN
Narrative, Realism and the Possibility of a Happy Ending

Reena Dube
SATYAJIT RAY'S *THE CHESS PLAYERS* AND POSTCOLONIAL THEORY
Culture, Labour and the Value of Alterity

John Anthony Tercier
THE CONTEMPORARY DEATHBED
The Ultimate Rush

Erica Sheen and Lorna Hutson
LITERATURE, POLITICS AND LAW IN RENAISSANCE ENGLAND

Jean-Jacques Lecercle and Denise Riley
THE FORCE OF LANGUAGE

Geoff Gilbert
BEFORE MODERNISM WAS
Modern History and the Constituency of Writing

Stephen Heath, Colin MacCabe and Denise Riley (*editors*)
THE LANGUAGE, DISCOURSE, SOCIETY READER

Jennifer Keating-Miller
LANGUAGE, IDENTITY AND LIBERATION IN CONTEMPORARY IRISH LITERATURE

Michael O'Pray
FILM, FORM AND PHANTASY
Adrian Stokes and Film Aesthetics

James A. Snead, edited by Kara Keeling, Colin MacCabe and Cornel West
RACIST TRACES AND OTHER WRITINGS
European Pedigrees/African Contagions

Patrizia Lombardo
CITIES, WORDS AND IMAGES

Colin MacCabe
JAMES JOYCE AND THE REVOLUTION OF THE WORD
Second edition

Moustapha Safouan
SPEECH OR DEATH?
Language as Social Order: a Psychoanalytic Study

Jean-Jacques Lecercle
DELEUZE AND LANGUAGE

Piers Gray, edited by Colin MacCabe and Victoria Rothschild
STALIN ON LINGUISTICS AND OTHER ESSAYS

Geoffrey Ward
STATUTES OF LIBERTY
The New York School of Poets

Moustapha Safouan
JACQUES LACAN AND THE QUESTION OF PSYCHOANALYTIC TRAINING (*Translated and introduced by Jacqueline Rose*)

Stanley Shostak
THE DEATH OF LIFE
The Legacy of Molecular Biology

Elizabeth Cowie
REPRESENTING THE WOMAN
Cinema and Psychoanalysis

Raymond Tallis
NOT SAUSSURE
A Critique of Post-Saussurean Literary Theory

Ian Hunter
CULTURE AND GOVERNMENT
The Emergence of Literary Education

Language, Discourse, Society
Series Standing Order ISBN 978–0–333–71482–9 (hardback)
978–0–333–80332–5 (paperback)
(*outside North America only*)

You can receive future titles in this series as they are published by placing a standing order. Please contact your bookseller or, in case of difficulty, write to us at the address below with your name and address, the title of the series and the ISBN quoted above.

Customer Services Department, Macmillan Distribution Ltd, Houndmills, Basingstoke, Hampshire RG21 6XS, England

Language, Identity and Liberation in Contemporary Irish Literature

Jennifer Keating-Miller
Carnegie Mellon University

palgrave
macmillan

© Jennifer Keating-Miller 2009

All rights reserved. No reproduction, copy or transmission of this publication may be made without written permission.

No portion of this publication may be reproduced, copied or transmitted save with written permission or in accordance with the provisions of the Copyright, Designs and Patents Act 1988, or under the terms of any licence permitting limited copying issued by the Copyright Licensing Agency, Saffron House, 6-10 Kirby Street, London EC1N 8TS.

Any person who does any unauthorized act in relation to this publication may be liable to criminal prosecution and civil claims for damages.

The author has asserted her right to be identified as the author of this work in accordance with the Copyright, Designs and Patents Act 1988.

First published 2009 by
PALGRAVE MACMILLAN

Palgrave Macmillan in the UK is an imprint of Macmillan Publishers Limited, registered in England, company number 785998, of Houndmills, Basingstoke, Hampshire RG21 6XS.

Palgrave Macmillan in the US is a division of St Martin's Press LLC, 175 Fifth Avenue, New York, NY 10010.

Palgrave Macmillan is the global academic imprint of the above companies and has companies and representatives throughout the world.

Palgrave® and Macmillan® are registered trademarks in the United States, the United Kingdom, Europe and other countries.

ISBN-13: 978–0–230–23750–6 hardback

This book is printed on paper suitable for recycling and made from fully managed and sustained forest sources. Logging, pulping and manufacturing processes are expected to conform to the environmental regulations of the country of origin.

A catalogue record for this book is available from the British Library.

A catalog record for this book is available from the Library of Congress.

10 9 8 7 6 5 4 3 2 1
18 17 16 15 14 13 12 11 10 09

Printed and bound in Great Britain by
CPI Antony Rowe, Chippenham and Eastbourne

For Nana

If the notion of "Ireland" seemed to some to have become problematic, that was only because the seamless garment once wrapped like a green flag around Cathleen ní Houlihan had given way to a quilt of many patches and colours, all beautiful, all distinct, yet all connected too. No one element should subordinate or assimilate the others: Irish or English, rural or urban, Gaelic or Anglo, each has its part in the pattern.

(Declan Kiberd, Inventing Ireland)

Contents

Acknowledgements	viii
Preface	x
1 A "Habitable Grief"?: The Legacy of Cultural and Political Strife in Ireland's Contentious Language Systems	1
2 A Republic of One: Individuality, Autonomy and the Question of Irish Collectivity in Seamus Deane's *Reading in the Dark* and Dermot Healy's *A Goat's Song*	24
3 Writing Republicanism: A Betrayal of Entrenched Tribalism in Belfast's Own Vernacular	58
4 The Misfit Chorus Line: Ireland from the Margins in Patrick McCabe's *Call Me the Breeze*	100
5 Casting Cathleen: Femininity and Motherhood on the Contemporary Irish Stage	136
Notes	176
Works Cited	179
Bibliography	182
Index	189

Acknowledgements

First and foremost I would like to thank James F. Knapp, Colin MacCabe and Stephen Carr at the University of Pittsburgh, and Paul Hopper at Carnegie Mellon University, who each contributed to the growth of this project, oversaw its development and supported me in my efforts to see it come to print. I am also in debt to individuals throughout Ireland who agreed to be interviewed in my research process, including Seamus Deane, Dermot Healy, Patrick McCabe, Gerry Adams, Danny Morrison, Lawrence McKeown and Pam Brighton. I benefited as well from library facilities at University College Cork, Queen's University Belfast, the University of Pittsburgh and the University of Rochester. Special thanks go to my godfather, Brian Allen, who assisted in scheduling interviews in Ireland while I was in the United States, to Anne-Marie Murray, formerly of Dubbeljoint Theatre Co., for assisting me in navigating Belfast, and to David Bleich and Beth Olivares, for numerous discussions as my research progressed over the last several years. I must also thank the Irish Nationality Room Committee at the University of Pittsburgh for a generous research grant in the summer of 2004 that enabled me to launch this entire escapade, and to the University of Pittsburgh for a Pre-Doctoral Andrew Mellon Fellowship in 2007–2008 to support my completion of this work.

I would like to thank Christabel Scaife, Christine Ranft and all of the editorial and support staff associated with Palgrave Macmillan. Additionally, I would also like to extend thanks to the following publishers for permission to cite from their authors' work: Declan Kiberd's *Inventing Ireland: The Literature of the Modern Nation*, published by Jonathan Cape, reprinted by permission of The Random House Group Ltd. Patrick McCabe's *Call Me the Breeze*, reprinted by permission from HarperCollins Publishers. Gerry Adams' *The Street* (1992) reprinted with permission from Brandon/Mount Eagle Publications. Dermot Healy's *A Goat's Song*, copyright 1994 by Dermot Healy. Used by permission of Viking Penguin, a division of Penguin Group (USA) Inc. Eavan Boland "A Habitable Grief" & "Mother Ireland": "A Habitable Grief", "Mother Ireland", from *The Lost Land* by Eavan Boland. Copyright 1998 by Eavan Boland. Used by permission of W. W. Norton & Company, Inc. "A Habitable Grief," "Mother Ireland" from *The Lost Land* by Eavan Boland. Copyright 1998 by Eavan Boland. Used by permission of Carcanet Press Ltd.

in UK/Commonwealth excluding USA/Canada. Seamus Deane's *Reading in the Dark*, copyright 1996 by Seamus Deane. Used by permission of Alfred A. Knopf, a division of Random House, Inc. Christina Reid, *Plays 1*, used by permission from Methuen Drama, an imprint of A&C Black Publishers who are also thanked for permission to quote from Martin McDonagh's "The Beauty Queen of Leenane". I would like to thank Danny Morrison et al. for permission to cite from "Binlids." Thanks also go to Pearse Elliott for permission to cite from "A Mother's Heart."

I would especially like to thank my husband Billy and my son Liam, who patiently support my work and reward me with their smiles and laughter. I would also like to thank my parents, John and Maureen, for their unyielding emotional, financial and intellectual support for each and every one of my endeavors. Thanks are also extended to all my family and friends in the US, Ireland and elsewhere, who have encouraged me throughout the years. Without you all, I am lost.

Preface

Language, Identity and Liberation in Contemporary Irish Literature is a study of literary movements in multiple genres connected to the political and social changes in Ireland and Northern Ireland since the early nineteen-eighties. As the region developed into a self-possessed member of the European Union, its new presence affected Irish writers' work. This study focuses on writers' representations of the region's contested language systems in Standard English, Irish and Irish-English that have been historically linked to political affiliation and cultural identity. As writers consider the effects that Ireland's rapid economic development and post-conflict resolutions have on various communities, I suggest their work may contribute to the region's continued development of democratic processes that challenge nationalist imperatives. While this survey is representative of contemporary trends in Irish literature, it is not comprehensive. Due to the limitations of space and time, many talented writers' work has not been addressed in the following pages. I believe this project can initiate a course of inquiry to invite further dialogue on the significance of Ireland's relationship to language, aesthetic representation and the region's developing democracy.

After conducting interviews with several of the writers whose work I analyze, including Seamus Deane, Patrick McCabe, Dermot Healy, Gerry Adams and others, I found their levels of conscious attention to portrayals of the region's language systems vary. But a common characteristic shared by these writers that is demonstrated in their respective work is an explicit focus on Ireland's contemporary and rapidly changing culture and politics. Their attention to the region's historical legacy and individual Irish citizens' participation in democratic processes at the turn of the twenty-first century is of paramount concern, a sentiment seemingly shared by other writers like Christina Reid, Danny Morrison, Pearse Elliott, Brenda Murphy, Christina Poland and Jake MacSiacais. Collectively, these writers illustrate a movement of compelling social significance, which demonstrates the region's cultural and political hybridity that challenges nationalist rhetoric of ethnic, linguistic or cultural purity. I only hope this subject will prove to be of interest to others to ensure that this discussion can and will continue in coming years.

1
A "Habitable Grief"?: The Legacy of Cultural and Political Strife in Ireland's Contentious Language Systems

> That is what language is:
> a habitable grief. A turn of speech
> for the everyday and ordinary abrasion
> of losses such as this:
>
> which hurts
> just enough to be a scar.
>
> And heals just enough to be a nation.
>
> (Eavan Boland, "Habitable Grief,"
> *The Lost Land*)

I

Since the Statutes of Kilkenny in the fourteenth century, language systems in Ireland have been inextricably linked to cultural and political affiliations. Throughout the nineteenth century as nationalism grew worldwide, linguistic and religious association came to manifest itself on national lines, developing into a Unionist and Nationalist divide, which has haunted the region for generations. The 1801 Act of Union that officially joined Ireland with England, Wales and Scotland under the British Crown, led to an association of eighteenth-century Enlightenment English with the colonial state, a language system believed to be associated with order, reason and power. In the early decades of the century, pockets of rural peasantry pushed to the West of Ireland by Cromwell centuries before, continued to speak Ireland's mother tongue. But by the century's end, only 13 percent of the population spoke Irish (Filppula 1999, 9). While the language continued to serve as a nostalgic symbol of Irish cultural purity it was rendered virtually useless in the wake of British imperialism, a tongue affiliated with poverty, ignorance and desolation.

Amidst the cultural shift from the sixteenth century onwards that saw significant Anglicization and slow industrialization, Ireland's contentious linguistic systems came to reflect the region's history. The contact language Irish-English gradually emerged and became substantially more prevalent throughout the nineteenth century as the predominantly uneducated masses were forced to adapt to the substantial cultural and political changes associated with British imperialism. As significant numbers of the population were compelled to learn the new master's language through informal techniques, Irish-English came to reflect the vocabulary of the super-stratum Enlightenment English and the grammatical structures found in the substratum system of Irish (Filppula). By the mid-nineteenth century some Irish ballads were translated into English in publications like *Nation* but by the century's end, Irish literature came to be written predominantly in English, betraying the cultural and linguistic revolution associated with one hundred years of direct British rule.

Despite its near extinction by the turn of the twentieth century, Irish remained a virulent symbol of Irish purity and rebellion under British colonization in political and literary imaginations. Writers from William Butler Yeats, Lady Augusta Gregory and John Millington Synge to James Joyce and Padraic Pearse mused on the historic and political significance of Ireland's contested language systems, weighing the benefits and costs of the region's bilingualism in their literary works. And gradually, Lady Gregory, J.M. Synge and James Joyce each began to portray Ireland's hybrid language system, Irish-English, in their work, exploring the notion that "language(s), rather than being disputed territory, might turn out to be the common ground upon which both agreement and disagreement are possible" (Crowley 2000, 11). Like the contradiction that is Irish history, at once colonized and "unionized" through the 1801 Act of Union, Irish-English mirrors Irish cultural and political hybridity. This study considers Tony Crowley's suggestion that Irish-English may be a "common ground on which both agreement and disagreement are possible."

As Irish-English serves as a living artifact, which at once affiliates and distinguishes Ireland from its Celtic and Anglo-Saxon linguistic and cultural influences, this investigation attends to the degrees to which literary representations of such language systems may catalog the historical precedents and political influences of Irish history evident in contemporary Irish literature. Through analyses of plays, short stories and novels, this study explores the significance of representations of Ireland's multifarious linguistic history, tracing the influence of Enlightenment English, Gaelic and the extant relic of Irish-English. This inquiry demonstrates how Irish writers of the contemporary moment negotiate visions of Irish identity formation amidst hybrid cultural and linguistic past and present influences, and how such explorations may in turn serve as models for individual activism in Ireland's ever developing democratic processes. The freedom to exercise political and cultural autonomy in Northern Irish versus Republic and rural versus urban communities can differ considerably, as depicted by contemporary authors. But the spirit of exploration that informs this study acknowledges an uneven development of freedom in Ireland's various and multi-faceted communities, elements that further illustrate the remarkable linguistic, cultural and political hybridity in this region.

II

Writers like Yeats, Gregory, Synge and Joyce initially breathed life into the potential "common ground" of language in Ireland as their work came to feed and water the "passions" of Irish Nationalism "instead of drying them up" (Plato 2004, 334). Serving as a catalyst for anti-colonial political movements at the turn of the twentieth century, literary works like "The Playboy of the Western World," "Cathleen ni Houlihan" and "Spreading the News," which represented language systems particular to Ireland, ennobled the once disenfranchised. As writers like Yeats, Synge and Gregory cataloged Ireland's cultural landscape through imitative representations of linguistic systems likened to "that of turning a mirror," they committed non-standard speech patterns to the page, elevating the most ignorant, desolate and poor of the population as national icons of Celtic purity (Plato 2004, 319). Joyce's work skillfully challenged such potent tropes in texts like *Dubliners* and *Ulysses*, as he refused to romanticize Irish poverty and dejection. Instead, his painstakingly detailed representations of Irish cultural paralysis and social and political hybridity set an alternative example for Irish letters for a new generation of writers.

While evidence of such artistic negotiation can be indentified in literary collections of Ireland's most prolific writers throughout the twentieth century, anecdotal evidence sometimes captures the profundity of Irish cultural, social and political rifts. In 1951, Eavan Boland, the daughter of an Irish diplomat, moved from Dublin to London. Only six years old at the time, she was offered a brief but poignant lesson on political tensions stretching across the Irish Sea that came to haunt her well into her adult years.

> I was in the cloakroom at school in the middle of the afternoon. A winter darkness was already gathering through one of the stubborn fogs of the time. A teacher was marshaling children here and there, dividing those who were taking buses from those who were being collected. "I amn't taking the bus," I said. I was six or seven then, still within earshot of another way of speaking. But the English do not use that particular construction. It is an older usage. If they contract the verb and the negative, they say, "I'm not."
>
> Without knowing, I had used that thing for which the English reserve a visceral dislike: their language, loaded and aimed by the old enemy. The teacher whirled around. She corrected my grammar; her face set, her tone cold. "You're not in Ireland now" was what she said. (Boland 1995, 46)

Boland describes this moment as the "day my tongue betrayed me out of dream and counterfeit into cold truth" (Boland 1995, 46). In this exchange she is propelled into a political chasm that has divided Ireland and England for centuries but often manifests itself in the seemingly mundane language of everyday life. Boland's "amn't," a sufficient catalyst to compel her teacher to "whirl around" and correct her grammar "her face set, her tone cold," with the chilling "You're not in Ireland now," compresses the vestiges of a flawed imperial legacy in Ireland. Boland's reflection on the symbolism of this contraction suggests that it threatened her teacher with the menacing notion of "their language [English], loaded and aimed by the old enemy." But if we are to understand "amn't" as an "older usage" as Boland suggests, a remnant of an archaic form of English exported to Ireland through colonialism and returning to haunt contemporary English subjects, would the language actually still be "their" language? Or have contemporary Irish-English speakers come to possess a language that is now particularly distinct from English as it is spoken in England?

In *Lost Land* Boland describes Ireland's English as the "habitable grief" of "another way of speaking." It is neither fundamentally native nor foreign, both familiar and strange. The teacher who scolds the young Boland responds to what she perceives as a foreign strand of English as she coldly reminds the child that she is "not in Ireland now." Boland's use of "amn't" ironically stems from a Union of English aggression that imposed a foreign tongue on an Irish population. As an adult, Boland can muse on the complex and often contradictory interactions that are Anglo-Irish relations. But as a child of six, the teacher's reprimand instills fear and shame. In the recount of this brief exchange, Boland crystallizes the complex power dynamics born from political tensions that have come to be aptly symbolized in the language systems of modern Ireland. As the work of contemporary Irish writers suggests, however, the non-standard form of English that Boland describes as a "habitable grief" may in fact be Ireland's after all. Irish-English at once stems from and differentiates itself from its Anglo-Saxon and Celtic parentage. And its representation in recent Irish literature serves as a striking symbol for the potential growth of democracy in Ireland, North and South, as writers resist traditional political binaries entrenched in Nationalist and Unionist divides. Ireland's language systems vary slightly in vocabulary usage, phonetics and syntax throughout the region, demonstrating marked variation in the system of Irish-English. But if Ireland's multiple voices form a collective of various tones, cadences and rhythms, how then does Ireland's political landscape reflect such diversity? If language is an organic, ever-changing entity, how then might identity-formation in Ireland mimic such characteristics?

While Irish and English continue to contend for linguistic dominance in contemporary Ireland, various systems of the modern contact language, Irish-English, have come to represent hybrid, multifaceted formations of Irish identity that continue to resist residuals of singular, nationalist visions of Irishness from the turn of the twentieth century. Tapping into such a link between modern politics and language, contemporary Irish writers' representations of "social networks," communicating through various systems of Irish-English, offer visions of complex, malleable, often contradictory Irish identities (Milroy 1980, 174).[1] This study will examine the political reverberations of language representation in a collection of literary works penned by Irish writers from various geographical, religious and political backgrounds, in an effort to examine contemporary Irish literature's potential to display alternative visions to lengthy historical stalemates in Irish, Northern Irish and English relations.

III

Although contradictions in Ireland's linguistic development are evident from the fourteenth century onwards, nowhere is the complexity more palpable than in the Irish Constitution for the Republic of Ireland

6 *Language, Identity and Liberation in Contemporary Irish Literature*

(Crowley 2000). Although the document itself was written in English, Article 8 stipulates that Irish is the privileged national language of Eire, with English serving as the second official language. Despite the decree, English remains the unofficial first language of Ireland. Although Irish is occasionally employed in everyday oral or written exchange outside of diminishing Gaeltachts, ranging from school instruction exclusively in the Irish medium, literary artistry and television programming to burgeoning revivalist movements predominantly in the North of Ireland, Irish has never been restored as the spoken language of Eire. Competency in Irish is mandated, however, for all civil service employment throughout the Republic and it is required in secondary school to the Junior Certificate level. As Irish-English has come to debunk the myth of inextricable links between purified language and culture, Irish and English populations alike have been challenged, much like Boland and her unsympathetic teacher, to embrace Ireland's contact language and culture.

Since Ireland's contemporary linguistic systems have been strongly influenced by historical factors, other elements of Irish culture continue to be impacted by the legacies of Anglo-Irish relations. In recent decades, strong Irish economic development both North and South of the border, the bloodshed of "The Troubles," and the often stalling peace negotiations developing from the 1998 Good Friday Peace Agreement have all contributed to a historically familiar quagmire in the ongoing Peace Process. Ireland's new relative wealth and political and cultural confidence, however, continue to re-write the age old "Irish Question." As the Republic grows into a significant international economic contender and Northern Ireland has finally erected a fledgling power-sharing government, the region demonstrates that it is no longer the quaint, agricultural back garden of the wealthy, industrial, English powerhouse. While Ireland and Northern Ireland have asserted themselves as international economic contenders, profiting from globalization with steady, reliable workforces, high levels of national education and tax relief for companies willing to relocate, England's perpetual symbolic presence in the Republic and literal presence in Northern Ireland continue to propagate Unionist and Nationalist binaries in the political landscape. Despite rapid modernization from the late nineteen-eighties onwards, Ireland's cultural and political contradictions of conservatism and progressivism have not been erased by rapid economic development and improved international influence. Instead, the region must now attend to historical legacies of British imperialism in addition to rapid influxes of immigrant populations, the development of legitimate democratic processes in Northern Ireland and almost fitful economic change North and South of the border.

While the influence of the Catholic Church in the Republic of Ireland has abated through the population's gradual abandonment of conservatism, and Northern Ireland's Protestant oligarchy has lost some of its power to demoralize and discriminate against its Catholic minority, Ireland still struggles to balance its contending, multifaceted identities of the past and present. Recognizing such a crossroads, Irish writers are attending to the inherently difficult questions of cultural and political identity formation as the region adjusts to a complicated and often contentious relationship with its British neighbor while rapidly advancing technologically and economically to participate in a growing international market. Analogous to writers of the Irish Literary Renaissance at the turn of the twentieth century, contemporary Irish writers from Seamus Deane and Patrick McCabe to Christina Reid and Brenda Murphy have approached representations of Irish identity formation with candor, asking audiences to scrutinize their contemporary cultural landscape and to imagine alternative political visions for the future of Ireland. But these writers distinguish themselves from their literary predecessors in their complicated visions of Irish hybrid culture, as they perpetually resist singular representations of Irish identity endemic to the work of many Irish Renaissance writers.

IV

At the turn of the twentieth century, Ireland's anti-colonial efforts to escape English political and cultural persecution in the colonial paradigm, although revolutionary, were relatively simple. Crafted by activists as diverse as Pearse, Yeats, Synge, Lady Gregory and Arthur Griffith, the premise was to undermine British imperial authority by introducing a mythic Irish pastoral untainted by Anglicization. Stemming from the precedent of a politicized effort to preserve Gaelic bard culture in Charles Gavan Duffy's and Thomas Davis' mid-nineteenth century publication *Nation,* which showcased English versions of Irish ballads and poems, anti-colonial activists of the early twentieth century also came to present Irish cultural opposition to colonialism in the language of the oppressor. Offering "images we construct of a privileged, genealogically useful past, a past in which we exclude unwanted elements, vestiges, narratives," the Irish anti-colonial movement positioned a mythic, Irish heroic narrative in opposition to British cultural and political hegemony (Said 1994, 15). Driven by the efforts of a relatively privileged middle class, Ireland's nationalist movement came to resemble hyper-polarization of identity formation characteristic of anti-colonial efforts worldwide. In opposition to imperial influence in Ireland that positioned Irish language and culture as subservient to and deviant from the superior British archetype, Irish nationalists were presented with the challenge of bolstering an Irish identity that could be conceived of as at least equal, if not superior to, the culture of the oppressor. Their presentation of an Irish pastoral, a mythic past that linked all Irish-born natives regardless of creed, had to offer confidence to a subjugated population in an effort to fuel the impending anti-colonial revolution.

In reference to the horrific decolonization process in Algeria, analogous to Ireland's decolonization process at times, Franz Fanon claims the revolution begins when

> the native discovers that his life, his breath, his beating heart are the same as those of the settler. He finds out that the settler's skin is not of any more value than a native's skin; and it must be said that this discovery shakes the world in a very necessary manner. All the new, revolutionary assurance of the native stems from it. For if, in fact, my life is worth as much as the settler's, his glance no longer shrivels me up nor freezes me, and his voice no longer turns me into stone. I am no longer on tenterhooks in his presence; in fact, I don't give a damn. (45)

Just as Boland's reflection on the linguistic slip that shamed her as a young child allowed her to realize that such language actually threatened her teacher, "loaded and aimed by the old enemy," the native's discovery of commonality between him/her and his/her colonial oppressor, "utterly" changes negotiations of political power.[2] As a child, Boland was mortified by the teacher's scolding but as an adult, she understands that the utterance of "amn't" actually serves as a moment in which the native and the settler see the *self* hauntingly reflected in the *other*.[3] The teacher's "glance" "shrivels" and "freezes" the young Boland but as an adult the teacher's voice "no longer turns [her] to stone." While Fanon speaks from the native's perspective, inference is given to the colonizer's reaction. Much like the teacher whose cultural authority is challenged by Boland's speech, which echoes the failure of complete colonial linguistic dominance in Ireland, Fanon's settler loses influence once the native "discovers that his life, his breath, his beating heart are the same as those of the settler." Just as the native's discovery "shakes the world in a very necessary manner" through his/her challenge to the established authority, Boland's utterance reminds her teacher that Irish-English is not just a deviation from English as it spoken in England. Instead, it is a linguistic system born from a failed imperial project that has fueled the literary work of artists from the twentieth century onwards.

Synge's work at the turn of the twentieth century played a crucial role in romantically redefining Irish identity within the colonial paradigm. Irish peasants were no longer a reduced population condemned by the colonial oppressor but were instead presented as authentic representatives of Irish culture whose poverty marked a refusal to comply with British capitalistic exploitation. Their quaint lack of technological advancement indicated resistance to English industrialization and the population's limited formal education was misinterpreted as a mythically pure oral tradition. Synge's work is an example of politically subversive art that helped to actualize Ireland's revolutionary anti-colonial movement. His principal focus on representations of an Irish-English language system would create an alternative to the former linguistic dominance of Irish and eighteenth-century Enlightenment English, respectively. Although Synge claimed to have little interest in the Irish nationalist movement of his day, his plays were absorbed by nationalist myth-builders, inextricably linked to the turn of the twentieth century anti-colonial effort.

Claiming to capture the system of English spoken in rural communities in the dialogue of his plays, Synge's representations of Irish-English significantly contributed to the myth of a singular Irish identity, shared at one time or another, by all who opposed British imperialism in Ireland. Attempting to offer Irish audiences a reflection of pure Irish culture through the language of his plays, Synge claims to have "used one or two words only that I have not heard among the country people of Ireland, or spoken in my nursery before I could read the newspapers" (Synge 1960, *Preface*). As he privileges the spoken language of particular regions of Ireland, Synge assists in redistributing cultural and linguistic sway, realigning negotiations of power in a pivotal period of Anglo-Irish relations. Synge's art, sharing in the spirit of most Irish literature of the Irish Literary Revival, sought to elevate Irish peasant culture to the position of high art. His work defines Irish national identity diametrically opposed to British imperialism as necessarily rural, nobly impoverished and illiterate, communicating solely in a bastardized language that "inevitably frustrates the claims of either of its parent languages, as the dominance of the one is deconstructed by the ghostly presence of its other" (Knapp 1987, 32). But this form of mimicry, an attempt to ground art in the grittiness of a language "heard among the country people of Ireland," ran the risk of severely limiting a mythically holistic vision of Irish national identity to the historical experience of a specific fraction of the population.

Synge's plays were received as a voice for those silenced in the colonial state by class disparity, lack of political representation until the mid-nineteenth century through the work of "The Emancipator," Daniel O'Connell, and lack of education. Although Synge's condescendence could be read as yet another example of a bourgeois figure speaking for rather than enabling the subaltern to speak, Synge was virtually unconcerned by the political reverberations of his work.[4] His was an aesthetic project, authenticated by the artist's capability to re-present real Irish-English speech. He claims,

> In a good play every speech should be as fully flavoured as a nut or apple, and such speeches cannot be written by anyone who works among people who have shut their lips on poetry. In Ireland, for a few years more, we have a popular imagination that is fiery and magnificent, and tender; so that those of us who wish to write start with a chance that is not given to writers in places where the springtime of the local life has been forgotten, and the harvest is a memory only, and the straw has been turned into bricks. (Synge *Preface*)

Invoking the natural flavor of the "nut or apple" to defend his representations of Irish-English speech, Synge attempts to justify his project as one in tune with nature. He claims representations of speech "cannot be written by anyone who works among people who have shut their lips on poetry," nor in environments where "the springtime of the local life has been forgotten." With these examples, he again points towards the pastoral, the provincial, as the bastion of pure speech patterns and therefore living culture.

Though he attempted to distance himself from political strife, evident in his relatively nonchalant reactions to the riots following the premiere of "The Playboy of the Western World," Synge's work inevitably contributed to the anti-colonial effort. From misinterpretation of his work as romanticizing Ireland's lack of technological advancement and industrialization to his emphasis on representing Irish oral traditions, Synge's work conveniently fed into a nationalist agenda. Unlike the work collected in *Nation*, however, which was not presented in colloquial forms, Synge suggests that his work is grounded in *the* real language of the "country people" of Ireland. He extends this assertion when he claims, "in countries where the imagination of the people, and the language they use, is rich and living, it is possible for a writer to be rich and copious in his words, and at the same time to give the reality, which is the root of all poetry, in a comprehensive and natural form" (Synge 1960, *Preface*). As he insists on the "natural form" that conveys "the imagination of the people, and the language they use," Synge's work lends itself to the anti-colonial agenda, which sought to empower "the people of Ireland," to loosen the shackles of colonialism, in turn reversing the supposed ill-effects of industrialization and modernization.

Synge's work demonstrates a rudimentary gesture towards democratization, which elevates the experience of the Irish peasant to that of the Irish icon. In this, Synge challenges the value system imposed through British imperialism that privileged the English "John Bull" as the prototype of humanity from which all other cultures and ethnicities deviated (Curtis 1996). In Synge's plays village idiots who are "slow at learning, a middling scholar only," like Christy Mahon or woeful widows who pay "a big price for the finest white boards you'd find in Connemara," for coffins to bury their fisherman husbands and sons, like Maurya, are not the dejected, vacant-eyed peasants of William Makepeace Thackeray's *Irish Sketchbook*.[5] Instead, they are presented as *real* representatives of the "people" of Ireland. Synge's plays position Irish peasantry as the archetype of "Irishness," encapsulating all that is both beautiful and tragic in the nation's history. And the significance of this trope is packed carefully into the plays' presentations of language. Synge's self-proclaimed mimicry of the language of the "country people of Ireland" serves as a subversive force, with the potential to symbolically undermine British hegemony. The spoken language of the "country people of Ireland" was neither that of their English oppressors nor that of their Irish-speaking ancestors. And Synge's work, along with the work of other writers of the Celtic Twilight, documents these dramatic changes that were underway by the mid-nineteenth century, feeding into the sociopolitical and linguistic reality of Ireland by the turn of the twentieth century.

Although Synge's work in plays like "The Playboy of the Western World," "Riders to the Sea" and "Deirdre of the Sorrows" is both tragic and comic, folkloric and realistic, his efforts to capture the *real* speech of the "country people of Ireland" resemble William Wordsworth's understanding of his work as "an experiment," that fit "to metrical arrangement a selection of the real language of men" (Wordsworth 2002, 241). While Synge and Wordsworth each claim to present the real language of men and women in an effort to authenticate their literary endeavors, neither Wordsworth nor Synge question the success of their respective efforts to accurately present such language in their work. Nor are they interested in interrogating the potential political reverberations of such work. But the political ramifications of such literary use of language were not lost on their contemporary audiences or on those who came in contact with their work in subsequent generations.

Synge's work assisted in the inspiration of a virulent Irish nationalist movement through imitative artistic representation that lifted the Irish peasant out of dejected anonymity to challenge the cultural value system associated with British colonialism in Ireland. His plays so closely resembled specific historical circumstances for particular communities that Synge's work plucked the nativist cords of the nationalist movement, offering voice (whether legitimate or not) to a population once silenced by language barriers. To protest such imitative artistry indicates the political potency of imitative representations likened to "turning a mirror" (Plato 2004, 319). But Synge's plays offered opportunity for an audience to scrutinize society at the remove afforded through the abstraction of representation. His work invited an Irish public (those who could afford to attend the National Theater) to bear witness to a rural, mythic native narrative all but lost in urban centers.

Nineteenth-century British colonial rhetoric, building on eighteenth-century Enlightenment principles, adopted the triumph of rationalism over watered "passions," extending dichotomy along lines of gender when referring to colonial subjects. Representations of Ireland as a defenseless motherland, susceptible to violence and exploitation, were common in the Victorian era. English reason was to tame and civilize Ireland's passionate hysterics, a policy supported and justified culturally by Ernest Renan's claims that "the Celtic Race...is an essentially feminine face," in *Poésie des Races Celtiques*, and further exploited by Matthew Arnold's *On the Study of Celtic Literature*. But work by a figure like Synge, a middle-class Anglo-Irishman, who wished to capture the language of "the country people of Ireland" by turning the "mirror" of poetic mimicry, came to "water the passions" of a rapidly emerging anti-colonial movement rendering British "rational principle" unfit "for the common good" in Ireland (Plato 2004, 334).

Synge's plays were particular in their capability to faithfully represent the harsh, Spartan-like fishing communities living on the Aran Islands in "Riders to the Sea." They were also notable for their ability to capture the playful spirit of raucous slaggings exchanged in small, rural villages like that introduced in "The Playboy of the Western World." But according to Declan Kiberd, Synge's work "went far deeper than a conventional flair for turning a piece of Irish poetry or prose into English," but instead "involved a capacity to project a whole Gaelic culture in English...an act of supreme translation" (Kiberd 1996, 626). Kiberd suggests that Synge's work may have actually delivered an Irish-English equivalent to the rhythm, wit and precision afforded in Gaelic expression in his "act of supreme translation," but one must ask, what exactly was translated? While Kiberd's reading of the revolutionary nature of Synge's work is useful, he does not address the manner in which Synge's representations indirectly betrayed the complexity of Irish identity in the wake of imperialism. Because the "language of his plays is based less on the English spoken in rural Ireland than on the peculiar brand of English spoken in *Gaeltacht* areas," Synge mislabels such language as that of the "country people of Ireland," instead of identifying it as one of various systems spoken in the budding nation-state. In the first scene of "The Playboy of the Western World," simple questions like "Where's himself?" when Shawn Keogh asks the whereabouts of Pegeen's father, Michael, and greetings like "God bless you. The blessing of God on this place," as Michael James, Philly Cullen and Jimmy Farrell enter Michael's public-house, are literal translations from Irish: "Dia duit leat. Dia duit an auile áit," and "Cén sé áit?" This English would have been the type of language system that was informally acquired throughout the nineteenth century or earlier, through trade or other forms of contact with the colonial language, once it became apparent that English was a "symbol for opportunity and success" (Filppula 1999, 9). Synge's "translations," therefore, capture the language spoken in particular regions of Ireland, a living artifact born from tumultuous Irish-English relations through which, Irish grammar is grafted onto English. But these "translations" are not necessarily accurate representations of Irish-English speech for the entire region. Instead, Synge's work marked the documentation of an emerging *heteroglossia,* a polymorphous language system pushing against the *unitary* language systems of Irish and eighteenth-century Enlightenment English, setting yet another precedent for the interrelationship between literature and politics in Ireland (Bakhtin).

V

Synge's presentations of Irish-English marked Ireland's modern culture born from the legacies of sixteenth century plantations, Catholic second-class citizenry and the failures of Irish and eighteenth-century Enlightenment English to serve the communicatory needs of its population. By the turn of the twentieth century Ireland faced a crucial crossroads. As momentum for the anti-colonial revolution gradually built, activists had to determine how Ireland was to differentiate itself culturally and politically from its neighbor. As indicated by Synge's strategic decision to work with Irish-English rather than eighteenth-century Enlightenment English or Irish to depict dialogue in his plays, Ireland's linguistic make-up had incurred significant alterations throughout the nineteenth century.

From 1771 to 1871, the national percentage of Irish-speakers gradually declined from 45 percent to 13 percent, giving rise to an increasingly bilingual community that gradually departed from Gaelic almost completely (Filppula 1999, 9). Irish

> was being promoted as the necessary center for a program of nationalist renewal which encompassed political, economic, cultural, and (sometimes) religious spheres. In the heated atmosphere of the campaign for the "de-anglicization" of Ireland, the authority of the Irish language was increasingly identified with heroic myths of origin and with an ideology of Celtic racialism. In Bakhtin's terms, Irish was striving to become a Unitary language, saturating the space of its society and shaping men and women according to a model which, if not eternal, was at least presumed to transcend the accidents of recent history. An Irish-speaking Ireland would once again be natural, whole. (Knapp 1987, 31–2)

Synge's privilege of Irish-English over Irish, despite his own involvement in Irish revivalism, embraced part of the linguistic reality of Ireland's cultural make-up, acknowledging the impossibility of mending the cultural fragmentation resulting from colonization. Synge's work compounded the notion that "an Irish-speaking Ireland," a virtual impossibility in its own right, could never turn back the hands of time. Anti-colonial activists relied on Irish language revivalism like that fostered by the Gaelic League, positioned in opposition to the eighteenth century Enlightenment English employed by the British colonial apparatus, to serve as a metaphor for the political and cultural strife coming to a head between England and Ireland by the early decades of the twentieth century. Synge's work, however, in presenting "translations" of specific forms of Irish-English from Gaeltacht communities was "a significant cultural gesture just insofar as it succeeds in calling into question the social and intellectual constraints imposed by language-as-myth" (Knapp 1987, 32). Proponents of the colonial project and the anti-colonial movement relied on the myth of essential, singular national identities opposed to one another in linguistic forms by the vying for power of *unitary* language systems. Synge's insistence on presenting the language of "the country people of Ireland" marked the gradual emergence of the *heteroglossia* of Irish-English, born from a culture emerging from colonial rule. Although susceptible to absorption in later nationalist mythologies, Synge's work challenged Irish and English populations alike to consider the cultural conundrum that was identity formation in Ireland, no longer fitting the paradigms of traditional conceptions of English or Irish cultures, respectively.

Although Synge's work complicates the link of national identities with specific languages through his emphasis on Irish-English, his depictions of Irish peasantry as figures of "Irishness," in opposition to British modernization and industrialization, continued to propagate nationalist mythologies less affiliated with the Gaelic League. The resonance of Synge's work rests, however, on his ability to identify a gradually emerging *heteroglossia*, a multifaceted language system emerging from the *unitary* language systems of Irish and eighteenth-century Enlightenment English. According to Bakhtin, unitary language

> constitutes the theoretical expression of the historical processes of linguistic unification and centralization, an expression of the centripetal forces of language. A unitary language is not something given [dan] but is always in essence posited [zadan] – and at every moment of its linguistic life it is opposed to the realities of heteroglossia. But at the same time it makes its real presence felt as a force for overcoming this heteroglossia, imposing specific limits to it, guaranteeing a certain maximum of mutual understanding and crystallizing into a real, though still relative, unity – the unity of the reigning conversation (every day) and literary language, "correct language". (Bakhtin 1981, 270)

As Gaelic Leaguers sought to push Irish into contention as a *unitary* language system in opposition to the eighteenth-century Enlightenment English employed by the established British power, Synge's work, along with that of other Irish Renaissance writers, inscribed a third contender in the *heteroglossia* of Irish-English. But was Synge's work merely identifying an emerging language system that threatened to compromise the dominance of eighteenth-century Enlightenment English and floundering Irish? Or was the *heteroglossia* of Irish-English gradually offsetting the dominance of both its parent languages, gradually emerging as the unitary language system of modern Ireland?

Bakhtin's vocabulary helps in analyzing these linguistic contenders as his work insists on the polymorphous nature of *unitary* language systems which are "not something given [dan] but is (are) always in essence posited," positioned in opposition to the "realities of heteroglossia." Although Synge's plays cannot necessarily fuel linguistic study, his perception that in "a good play every speech should be as fully flavoured as a nut or an apple," indicates that Synge believes his work actually captured and re-presented a linguistic reality in his contemporary Ireland. As he attempts to circumvent the mediation of artistic representation by closing down the space between the natural and the contrived in the language of his plays, Synge attempted to ensure his literary works portrayed his interpretation of real speech patterns. Like Wordsworth, however, Synge only seems to think that he faithfully re-presents the language he heard "spoken in my (his) own nursery" without actually doing so. Although Kiberd suggests Synge's genius lies in his translation capabilities, Synge's representations of Irish-English do not necessarily reflect the organic complexity or growth likened to the nut or apple of his metaphor. His work was certainly revolutionary in its demarcation of distinctions in Irish-English language systems that distinguish them from their English and Irish counterparts, but his presentations of the "real" language of the country people of Ireland were unitary and static, failing to present the complex and ever changing *heteroglossia* of Irish-English. While Synge's work initially instigated riots from Republican communities such as those emerging from the debut of "The Playboy of the Western World," his privileging of the Irish rural pastoral and his representations of Irish-English assisted the myth-making of Irish nationalism, which later stifled artistic and political expression that attempted to debunk such potent mythologies.

VI

Synge's work demonstrates an important development in representations of an Irish-English language system, challenging the cultural hegemony of British colonialism. After him, James Joyce's work in *Ulysses* set a new precedent for representing the tangled relationship between Irish identity formation and the *heteroglossia* of Irish-English. His work builds from Stephen Dedalus' lament in *A Portrait of the Artist as a Young Man*, "The language in which we are speaking is his before it is mine... His language, so familiar and so foreign, will always be for me an acquired speech... What did he come here for to teach us his own language or to learn it from us?" In *Ulysses* Joyce parses out the political power affiliated with various language systems, eventually demonstrating an effort to "teach" Stephen's Dean of Studies an altered version of "his own language." His democratizing performance that presents high art as a collection of the details of everyday life, deflates the heroic grandeur of decolonization evident in literary work by other artists like Synge, Yeats and Pearse. *Ulysses* illustrates a complex vision of Ireland that is neither static nor predictable, painting an alternative vision of Irish culture to the Irish pastoral unflinchingly privileged by most artists of the Celtic Twilight.

Under the guise of capturing each detail of Stephen Dedalus' and Leopold Bloom's "social networks" as they traverse the streets of Dublin on 16, June 1904, Joyce's *Ulysses* examines imitative art. Introducing a mirror metaphor early in the text, in the hand of Buck Mulligan, Joyce immediately asks his audience to consider the significance of reflection and mimicry in Irish letters. "Look at yourself... you dreadful bard. Stephen bent forward and peered at the mirror held out to him, cleft by a crooked crack, hair on end: As he and others see me. Who chose this face for me?" (Joyce 1990, 6). Through these various mitigating factors, Joyce distances his work from simplistic anti-colonial movements attempting to turn back the hands of time in an effort to eradicate British imperialism from Ireland's political future. Joyce's image may instead ring true in its candid portrayal of every day detail. The crack in the mirror can discourage interpretations of Joyce's work as simply turning a cultural "looking glass" for scrutiny to propagate reactive political change. Instead, Joyce may ask his audience to attend to the contradictions of cultural imperialism, colonial occupation, Irish cultural and linguistic degeneracy and political hypocrisy in a work that only *seems* to faithfully reflect Dublin on 16, June 1904.

The multiple layers of mediation offered in this symbol may actually betray Joyce's suspicion of political manipulation through imitative art. The looking glass belongs to a servant, absent and notably silent in the scene. The mode of transmitting the image is fundamentally flawed through the crack. It is held by the middle-class Mulligan, for the educated though penniless Stephen to peer at his skewed image. Tapping into the Shakespearean precedent of a native subject engaging with the judgment of its colonial counterpart, Joyce reviews the role of Irish imitative art in the decolonization process with the ensuing exchange: "The rage of Caliban at not seeing his face in a mirror, he (Mulligan) said. If Wilde were only alive to see you. – It is a symbol of Irish art. The cracked looking glass of a servant" (Joyce 1990, 6). Buck Mulligan, an Irish medical student holds the cracked looking glass to reflect Stephen's image, demanding self scrutiny and analysis that are further complicated by the "crooked crack." Aware of visions of racial supremacy, class distinction and aesthetic values, Joyce's "cracked looking glass of a servant" may serve as a metaphor that distinguishes his work from that of the artists of the Irish Literary Renaissance.

Unlike Synge's work that attempts to turn "a mirror," Joyce's fragmentary image of Dublin demands recognition of Ireland's hybrid culture and language. Leopold Bloom's and Stephen Dedalus' journeys throughout the city introduce the complex yet stagnant communities of Joyce's Dublin, not only through detailed imagery but also through Joyce's careful construction of dialogue. Although he is not the literary linguist Synge wishes to be, Joyce's awareness of language rejects any simple relationships between Irish politics and culture that are already wrapped up in the language debate at the time. Joyce's polymorphous vision of Irish identity, which serves as an example of the hybrid nature of Irish communities, challenges the cultural precedence offered by artists like Synge. His focus on urban Dublin as a cultural, linguistic, intellectual and political cross-section, which has not necessarily escaped the paralysis endemic to colonized Ireland, exemplifies the social, political and cultural hybridity that is imprecisely branded "Anglicization" by other anti-colonial activists of the same period. Joyce's "cracked looking glass of a servant," which Stephen claims represents Irish art, carves a caveat in notions of realistic art necessarily based on imitative principles. Joyce's *Ulysses* engages the historical particularity of Dublin in June of 1904, in a playful manner, which enables imagined pathways to escape the political, cultural and social stasis plaguing Ireland at that time.

Joyce's presentation of Stephen Dedalus' and Leopold Bloom's interactions with characters as they journey through an ordinary day, offers a vision of literary representations of the "social networks" that Milroy identifies as her subject of study in Belfast in the early nineteen-eighties. Irish speech patterns are numerous throughout the novel as Joyce works with the English language Ireland inherited from the legacy of colonialism. His writing highlights a complex relationship between written and spoken language that becomes inherently more complicated given the "centripetal forces" of Enlightenment English and Irish, and the opposing forces of the *heteroglossia* in various dialects of Irish-English. He touches on the complexity of Ireland's linguistic history in Stephen's interactions with the dairywoman early in the text. Haines speaks to the old woman in Irish, in a condescending effort to show how a foreigner is more adept at speaking Ireland's mother tongue than the nation's own population. "Is it French you are talking, sir?" she replies (Joyce 1990, 14). Contributing to the mockery, Haines replies "Irish... Is there no Gaelic on you?" His all but staged rendition of asking the dairywoman if she speaks any Irish echoes Synge's portrayal of Irish-English as it spoken in Gaeltacht regions.

Joyce's depiction of Stephen's social networks brings together the economically and politically privileged English student, Haines, the middle-class Irish in Buck Mulligan and the urban Irish poor, in the nameless dairywoman. Her ignorance of the sound of Irish, which she initially mistakes for French, not only gestures towards the dying Irish language only existing in pockets of the West, from where she presumes Haines is visiting, but also positions Ireland in a wider European collective. But Mulligan's question, "Is there no Gaelic on you?" suggests Joyce's sarcastic disapproval of the nationalist agenda as he scathingly mimics representations of speech that only privilege the Irish-English language systems of the Gaeltachts, represented by artists like Synge. Joyce seems to reject romantic notions of Irish mending the cultural and political fragmentation born from imperialism as the dairywoman responds to Buck Mulligan's comment on Haines' linguistic prescriptions. "Sure we ought to (speak Irish), the old woman said, and I'm ashamed I don't speak the language myself. I'm told it's a grand language by them that knows" (Joyce 1990, 14). Joyce seems to have no taste for utopian visions offered by the Gaelic League and Nationalist activists who claimed that Irish would heal the wounds of colonialism. Additionally, the dairywoman could represent a population that would most likely remain impoverished, regardless of the language spoken in Ireland, unless such linguistic change was matched with equally successful economic and political redistribution of power and resources. Stephen's role as mediator may be a satire of the complex power struggles involved in the politics of language in Ireland. As Stephen attempts to protect the disenfranchised dairywoman from Mulligan's sarcasm and Haines' arrogant prescriptions, Joyce presents a vision of Ireland's material reality that dispels myths that Irish would enable a retrieval of pure Irish culture decimated by imperialism. Instead, Joyce's work suggests that Ireland must develop a more realistic sense of its historical context, if the nation is to ever emerge from the degenerative paralysis of colonialism.

Rather than prescribing a solution to the conundrum of Irish politics represented in language debates, Joyce's focus on the dairywoman's interactions with Stephen, Mulligan and Haines offers a scenario of Irish cultural and linguistic conflict that is not necessarily mimetic art but instead serves as a significantly more complicated representation, likened to visions reflected by the "cracked looking glass of a servant." Joyce's work differs from Synge's in that his characters attend to the complexity of Irish versus English debates through representations of language systems that raise the issue of Irish-English, exemplified in Buck Mulligan's staged question, "Is there Gaelic on you?" While Joyce writes in an Irish-English that intertwines and points to various European languages throughout the text, his heavy-handed satire highlights the shortcomings of each political faction engaged in early twentieth-century language battles. This betrays the "crack" in Joyce's *realistic* vision, which distances his work from the "real" language that Synge and Wordsworth seemed to believe would authenticate their work.

In "Cyclops," Joyce criticizes Republican tunnel vision with his representation of the Citizen, the contradictory, medieval culchie, fashioned as a twentieth-century instantiation of the Irish Literary Renaissance's icon of the heroic pastoral. Joyce's representation of the social network that places the Citizen, Leopold Bloom, Joe Hynes, Rob Doran and the nameless narrator in dialogue, offers rich sounds of various colloquial language systems, placing the Citizen's dangerously xenophobic nationalism in its historical context. Joyce opens the chapter with a nameless narrator who "speaks" in a version of Irish-English that demonstrates the use of Irish-inspired metaphors like "to let him have the weight of my tongue," similar to 'Thug sé an teanga dó,' to signify verbal abuse (Joyce 1990, 292). And Joyce carefully punctuates the narrator's account of an afternoon at Barney Kiernan's with basic characteristics of Hiberno-English like "and + NP + V_{ing}"[6] to indicate that two actions occurred at the same time with sentences like, "so we turned into Barney Kiernan's and there sure enough was the citizen up in the corner having a great confab with himself and that bloody mangy mongrel, Garryowen, and he waiting there for what the sky would drop in the way of drink" (295). But the complexity of this representation of language intertwined with identity formation becomes much more apparent as the individuals convene in the pub to satiate their "thirst," engaging in spirited conversation.

Throughout this chapter conversation continually oscillates around Joyce's Citizen, suggesting the cultural and political centrality of Irish Republicanism in Dublin at the turn of the twentieth century. Joyce positions the Citizen as an idiotic anomaly caught between ancient heroic mythology and cosmopolitan Dublin, intoxicated by nationalism and inebriated by "drink." The Citizen, fashioned as "broadshouldered deepchested stronglimbed frankeyed redhaired...seated on a large boulder at the foot of a round tower," simultaneously sits at Barney Kiernan's in the company of Joe, Rob Doran and our nameless narrator (Joyce 1990, 296). Like a projector strip stalled between frames, Joyce presents the Citizen in his own contradictory duality, resting between the comic and the direly serious. He is not necessarily dismissed as a simple fool or a clown, but instead presented in a darkly humorous form, to be reckoned with as a contentious political and cultural force, capable of irreparable damage.

In the heroic frame the Citizen appears in ancient garb, as though the highly idealized figure Pearse, Yeats and Synge imagined, emerged from their lofty descriptions and stepped onto the streets of Dublin. Working with costume alone, Joyce offers a literal working of the Citizen's fantasy of Ireland freeing itself from all modern threads, wearing only skins stitched with gut, and girdles composed merely of "straw and rushes" (296). The Citizen's garb resists every form of modernization from woven linen to soled shoes, to lodge his misguided protest of British imperialism: To be modernized is to be Anglicized. Despite his vulgar appearance, Joyce attends to the dangerously tempting ideology of Irish racial supremacy, which the Citizen espouses as he engages in dialogue with the narrator, Bloom and Joe, continuously moving from Irish-English to Irish throughout the conversation.

Once Joe and the narrator enter the pub, Joe greets the Citizen with, "how's the old heart, citizen?" to which the Citizen responds with an Irish term of endearment, "Never better, *a chara."* Indicating a mixing of linguistic systems hearkening back to the image of a projector stalled between frames, Joyce's depiction of the Citizen suggests that Ireland cannot abandon its material reality of historical circumstance. The Citizen, who advocates a pure Irish mythic pastoral converses in English himself, now and then reverting to Irish to hush his mongrel of a dog with, "Bhi i dho husht" (Joyce 1990, 290). The nameless narrator's voice offers a steady flow of information in colloquial form placed in continual juxtaposition to the Citizen's mixed linguistic system and the complexity of Bloom's rationalism captured in interjections like "That can be explained by science...It's only a natural phenomenon, don't you see, because on account of the..." in regard to the physiological post-mortem effects of Joe Brady's hanging at Kilmainham jail, and the *"but don't you see?"* and *"but on the other hand"* recounted by the narrator. Rather than representing one strand of the *heteroglossia* of Irish-English that is positioned in contention with the unitary systems of Irish and English outside of the literary text as Synge was inclined to do, Joyce actually places these contending linguistic systems in conversation with one another. Bloom's eighteenth-century Enlightenment English in dialogue with the Citizen's Irish and Irish-English phrases, push against the steady monologue of the Irish-English narration offered by the nameless narrator and intermittent phrases from characters like Joe who claims he has "a thirst on me I wouldn't sell for half a crown." In this, Joyce seems to ask his reader to examine his cross section of identity formation through language in Ireland.

VII

While Ireland's anti-colonial movement at the turn of the twentieth century was certainly fueled by the Celtic Literary Revival's myth making, the precedent of Joyce's groundbreaking work that privileges the hybridity of Ireland's language and culture paved the way for a contemporary generation of Irish writers to consider the cultural legacies of Ireland's partition, which has further complicated political relations between Ireland (North and South) and England. Irish-English still serves as the living artifact of a long, tangled, cultural and political Anglo-Irish history well documented in Joyce's work where literary representations of this contact language, mediated through the artist's cracked looking glass, may offer imagined patience with hybridity and historical realities, often resisted in polarized modern Irish politics. Joyce's depiction of the Citizen – a "figure seated on a large boulder at the foot of a round tower...broadshouldered deepchested stronglimbed frankeyed redhaired freely freckled shaggybearded widemouthed largenosed longheaded deepvoiced barekneed brawnyhanded hairylegged ruddyfaced sinewyarmed hero" – as a committed though tragically misguided Republican patriot whose answer to the colonial travesty is a return to a non-existent mythic pastoral, offers Joyce's cutting criticism of a highly romanticized anti-colonial movement. As he places this comic version of the frighteningly real turn of the twentieth-century Republican in conversation with the Jewish cosmopolitan Bloom, Joyce illustrates their equal susceptibility to Irish cultural paralysis despite marked differences in class, educational attainment and political affiliation. Similarly, Irish writers of the contemporary period are addressing the cultural effects of partition, globalization and ongoing residuals of British colonization in Ireland through literary representations of Irish-English language systems in order to explore various forms of Irish identity.

Languages have come to represent cultural and national distinctions connected to geographical territories, and contention between various language systems has come to resemble national conflicts. But as unitary linguistic systems vying for power are then challenged by emerging *heteroglossias* born from conflict like in the case of Irish-English, how then do citizens negotiate the relationships between hybrid language systems and mythologies of cultural purity associated with nationalist agendas? Does Irish-English exemplify a "common ground upon which both agreement and disagreement are possible?" Or can contact languages ever carry the cultural and political resonance associated with unitary linguistic systems of another historic period? The following chapters will engage with literary work that attends to Ireland's complicated cultural hybridity born from the legacy of British colonialism and modern globalization, represented in the various language systems through which each writer chooses to explore Irish identity formation in the contemporary period. Reaching across generations, gender lines, geography and religion, writers are engaging with Irish identity formation through mediums of language that challenge nationalist and colonial visions of political landscapes, exploring portrayals of citizens in the North, the Republic, in the provincial, the cosmopolitan, the rural and the urban enclaves of Ireland, all in an effort to portray the complicated beauty of a people and their country.

2
A Republic of One: Individuality, Autonomy and the Question of Irish Collectivity in Seamus Deane's *Reading in the Dark* and Dermot Healy's *A Goat's Song*

> Nothing is more monotonous or despairing than the search for the essence which defines a nation.
>
> (Seamus Deane, *Celtic Revivals*)

I

In *Celtic Revivals* Seamus Deane claims "nothing is more monotonous or despairing than the search for the essence which defines a nation." It is an exhaustive task that in twentieth-century Ireland has led to violent conflict, bloodshed and the undermining of democratic processes. If energy could be refocused to create or mould a multifarious national identity as individuals reach outward and forward rather than delving inward to the depths of a mythical past, Irish citizenry may garner the power to define a nation through multifarious cultural innovation and change rather than through a stagnant, enigmatic essence that has been the bane of twentieth-century nationalism. Seamus Deane's *Reading in the Dark* and Dermot Healy's *A Goat's Song* attend to two distinct periods of twentieth-century Irish history, particularly marked by Irish nationalist agendas: post-partition Derry from the late nineteen-forties to the opening of 'The Troubles' in 1968 and the period of 'The Troubles' from the late nineteen-sixties to the nineteen-eighties in Belfast, Dublin and the West Coast of the Republic. These texts, whose central plots address the politically polarizing effects of a continued British presence in Ireland and the violent legacies of the IRA in two periods of paramilitary activity, represent some of the political and cultural effects of Irish efforts to define a nation. While the themes of these novels are familiar subjects addressed by Irish writers from Joyce to Heaney, Deane and Healy present the most complex questions of identity-formation in Ireland through the metaphor of the region's various (and sometimes contesting) language systems (Milroy 1980).

Deane's and Healy's works follow a twentieth-century tradition of consciously representing the political effects of Enlightenment English associated with the rationalism employed to justify British colonization of Ireland and the ghostly presence of Gaelic, in continued conversation with various forms of Irish-English associated with particular regions of the country. But their work does not follow an anti-imperial imperative like that of some of their literary predecessors, a reactionary relationship that was fractured by the legacy of the Anglo-Irish treaty. Instead, Deane's and Healy's works attend to an inherently more complex cultural terrain of contemporary Ireland, plagued by violence, fragile democratic processes and legacies of economic depravity, as they engage with the challenge of presenting imagined visions of Irish collectivity that stem from the autonomy and empowerment of Ireland's citizenry. As they garner the political potency of literature in Irish culture, Deane's and Healy's representations of Ireland's hybrid linguistic systems represented in dialogue between respective characters, fashion glimpses of an Ireland that may serve as an example of cultural tolerance, liberty and political agency that embraces difference and celebrates diversity, as it abandons a fruitless search for the "essence which defines a nation."

Seamus Deane's *Reading in the Dark* was published at a particularly bleak and uncertain time in the slow progression of Northern Ireland's peace process. In February of 1996 the IRA broke an eighteen-month ceasefire by bombing the Docklands of East London. The ceasefire would not be reinstated until 20, July 1997, almost a year after the initial release of Deane's novel in 1996. Although Deane's work attends to Protestant-dominated Derry in the mid-twentieth century just before the eruption of "The Troubles," the novel's spirit of tolerance, patience and resistance to traditional Irish nationalism was particularly prescient at the time of the work's release. Deane's novel enters a tradition "that emerges to impose a continuity on this shattered narrative and that 'tradition' [which] is as much answerable to the political and social needs of the moment of its production as to its content-matter" (McCarthy 2005, 235). As McCarthy claims, Deane's work imposes order on successions of events in Irish history that may only have loose affiliation to the localized focus of his work. As his novel hones in on the microcosmic narrative of familial mysteries in Catholic Derry, Deane intertwines strands of historical events of national consequence and mythic legends in his concentration on a subset of Derry's community. In this imposition of a narrative of "continuity" Deane can attend to questions facing contemporary and historic Ireland through the content-matter of his art. Deane's novel can, therefore, come to serve as a mode for exploring Ireland's national history, specifically through individual characters' relationships to the political binaries of British Unionism and Irish Nationalism. Intertwining a national legacy in the mysterious history of the young boy's family, Deane writes through polarities of identity formation so strongly affiliated with Northern Ireland's sectarian divides. His work explores how the empowerment of individuals to exercise and perpetuate autonomy as a means towards the development of social equity, community and potential national collectivity, may serve as a political model for Ireland North and South. Through representations of some of Ireland's most pressing social and political questions, in the safe distance of relatively recent history, Deane's novel asks how Ireland's recent and mythical pasts may inform the nation's contemporary circumstances.

Unlike Benjamin's Angel of History, mouth agape and horrified by "a chain of events he sees [as] one single catastrophe which keeps piling wreckage upon wreckage and hurls it in front of his feet," as he is helplessly propelled forward by a storm that "we call progress," Deane's work demonstrates a catalog of the "wreckage" known as Irish history in an effort to gradually mold and eventually embrace a new Irish collective (Benjamin 1968, 259–60).[1] As Deane attends to Ireland's mythic pastoral in continued juxtaposition to Ireland's true historical reality, his work comes to rely on representations of Ireland's hegemonic culture through presentations of language. Deane represents Ireland's hybrid linguistic make-up to demonstrate considerable variation in cultural, educational, socioeconomic and political identity formation throughout Ireland, enabling his work to serve as a distinct challenge to Nationalist mythologies.

Reading in the Dark challenges the legacies of language in Ireland that have grown directly out of the nation's tumultuous history as Deane places multiple strands of Ireland's language systems adjacent to one another. As it presents systems of Standard English in dialogue with Irish-English, the legacy of Gaelic, and Enlightenment English associated with British imperialism, Deane's novel relies on language representation to serve as a symbol for historical and contemporary political contestation. Although Deane's work is not unique in this manner, his decision to represent Ireland's multiple language systems in literary form challenges the classification of Irish-English as a spoken language only. In *The Grammar of Irish English: Language in Hibernian Style*, Markku Filppula writes,

> In a similar vein, Bliss (1979: 173), writing on the situation in the seventeenth and early eighteenth centuries, states that "Hiberno-English was never a written language: the few Irishmen able to write English would aim to write standard English." There is little support for the notion of StIrE in research in later stages of HE either. (19)

This classification becomes complicated, however, when considering the precedent offered by Maria Edgeworth's novels and short stories at the turn of the nineteenth century, the mid-nineteenth century collections of *Nation*, the work of Yeats, Gregory and Synge, and of course, that of James Joyce. Deane's work extends this tradition as it pays tribute to such literary precedence. But this novel demonstrates a re-writing of this tradition as well, as Deane attends to an infinitely more complex cultural terrain than his predecessors in post-partition Ireland.

In the literary vein, "Hiberno-English" has served as a highly politicized "written language," fueling anti-colonial efforts from the mid-nineteenth century onwards. Deane's representation of this multifaceted language system, in contact with representations of Gaelic and Enlightenment English, compresses Ireland's political and historical context in the novel, which enables readers to witness tensions centuries in the making. In this, Deane maintains a literary tradition of committing Irish-English to the page, preserving elements of an oral tradition, while his work challenges the established linguistic traditions of Gaelic and English in Ireland. Resisting notions of cultural or linguistic purity associated with Unionist or Nationalist politics, Deane's work reveals Ireland's hybrid linguistic and cultural history. He thereby writes out of polarities of Irish-identity formation endemic to the island's "shattered" historical narrative.

Early in the colonization process, Irish-English served as the only medium of communication for populations dispossessed of their native tongue and for whom the formal education necessary to master Standard English was nothing short of an impossibility. As Bliss and Filppula suggest, "Hiberno-English" was not initially a "written language: the few Irishmen able to write English would aim to write standard English."

It is significant, therefore, that this language came to symbolize Irish cultural particularity under British rule. And as Knapp claims, Irish-English "inevitably frustrates the claims of either of its parent languages, as the dominance of the one is deconstructed by the ghostly presence of its other." Irish-English, therefore, came to serve as a symbol of contemporary Irish cultural hybridity, resisting notions of cultural essence on either side of the Irish nationalist/English imperialist divide. When writers like Deane aestheticize political precedents through literary representations of such linguistic particularity, placing representations of various strands of Irish-English in conversation with twentieth-century legacies of Gaelic and Enlightenment English, they challenge polarized notions of identity affiliated with English imperialism and Irish nationalism. This can in turn potentially re-write Irish identity through Ireland's multi-faceted contact language.

II

Deane's novel is particularly striking in its focus on resisting traditional categories of social and political affiliation in mid-twentieth century Ireland. Although Deane's protagonist is a young Catholic boy raised in a working-class family his educational goals and accomplishments are not compromised by poverty, sectarian prejudice or familial tragedy. The boy's narration certainly includes classic tropes of Catholic Northern Irish hardships ranging from disease, childhood mortality, poor nutrition and police brutality to an overpowering Catholic church, sectarian discrimination and paramilitary activity, but Deane refuses to let these characteristics crowd the novel's central trajectory. While this mystical novel is certainly grounded in uncovering the details of Uncle Eddie's disappearance and death, and McIlhenny's sinister exile, the overarching theme of the novel seems to be one of survival and growth in Ireland's paralytic political and social circumstances. As the nameless narrator comes of age while Derry slowly deteriorates into "The Troubles," sectarian lines become even more starkly defined as rhetoric and propaganda continue to separate already disparate communities. The narrator seems to serve as an example of innocent tolerance in a particularly tenuous moment in Irish history. As the North teetered on the brink of possible peace in the mid-nineties, Deane's novel suggests it is time for the North to come of age, and to allow its citizens to finally shape the region's identity accordingly.

In "Blood: October 1949," as the boy describes his paternal aunt Ena's passing, Deane's language is laden with metaphors and symbols of contrast that are set against the simple sentence structures represented in dialogue between guests at the subsequent funeral.

> She coughed. Crimson sparks landed all over her grey nightdress and the bedclothes. She looked at me, her eyes wide. I couldn't move, my legs were so leaden and a pulse passed up and down from my head to my toes as though someone had slashed me from behind. Before I could reach the door, it opened and Aunt Bernadette came in. She looked at us and her face went furtive with shock.
> "Sacred Heart," she whispered, "Ena". (Deane 1997, 39)

Deane's "crimson sparks," droplets of blood spattered on "her grey nightdress," seem to echo as they land in the silence of the boy's motionless shock. His immobility, his description of Aunt Bernadette's face that "went furtive with shock" reflects a sophistication of language that eventually brushes up against the dialogue of the "men who were standing around in knots, talking" at the subsequent funeral. And his Aunt Bernadette's "Sacred Heart," a humble prayer for mercy as she absorbs the blow of her sister's impending death, serves as a curt, immediate reaction to the scene mapped out in lengthy description just sentences before.

In marked tension to the previous scene, Deane's representation of guests conversing at Ena's funeral introduces another element of the boy's social network:[2] "We would listen and then move away, choking with laughter at their accents and their repetitions. For it wasn't talking; it was more like chanting."

> "Man dear, but that's a sore heart this time o' year, wi' Christmas on top o' us and all."
> "It is that, a sore heart indeed."
> "Aye, and at Christmas too."
> "Och ay, so it is. Sore surely."
> They would tug their caps forward by the peak and nod their heads in unison, shuffling their feet slowly.
> "Did ye see Bernadette, now; the younger sister?"
> "Was that Bernadette? She's far changed now."
> "Far changed indeed. But sure she'd be shook badly now by that death."
> "Aye, the manner o' it. So quick."
> "Still, you can see the likeness to the brother. The dead spit o' him."
> "Which brother d'ye mean?"

"The lost one. Eddie. The wan that disappeared."
"I never saw him. Is that who she's like? Isn't it strange now, the way families..."
Liam and I stopped laughing. We both listened, but they said little before my father appeared. He motioned us over to him.
"Now there's a double sore heart," said one of them as we moved off. "The oldest boy gone, God knows where, and now the youngest sister. Never had good health, God help her." (Deane 1997, 41)

While the boys' reaction to the men, "choking with laughter at their accents and their repetitions" may indicate naïve judgments, their reactions suggest elements of linguistic difference. But as Deane describes the conversation that "wasn't talking; it was more like chanting," he not only highlights linguistic particularity differentiated by regional, historical and educational attainment factors, he also betrays a vocabulary that may be associated with Catholic ritual. The boy's emphasis on characteristics of repetitions associated with chanting in Catholic ceremonies may again hearken back to differentiation in Northern Irish communities along sectarian lines.

The cadence of the language, its rhythmic flow that is also highlighted in the boy's description of the conversation as "chanting," indicates particular sounds of spoken language that initially seems foreign to the young boys and reveals Deane's light formalistic touch with echoes of a sestina. But with measured linguistic distinctions from the Standard English employed for the narrator in sections like, "we would listen and then move away, choking with laughter at their accents and their repetitions," in comparison to; "this time o' year, wi' Christmas on top o' us and all" and "Och ay, so it is. Sore surely," in addition to "Did ye see Bernadette, now; the younger sister?" Deane focuses on specific characteristics of language which are particular to Irish-English. Writing in regard to such particularities Filppula states:

> The grammar of HE presents a much more multifarious picture, because social and regional considerations, alongside time, play a significant role here. While present-day "educated speech" strives toward the StE norm in all essential respects, the speech of those with less formal education in rural settings especially, but also in urban working-class contexts, abounds in grammatical features which are sometimes far removed from the norms and usages of StE grammar... At that level, there is a lot of evidence of usages which differentiate HE from other dialects of English, and from what we

know of the earlier forms of HE speech we can assume that these differences were even sharper in the past. (Filppula 1999, 12)

Considering the "multifarious picture" of Hiberno-English that Filppula describes, Deane's representation of this particular strain of Irish-English that seems strange to the narrator and his older brother comes to symbolize disparities in Irish identity amongst a predominantly undereducated, Catholic population. In this, Deane fractures simplistic notions of singular Irish identity based on religion, class or language, which is often affiliated with nationalist rhetoric, north and south of the border.

Deane quickly checks the supposed hilarity of the situation by representing language that gestures towards politically voiceless populations, limited by access to education, economic sway, civil liberty and limited political representation. As the dialogue opens with:

> "Man dear, but that's a sore heart this time o' year, wi' Christmas on top o' us and all."
> "It is that, a sore heart indeed."
> "Aye, and at Christmas too."
> "Och ay, so it is. Sore surely."

Deane points directly towards Derry.[3] The boys' amusement at such language use indicates generational gaps, which translate into access to formal education, experience, and therefore language usage. Although the boys' family and Ena's funeral guests are presumably from comparable socioeconomic backgrounds, the narrator and his brothers are afforded access to public education and are encouraged to pursue such opportunities, which may have been unavailable to this cluster of men.

In the remainder of the exchange, elements specific to Irish-English emerge, from the forms of questions and responses to the use of the English article, *the*.

> "Did ye see Bernadette, now; the younger sister?"
> "Was that Bernadette? She's far changed now."
> "Far changed indeed. But sure she'd be shook badly now by that death."
> "Aye, the manner o' it. So quick."
> "Still, you can see the likeness to the brother. The dead spit o' him."
> "Which brother d'ye mean?"

"The lost one. Eddie. The wan that disappeared."
"I never saw him. Is that who she's like? Isn't it strange now, the way families..."

Deane's construction of the use of the English article, *the*, indicates representation of Irish-English particularly in sections like "the younger sister" and "likeness to the brother." In these instances, Deane chooses to employ "the" rather than "her" to refer to the sibling's relationship which, according to Filppula, is indicative of the influence of Irish (the substratum) on the contact language, Irish-English. He writes,

> From the earliest writers like Joyce, the Irish substratum is the self-evident source for the peculiarities of HE article usage, as can be seen from the following statement:
> In Irish there is only one article, *an*, which is equivalent to the English definite article *the*. The article (*an*) is much more freely used in Irish than *the* is in English, a practice which we are inclined to imitate in our Anglo-Irish speech. (Filppula 1999, 64–5)

Additionally, Deane employs phonetic inflections like "Och," "aye," "d'ye," and "wan" to mark distinctive sounds in this system. The frontal open to open-mid ae sound in "wan" pushes against the open-mid, rounded back sound of the "o" associated with the Standard English pronunciation of "one" (International Phonetic Alphabet 2005). Additionally, "ye" serves as a non-standard signifier of the plural "you" form, to mark characteristics that distinguish Irish-English from one of its parental standardized forms.

The cited passage also introduces question and response characteristics particular to "HE usage" (Filppula 1999, 160).

> Responses to Yes/No questions form a potentially interesting area because Irish has no exact equivalents of the affirmative and negative particles *yes* and *no*. Indeed, there are observations in the literature on HE usages which are said to reflect the Irish system to a certain extent. Thus, Hayden and Hartog (1909: 934–5) claim that the 'Irish use of the particles "Yes" and "No" very sparingly, and even then add a short sentence of affirmation or denial'... Another early writer commenting on HE usage in responses is Joyce (1910/1988: 130), who, however, gives a slightly different description: for him, the special nature of HE responses manifests itself in the 'redundant' use of full statements besides the *yes* or *no* indicating the polar choice...

Mac Eoin (1993: 141) states the basic facts about Irish responses in a very succinct form: instead of the words for 'yes' or 'no', Irish repeats the verb of the question, usually in the shortest available form. (Filppula 1999, 160–1)

Deane's formulation of such an exchange emphasizes the element of repetition that is exacerbated through the narrator and his brother's reactions to these linguistic traits. In the lines, "Did ye see Bernadette, now; the younger sister?" / "Was that Bernadette? She's far changed now." / "Far changed indeed. But sure she'd be shook badly now by that death," the influence of the Irish substratum is evident. Instead of answering "Yes" or "No," the question is answered with a question. The ensuing comment "she's far changed now," indicates the question is answered affirmatively (Bernadette was seen) without directly saying so. Additionally, the phrase, "she's far changed," is repeated by yet another participant in the conversation to imply affirmation in response to the first question, in addition to agreeing with the original response to the first question. Considering Derry's proximity to Donegal (and Deane's construction of links between his Derry characters and their extended family residing in Donegal) the linguistic vestiges of that region's Gaeltacht may emerge in such representations of speech.[4]

While language is not the central metaphor for Irish-identity formation throughout *Reading in the Dark*, Deane draws on several language systems as something of a soundtrack to Ireland's multi-faceted cultural landscape. The region's multiple language systems serve as tangible, easily recognizable characteristics of cultural and social influences from a variety of sources. In the opening pages of the novel, where "on the stairs, there was a clear, plain silence," Deane suggests that silence and absence are as much of a *presence* in Irish history and culture, as language (Deane 1997, 3). Considering the virtual silencing of Ireland's native tongue, "silence" in British Parliament until the late nineteenth century and quiet obedience to the Catholic church until the late twentieth century, absence of voice factors into the text almost as strikingly as Deane's representations of language. Such tension also emboldens Deane's meditation on language, suggesting the profundity of its complex influence on identity formation in Ireland. The opening lines read:

It was a short staircase, fourteen steps in all, covered in lino from which the original pattern had been polished away to the point where it had the look of a faint memory. Eleven steps took you to the turn of the stairs where the cathedral and the sky always hung in the window frame. Three more steps took you on to the landing, about six feet long.

"Don't move," my mother said from the landing. "Don't cross that window."

I was on the tenth step, she was on the landing. I could have touched her.

"There's something between us. A shadow. Don't move."

I had no intention. I was enthralled. But I could see no shadow.

"There's somebody there. Somebody unhappy. Go back down the stairs, son." (Deane 1997, 3)

The lino, "from which the original pattern had been polished away to the point where it had the look of a faint memory," demonstrates Deane's lyrical skill as he muses on poverty, pride in cleanliness and the slow passage of time in working-class Ireland. The cathedral looming in the sky that "hung in the window frame," the family's silence on their turbulent history and the ghostly haunting that comes "between" the child and his mother, also prove to be influential symbols. Despite the cultural potency of these striking tropes, Deane's choice to utilize educated, sophisticated, impeccable standardized English for his young Catholic protagonist readily challenges polarized notions of identity based on class, political or religious affiliations in Northern Ireland.

While the narrator quite capably navigates dialogue with teachers and classmates at school, with his parents who have limited education and even with authorities like Sergeant Burke and the Bishop, all of whom employ varied forms of Enlightenment English, Irish-English or Standard English, his utility of Standard English should not and simply cannot be considered an anomaly. Deane's narrator is not unlike many Irish or Northern Irish citizens attempting to take advantage of educational opportunities while nonetheless having to navigate their various social networks. In this, the profundity of Deane's linguistic metaphor is in its seemingly obvious nature. The conundrum of language in Ireland is that it is always deeply connected to a history that is ever-changing. Although the family will deal with "a shadow" of familial mystery and betrayal, and superstition will be slow to abate its cultural influence in Ireland in the coming decades, Deane's narrator's immersion in Ireland's varied language systems demonstrates a certain cultural agility that may very well undermine stale traditional notions of affiliation.

The narrator's candid fascination with language enables Deane to imply his painstaking coming of age. Early in the text, when Una falls ill with meningitis, the boy muses,

This was a new illness. I loved the names of the others – diphtheria, scarlet fever or scarlatina, rubella, polio, influenza; they made me think of Italian football players... Meningitis. It was a word you had to bite on to say it. It had a fight and a hiss in it. When I said it I could feel Una's eyes widening all the time and getting lighter as if helium were pumping into them from her brain. They would burst, I thought, unless they could find a way of getting all that pure helium pain out. (Deane 1997, 13)

In this passage, the narrator's childlike innocence breathes life into language. Here, bacterial and viral invasions remind him of foreign "football players," invading his consciousness from a realm beyond. The hiss of "meningitis," its "fight" and "bite," offer metaphorical symbols of an ominous agent pumping the narrator's young sister full of "helium pain." The novelty of these deadly disease names embodies the boy's innocence at the beginning of the novel, where language is as much of a curiosity as haunting, death and family history. But as the novel progresses the boy's language, as much as his untamable imagination and curiosity, comes to serve as a point of contention as his ability to navigate various social networks comes to undermine traditional notions of affiliation in his community. From relatively early in the text Deane demonstrates that the narrator will transcend convenient categories of identification through immersion in Ireland's multifarious linguistic landscape. As Deane constructs the boy's rapidly evolving vocabulary and comfort with the spoken and written word of Standardized English, Irish-English and eventually Gaelic, the boy becomes an embodiment of the region's history that demonstrates the cultural, social and political complexity of a fledgling contemporary Ireland.

Deane's narrator is a literate creature. In "Reading in the Dark: October 1948," we learn "the first novel I read had a green hardboard cover and was two hundred and sixteen pages long" (19). Reminiscent of Joyce's Stephen Dedalus in *Portrait of the Artist As A Young Man*, the narrator is a sensible being, intuitively critical of his cultural surroundings.

The novel was called *The Shan Van Vocht,* a phonetic rendering of an Irish phrase meaning The Poor Old Woman, a traditional name for Ireland. It was about the great rebellion of 1798, the source of almost half the songs we sang around the August bonfires on the Feast of the Assumption. In the opening pages, people were talking in whispers about the dangers of the rebellion as they sat around a great open-hearth fire on a wild night of winter rain and squall. I read and re-read the opening many times. Outside was the bad weather; inside was the fire, implied danger, a love relationship. There was something exquisite in this blend, as I lay in bed reading while my brothers slept and shifted under the light that shone on their eyelids and made their dreams different. (Deane 1997, 20)

In this passage Deane distinguishes the narrator's responsibility as storyteller from his position as character. As his levels of literacy develop, the narrator's vocabulary changes. Language becomes less a curiosity and more of an instrument to access the "exquisite blend" of polarization represented in "a great open-hearth fire on a wild night" in addition to freedom from a crowded bedroom with brothers who "slept and shifted under the light." The narrator no longer plays with words phonetically as he does in earlier passages. Instead, his literacy provides intellectual entry to a national narrative – mystic, tragic, violent – offering the boy an initial opportunity to negotiate his relationship with these legacies.

Deane presents *The Shan Van Vocht* not only as a novel but as a problematic Irish symbol, "The Poor Old Woman, a traditional name for Ireland." He positions the trope as the mythic instantiation of Irish nationalism, inextricably linked to the rebellion of 1798, as well as one of several symbols of traditional nationalism that the boy repeatedly resists. Deane crafts this very carefully, positioning his resistance specifically through an innocent reading of the novel. As he falls in love with the novel's heroine, Ann, who was "too good" for Robert, the rebel hero, Deane's narrator becomes impatient with romantic nationalism and its reverence for blood sacrifice.

When they whispered, she did all the interesting talking. He just kept on about dying and remembering her always, even when she was there in front of him with her dark hair and her deep golden-brown eyes and her olive skin. So I talked to her instead and told her how beautiful she was and how I wouldn't go out on the rebellion at all but just sit there and whisper in her ear and let her know that now was forever and not some time in the future when the shooting and the hacking would be over, when what was left of life would be spent listening to the night wind wailing on the graveyards and empty hillsides. (Deane 1997, 20)

Wrapped up in his own romance, wanting to tell Ann "how beautiful she was and how I wouldn't go out on the rebellion at all but just sit there and whisper in her ear," Deane enables the narrator to choose which elements of the national romantic narrative to whch he will ascribe. Deane offers the child agency in this literary world, an exercise that is almost unavailable to him in the confines of politically corrupt Derry. As he "Reads in the Dark," the narrator is liberated by language, enabled to scrutinize "the source of almost half the songs we sang around the August bonfires on the Feast of the Assumption" with an innocence only allowed in the peaceful darkness of youth (Deane 1997, 19). He cannot so candidly dismiss nationalist romanticism in conversations with his maternal grandfather or in discussions about his paternal Uncle Eddie. But when he reads in the confines of a crowded, though relatively safe bedroom, Deane arms the narrator with scrutiny to resist a national mythology.

The narrator's eventual isolation, foreshadowed in his shadowy literal and symbolic reading practices, enables Deane to demonstrate cultural and social tension in a community divided on traditional, yet sometimes unpredictable, lines. Although Deane's Derry displays sectarian divides endemic to post-partition Ireland that bleed into political affiliation, discrimination and disenfranchisement, there are also significant disparities in educational attainment, socioeconomic position, employment opportunity and cultural and spiritual values within the community. Deane demonstrates such tension through detailed imagery, plot trajectory and snippets of historical information. But as the narrator's language system pushes up against multiple strands of Irish-English, represented in dialogue throughout the text, Deane's seeming criticism of stagnant, static notions of Irish identity garners legitimacy. According to Conor McCarthy:

> Deane's sense of culture as a realm of ideological contest is derived in part from his sense of outsiderhood in Northern Ireland; his sense (and that of his community) that the state did not belong to them, that they lived outside "official" culture (which was self-consciously British). In addition, Deane has spent most of his working life as an academic critic in the Republic, where, to a politicized member of the Northern nationalist minority, the mainstream political rhetoric of unity will have seemed hollow and mendacious. (2005, 233)

McCarthy's understanding of Deane's "sense of culture as a realm of ideological contest," manifests itself in the narrator's tenuous relationship to *The Shan Van Vocht*. As the narrator resists violent martyrdom, it becomes apparent that Deane's narrator will not only resist the "'official' culture (which was self-consciously British)" from which he was estranged in the Northern Irish state but he will also resist romantic Irish nationalism. His imagined reluctance to participate in the "rebellion" is influenced by infatuation with the fictional Ann. But the narrator's "reading" of the circumstances Ann and Robert face may serve as an early indication that his views could lead to isolation in Derry's Republican Catholic districts. McCarthy claims Deane's "sense of culture as a realm of ideological contest is derived in part from his sense of outsiderhood in Northern Ireland." But Deane's crafting of the narrator's impatience with the valorized rebellion, in addition to his isolation in Derry by virtue of his ethnicity and religion, suggests that the boy may serve as a fulcrum on which a new vision for Ireland may hinge. At once inside and outside of the dominant cultural tropes, Deane's narrator muddies traditional affiliation based on specific cultural, political or social traits, literally re-inscribing notions of identity formation in Ireland.

While Deane's novel does not offer direct representations of Irish, as Joyce does in the satiric "Cyclops" chapter of *Ulysses*, Deane attends to Ireland's dispossession of its native tongue through English. This comes to serve as an interesting cross-section of political tension as the narrator comes to tell his parents their family secrets in a language unavailable to either of them. Gaelic, therefore, comes to serve as the medium through which truth is revealed. But the revelation is rendered useless for the narrator's father, who seems to be most in need of this pertinent information. "In Irish: October 1955," attends, in part, to Ireland's contentious relationship with Gaelic, a symbol of perceived cultural purity inaccessible to most of the population. The narrator states:

> My mother knew no Irish, but she had dismembered bits and pieces of poems and songs that were from the Irish. (Deane 1997, 202)

Interestingly, Deane constructs this sentence with the particular article use of *the*, in "from the Irish," characteristically used in Hiberno-English (Filppula 1999, ch. 5, 55–89). But the significance of this passage lies in its content. Because the narrator's mother knows no Irish, and the father presumably also has limited knowledge of the language, the circumstances lend the young narrator authority over his parents. Although he is rendered virtually helpless by the burden of his family's secret, and he struggles to interact with his parents, the narrator is nonetheless put in the particularly uncomfortable position of knowingly overpowering his parents by virtue of their lack of education. Fearful of revealing his knowledge, conscious of his mother's distrustful silence, he states:

> I decided to write it all out in an exercise book, partly to get it clear, partly to rehearse it and decide which details to include or leave out. But then the fear that someone would find it and read it overcame me. So, with the help of a dictionary, I translated it all into Irish, taking more than a week to do it. Then I destroyed the English version, burning it in front of my mother's eyes, even though she told me I would clog up the fire with the paper. (Deane 1997, 203)

Gaelic frees the boy from the burden of truth and veils the story from his parents. Contested as the symbol that would once again make Ireland whole or that which would handicap the nation's development throughout the late nineteenth century and the early twentieth century, Deane's representation of Gaelic through English addresses the precarious role of the language both integral and extrinsic to the region's future. Without such a sophisticated level of literacy, the language would be all but unavailable even to the boy. He struggles to translate his family's dark history, "with the help of a dictionary...taking more than a week to do it." But his struggle is a success, although Deane chooses to engage in this representation in a limited fashion. After all, the translation appears only as an action described in English in the text, never actually revealed in Gaelic.

Ironically similar to Article 8 of the Irish Constitution, the role of Gaelic in Deane's novel is described in English. Ireland's relationship to its mother-tongue is estranged in the wake of colonialism, further exacerbated by Britain's prolonged presence in Northern Ireland. But various linguistic strands serve as a metaphor for the nation's relationship to its multiple sources of social, political and cultural influence. The narrator states,

> I waited for a few days. Then, one evening, when my father was there, reading his way through *Pear's Encyclopedia,* his hand-held education, as he called it, and I was sitting at the table doing homework, I read it all outright in Irish to him. It was an essay we had been assigned in school, I told him, on local history. He just nodded and smiled and said it sounded wonderful. My mother had listened carefully. I knew she knew what I was doing. My father tapped me on the shoulder and said he liked to hear the language spoken in the house. (Deane 1997, 203)

Resisting nostalgic presentations, Deane's representation of the role of Gaelic in Ireland considers inaccessibility to the language by a complete generation of working-class individuals, symbolized in the parents' ignorance. The complexity of this dynamic grows in the child's ability to please his father, who "liked to hear the language spoken in the house." In this, Deane comments on a loss. Despite the layer of deception involved in telling the story in a manner that the narrator knows is inaccessible to his parents, he does so in an effort to protect them as well as to heal his own troubles. Although his mother "listened carefully" and "knew what I [he] was doing," the boy's literacy enables him to negotiate a position of power. Much like in the chapter, "Reading in the Dark," the boy's educational development is symbolized through language, allowing him to negotiate a small degree of freedom in an otherwise limited position. To read this symbol as a national allegory may be beside the point, as Deane suggests the relationship to national legacies is continually redefined on individual levels. But in this chapter Deane certainly attends to the tumultuous historical symbol of Gaelic in Ireland, challenging simplistic notions that the language will either imprison or free the Irish population.

In the next chapter of the novel, Deane addresses Ireland's other linguistic parent, as the narrator and his classmates are asked to welcome a visitor to their "school, introduced by the President, sent by the Ministry of Education" (Deane 1997, 206). In "Political Education," "the speaker, a priest in British army uniform, a chaplain, a smooth and tall man, with a tall and smooth accent," comes to speak to the children about a common enemy: Communism. He begins:

> Were you to view the Foyle Basin from Binevenagh, almost twelve hundred feet above the sea, with the bird-haunted mud flats of the River Roe at its foot, you would begin to appreciate both the beauty and the strategic importance of the dramatic landscape and seascape in which your city rests. This was the city that, even today, still commands the eastern approaches of the North Atlantic, that is still a vital port for the great NATO fleets that regularly put in here during those exercises that are part of the Western world's preparations for the defeat of the international Communist threat. That threat is as real now as once was the threat of those German submarines that surrendered here at the end of the war and now lie rusting on the ocean floor, their scuttling a symbol and reminder of our determination to defend the cause of democracy and freedom, of the might and resolve with which we shall always mobilise our resources to maintain that democratic system in which we all have the good fortune to live. (Deane 1997, 206)

Deane's configuration of the chaplain's ornate language rivals the Standardized English system employed for the narrator. His majestic description of the Foyle Basin from the precipice of Binevenagh, its "bird-haunted mud flats of the River Roe at its foot," and the "strategic importance of the dramatic landscape and seascape" of Derry, are tools of flattery in an effort to woo his audience. He enters the classroom cognizant that it is "strange country," culturally disparate from the State and faith he represents (Deane 1997). Nonetheless, the chaplain makes no attempt to temper his language. Instead, it serves as a marker of his power and authority that proclaims Derry a "democratic system in which we all have the good fortune to live." The chaplain's long, verbose, elaborate sentences in Standardized English speak for the colonial State. His language serves as a relic, a reminder of the colonial power whose legislature and policy was delivered in Enlightenment English, a system associated with rationalism that justified occupation. If the chaplain claims that "our determination to defend the cause of democracy and freedom, of the might and resolve with which we shall always mobilise our resources to maintain that democratic system in which we all have the good fortune to live," his tone suggests that it will be done.

The environment in which the chaplain launches his mission to unify the community in opposition to a common enemy is significant. He is a Protestant figure employed by the State, a representative of the powerful Northern Irish majority, entering an adolescent classroom of the next generation of male Irish Catholics, the minority and potentially "troubling" sort. He appeals to his audience through praising familiar Irish landscapes – the natural cove of Foyle Basin or Lough Foyle – in grandiose terms, which shortly thereafter enable him to move towards the subject of a linked fate in heroic terms through the battle of democracy versus communism. But the irony of this effort is not lost on the audience, despite the chaplain's linguistic pageantry. " 'Propaganda,' Irwin said" in the wake of the chaplain's presentation.

> That's all that is. First, it's the Germans. Then it's the Russians. Always, it's the IRA. British propaganda. What have the Germans or Russians to do with us? It's the British who are the problem for us. McAuley's a moron. (Deane 1997, 210)

Irwin's take on the chaplain's presentation offers an interesting interpretation of the language associated with the state. As Irwin claims, "It's the British who are the problem for us," he resists the "global vision" the chaplain tries to sell. Irwin is uninterested in affiliation with anyone audacious enough to claim Derry, or Northern Ireland in general, a "democratic system" (210). Thus, language comes to serve as the medium through which this batch of propaganda is disseminated. The chaplain's language, affiliated with the State and religion he represents, is tainted with the same distrust reserved for all interactions with the British government.

Initially rendered "curiously silent," the narrator attempts to personalize the chaplain's message. He is apprehensive about dismissing a speech from someone he first believed to be "exquisite" (205).

> I remembered the teenage German my father had brought extra lunch to when he was in the prisoner-of-war compound down at the docks and who had, I had been told, given my father the German pistol as a thank you – the pistol that had disappeared into the police barracks years before and ignited so much since. But that was a petty squabble, perhaps. I was beginning to catch on at last. Global vision. I needed that. (Deane 1997, 210)

Herein lies the complexity of Deane's narrator: neither quick to join or oppose the chaplain or Irwin, he rests somewhere in between. While he is intrigued by the chaplain's speech he is suspicious of any affiliation with the State. And although he is familiar with Irwin's criticisms he remains unconvinced of its substance. Could the "British who are a problem for us," be nothing but a "petty squabble" in a global perspective or are grievances like sectarian oppression, police brutality and inaccessible democratic processes global troubles nonetheless?

Deane's polymorphous novel suggests that democracy in Ireland can be re-imagined if individuals can break free from polarized notions of identity that have plagued the region since the inception of colonialism. In *Imagined Communities*, Benedict Anderson writes, "for it shows that from the start the nation was conceived in language, not in blood, and that one could be 'invited into' the imagined community" (2003, 145). In the spirit of this "imagined community," shaped by affiliation between language and nation, it seems novels like Deane's *Reading in the Dark* may serve as intellectual exercises that imagine nation formation linked not to ethnic or territorial ties but instead to shared language systems. Considering Ireland's contentious history affiliated with language, from Gaelic to Enlightenment English to the contact language Irish-English, it would seem Ireland's conception of nationhood would be understood as a heterogeneous, organic entity, continually growing in complexity through time. As Deane orchestrates such cross-sections of dialogue, collective Irish identity may be linked to Ireland's heterogeneous language, Irish-English, rather than a mythic Gaelic culture affiliated with nationalism or English colonial/settler culture associated with Unionism. Ireland's contact language, therefore, would not serve as "an instrument of exclusion," but as Benedict Anderson suggests, would be "fundamentally inclusive, limited only by the fatality of Babel: no one lives long enough to learn *all* languages" (134). Deane's representations of Irish-English document vestigial traces of Gaelic and Enlightenment English in mid-twentieth century Northern Ireland, while simultaneously erecting Irish-English as the medium through which Ireland's past and present coexist, setting Ireland's linguistic systems in a dialectical exchange. As Deane represents such linguistic trajectories in dialogue between characters, he presents distinctions between spoken and literary language. But if we were to accept that "print-language is what invents nationalism, not *a* particular language per se" as suggested by Benedict Anderson, how then could one classify Deane's political vision of Irish collectivity through representations of heterogeneous language (134)? If "print-language is what invents nationalism" then could Deane's representations of language challenge twentieth century notions of Irish nationalism North and South?

Anderson's discussion of course focuses on the newspaper industry, not necessarily novels attending to national crises of identity. Nonetheless, Deane's and Healy's works are situated in the meta-region of language, nestled between oral and written communication. While Deane's "print-language" attends to the role of multiple language structures that betray various cultural and political affiliations that oscillate between oral and written communication, Healy's novel continually marks distinctions between the specific sounds of oral communication and the reification of such communication through the process of writing. Just as Jack Ferris reconfigures Catherine with the opening of a "spiral bound notebook" and thinks to himself, "Here it begins," Healy's novel self-consciously attends to a re-writing of contemporary Ireland indicating that "print-language," not only that of newspapers but especially that written by the artistically inclined, may in fact "invent" a new incarnation of "nationalism." Deane and Healy's novels suggest that Ireland's national collective may very well be forged not in "*a* particular language per se" but in the multifarious linguistic fabric that is Ireland today.

III

Dermot Healy's *A Goat's Song* follows the seemingly simple formula of a romance between a Northern Irish born, Catherine Adams, and the Republic of Ireland born, Jack Ferris, as the foundation for his exploration of Irish identity-formation in the late twentieth century. In the heartache that comes to be their dysfunctional romance, Healy negotiates the stark cultural, linguistic and political differences that have distanced the Northern Irish province from its Southern neighbors for generations preceding the Anglo-Irish treaty. But Jack's vision, "the only way I can free myself is to imagine her, not as herself, but as someone else, someone different, for then I can think of her without resenting her," before he "opens a spiral notebook and thought, Here it begins," serves as a moment where Healy winks at a national allegory (Healy 1994, 84). As Jack attempts to mold an alternative Catherine, "someone different, for then I can think of her without resenting her," Healy suggests the act of writing may serve as a particularly apt tool in reshaping our perceptions of material realities. While Jack attempts to re-imagine Catherine through writing a play on their tumultuous love affair, distancing the pain by restructuring the narrative, Healy's novel introduces a refreshing interpretation of Ireland's political and cultural landscape in a gesture towards imagining a new vision of Irish collectivity that celebrates, rather than dismisses, the region's multifarious culture and deeply contentious political differences.

One of the most striking elements of Healy's work is the novel's delicate balance between the intimacy of Catherine's and Jack's relationship to one another and their respective territorial affiliations. Northern Irish violence and Southern provincialism crowd and sour their relationship as readily as alcohol and seething tempers. Whether they live on the Mullet or in Belfast, national legacies invade their domestic interior ranging from bricks thrown through a window to Mr Adams' appearance on RTE news amidst riots in Derry. Just as Jack and Catherine strive and continually fail to coexist in a romantic relationship, Healy's work suggests drastic cultural, social and political changes will have to emerge if Ireland is to ever see peace with justice. And rather than reporting on such bleak realities, Healy's novel attempts to restructure the national narrative as he crafts a chorus of Ireland's multiple language systems, shattering notions of a singular Irish identity.

Anderson's suggestion that "print language is what invents nationalism" rests heavily on the commodification of language in print journalism. As language is reified through the capital exchange associated with the rise of newspaper industries in the nineteenth century, language comes to serve as a chief characteristic in the negotiation of identity. Oral communication and historical preservation fall secondary to the potency and static reliability of the reified written word that comes to serve as the chief medium through which a national identity can be expressed and preserved. Healy draws on the legacies of this nineteenth-century revolution in his crafting of Jack's day-to-day routine in war-torn Belfast. After a visit to the Pakistani market, the off-license and a knick-knack shop:

> lastly, he'd buy a copy of the *Belfast Newletter* – the proper Unionist paper – at George's newsagents. Only one copy of the Catholic newspaper was ever on sale there. It was still there in the afternoon when he came to collect the *Evening News*, which was bought by both religions.
> "Don't be tempted by it," advised Catherine. "There's not a soul in this area would be seen dead buying the *Irish News*."
> "I won't, don't worry."
> "It's left there deliberately to trap a body. That's how they'd know who you are. You've got to take care," she said adamantly. "I feel responsible for bringing you here."
> "I want to get to know these people" replied Jack. "I'm sharing this island with them."
> "But they are not inclined to share it with you," she said coldly. "Remember that." (Healy 1994, 282)

In late twentieth-century Northern Ireland, newspapers, like the bunting, flags and painted curbs that mark Catholic and Protestant enclaves, erect high standing walls in the smallest of communities. They are the mouth pieces of xenophobic notions of identity formation in Northern Ireland, saturating already divided communities in rhetoric of suspicion, distrust and verbose claims of righteousness in the integrity of either Republican or Unionist endeavors. Catherine's angst over something as seemingly mundane as Jack's choice between newspapers confirms Anderson's interpretation of "print language" as that which "invents nationalism." Just as the *Irish News* serves as a booby-trap, "deliberately" poised to snare a wandering Fenian in Catherine's predominantly Protestant, working-class neighborhood, the *Belfast Newsletter* may as well be a badge of honor for Ian Paisley's Democratic Unionist Party. The *Evening News* suggests a middle ground, a meeting place "bought by both religions" though it is positioned as a secondary authority, legible only in the shadows of sundown. Jack visits the newsagent where he is christened *the Irishman* by the "old lady" who didn't know his name but marked his identity on the strangeness of his accent. As he reads Unionist newspapers in an effort to "get to know these people" since he is "sharing this island with them," Jack's enthusiasm is checked by Catherine's chilling reminder that *they* are "not inclined to share it" with him.

While newspapers darken the lines between identities in Northern Ireland, widening chasms and feeding generalizations on either side of the Nationalist and Unionist divide, Healy's work suggests such polarities are both that which divide and align the multiple populations who share the "island." Healy's novel is situated in the realm of language, sliding between oral and written traditions in the writing and re-writing of Catherine's family history and her relationship with Jack. In this it seems to cycle in and over itself continually as Healy shifts from collections of Ireland's multiple language systems sounding off the page in character dialogue to Jack's collecting and writing such utterances in his plays, back again to Healy's writerly endeavor of drawing continual attention to the sounds of Ireland's language systems, North and South. McCarthy accurately describes this form as seemingly "urobic – that of the serpent with its tail in its mouth" (McCarthy 2000, 148).

> The narrative re-formation of Ferris's experience by the mind that creates serves the therapeutic reformation of the man who suffered. What makes this novel such a tale of wonder is how it shows this therapeutic reformation in the process of narrative poeisis itself, the process which gives to experience mythic form, and through that form, mythic significance. Poeisis re-forms the self after the deformation of melancholia. (148)

This forced continuity, "the serpent with its tail in its mouth," is a tightly wrought conundrum from which escape seems impossible. McCarthy's analysis attends to the content of the novel, namely Jack and Catherine's romance. Since Jack cannot distance himself from Catherine, he writes her. Through poeisis, transposing and therefore transporting her from his psyche to the page, pushing her from the annals of their history to the mythic heroic of his play, he can finally escape her. His cathartic process, writing through the real Catherine to the reified object that is his work, enables Jack to negotiate distance through proximity. The serpent's circular configuration is forced. He mouths his tail as a posture. Likewise, Healy adapts such a form to negotiate the seeming puzzle that is Irish identity formation through the most rudimentary form of asserting the sometimes contradictory conflation of individuality and collectivity in language. As Healy catalogs, identifies and reconfigures Ireland's multiple linguistic systems and constituencies he suggests that the responsibility may lie with the individual, rather than a national government, to re-write the nation's trajectory. Just as Jack must re-write Catherine to distance himself from the heartache that was their relationship, Healy's novel suggests Irish citizenry must re-inscribe the national history if the nation is to ever emerge from the confines of its politically potent mythologies.

Jack and Catherine's impossible affair, their similarities and differences, crowd in on them in their close proximity both on the Mullet and in Belfast. Their doomed relationship often mirrors the seeming impossibility of Ireland's populations sharing the "island." Healy's work demonstrates the inherent difficulty of various factions of Ireland's population sharing a limited territory in the context of such contentious strife as is evident by the late twentieth century. But the novel also serves as an exercise in the negotiation of individual autonomy in this contrived system. Through seeming ruptures in this system in violent outbursts, distinctions in speech, history and the exercise of political will, *A Goat's Song* suggests a shift in narrative structure may enable a fresh relationship with a seemingly familiar entity. Just as Jack Ferris can reinvent his relationship to Catherine by re-writing her, Healy too renegotiates the individual's relationship to the Irish state as he reconfigures the familiar in a new form.

Although Healy's marks of cultural, socioeconomic, historical, political and religious differences are often signified in language either through presentations of varied vocabularies, word order or phonetics, his work also relies on well-nurtured prejudices and carefully crafted slurs to depict strained interactions between Ireland's various populations. As Healy's novel canvases the Northern Irish–Southern Irish, Catholic–Protestant, Unionist–Nationalist binaries, as essentially dependent on one another as the means for defining self, he catalogs such divisions through violent outbursts.

> First the Angelus rang out, then came the news from RTE on the black-and-white TV. The Sergeant took no notice till he heard sounds and names that gradually grew familiar. He looked up with terror and saw they were re-running an account of the march. This came as a shock to Jonathan Adams. He had seen no TV men there, nor was

he used to them. It showed the Catholic gathering in Duke Street. Then the chaotic start of the march. The shouts for the police to give way were raised. With great religious zeal the Catholics called to the policemen. Within seconds a protester was being batoned. What happened next was seen by Jonathan Adams with blinding clarity. To the left of the picture could be seen a grey-haired policeman, hatless, chasing after a youth. When he lost him among the other marchers, he turned and batoned a middle-aged man who was already pouring blood.

The crowd in the bar shouted "bastards."

On the TV the old policeman had found his hat. As he put it on, he looked round for someone else to hit. Seeing no one he turned back and hit the screaming man again. A woman crouched low as she pulled her man away. The old policeman charged past the camera. Then, wild-eyed and wielding a baton he stared remorselessly straight at the lens. Jonathan Adams had become a witness to himself. He saw the mad look of fury in his own eye. He looked round the bar but no one was taking any notice of him. (Healy 1994, 121)

In this moment Healy pushes Adams into the historical trajectory of Northern Ireland and the "Troubles," and its dissemination throughout the Republic. As Jonathan Adams becomes "a witness to himself" telecast by RTE on a black-and-white TV in the West of Ireland, he is at once forced to rectify his own perception of self, with "the mad look of fury in his own eye," plastered on the screen. Although Healy, through Ferris, carefully documents Adams' pervasive distrust of all that is Roman Catholic throughout the novel, this moment serves as a rupture in the sergeant's code of behavior. Normally quiet, pensive, almost stealthy in his cataloged hatred of his Catholic counterparts, Adams' fury is unleashed in his reaction to the news broadcast. Immediately ashamed, frightened and appalled with the echo of "bastards" from the Southern audience collected in the pub, Adams must not only confront his own image, he is also forced to reckon with the judgment of those with whom he must share the "island." Adams can beat defenseless marchers without remorse in an environment where the Unionist Protestant majority is rarely held accountable for bullying the minority population. In the South, however, Adams discovers he is in the minority. It is merely a matter of posture and position – the head is the tail, the tail the head.

In the domestic plane, Maisie espouses her husband's prejudice with a rant on Catholic home décor and personal upkeep as she turns on her neighbors once they depart from her home on the Mullet. Again held unaccountable, she speaks freely:

> How could a man interest himself in them? She'd ask. And so gross! So overweight! Her condescension towards them had a hint of hysteria which she tried to subdue. "Did you ever notice," she'd repeat to the girls, "how tasteless they are? Look at their carpets! How could you – paisley on paisley?" She smirked ungraciously. "Those RCs are sad. They have no idea of patterns. Not an earthly. What I'd like to know is how they sleep in those rooms! And the way they spend money – it's a sin." (Healy 1994, 216)

In these instances, Healy offers glimpses of imagined Unionist psyches, defining the self through that which they are not – tacky Roman Catholic housewives and insubordinate Fenian zealots. Healy relies on such instances to demonstrate the national and individual instances of such ruptures and outbursts. Adams' violent acts, which propel him into a national narrative of persecution and discrimination and Maisie's chilling slurs, muffled in the domestic interior, sound the panic affiliated with settler populations. Desperate to prove they belong and that their culture is in fact superior and seemingly more natural than the Catholic population, Healy invites the reader to consider such self-consciousness, while opening up an exchange of values as the Adams family embarks on their cultural journey living on the Mullet and learning Irish.

Jack's retelling of the Adams' family history undermines traditional power structures in the Republic of Ireland and Northern Ireland, respectively. In Fermanagh, the Adams family is protected by the code of privilege afforded the Protestant majority, even after Sergeant Adams becomes a target of the IRA. But in the South, Irish born Protestants are an endangered race.

> The South was a museum in which Jonathan Adams, at least, wandered as a stranger. It stored quaint phrasing, soft vowels, superstitions, unpunctual tradesmen, maddening longueurs, stray donkeys. Shouts at midday, cheers at midnight. And no violence. Goats strolled the village. Turf went over and back. Swans flew. And the price of goods changed every day. (Healy 1994, 148)

Because of his "fluency in the world of figures – exact figures," the Sergeant is unaccustomed to the fluidity of the South (Healy 1994, 107). Frustrated by the seeming softness of "vowels" and commitments to the rigid order he associates with everyday life, Adams flounders on the Mullet. He yearns to domesticate and categorize the Southern landscape and population, virtually unscathed by the pervasive violence of the North. He is rendered all but helpless with a loss of authority and control, so he strives to find an entry-point into the culture.

> Jonathan Adams stomped round the townlands drawing maps and marking in the boundaries of the old landlords' houses while Maisie sat in the car reading gardening books. Each place name had a different resonance and sound depending on who was talking. He wrote down the different versions and then tried them out on his neighbor Joe Love, who would guess their meaning. He watched Bernie Burke heading past the house with plastic bags of fish. A greeting in Irish was called. His lack of Irish began to infuriate him. Every door to the peninsula's past was closed to him. The Irish language was denying him entrance.
> "I need books," he told Maisie, "and I need maps that are not Catholic maps." (Healy 1994, 163)

Adams' heavy footed quest to map and mark the Mullet, to uncover property lines of long ago dismantled big houses, "while Maisie sat in the car reading gardening books" to discover tricks to manipulate the seemingly untamable wild gardens of The Dwellings, serve as meeting points where the couple attempt to domesticate the public and private spheres of the Republic. As their authority over land, language, politics and culture disintegrates in the North, Jonathan then brings such sentiments to the South. But in order to enter the South in any meaningful way, Jonathan senses a need to master "the Irish language." As he attempts to dissect the South, with "maps that are not Catholic maps," Adams tries to parse out the strands of Catholic Irish culture that he can tolerate. Still a Protestant Loyalist, he refuses to embrace the Catholic majority in the South. He is willing, however, to enter a mythic pastoral, readily armed with the Irish language.

Although Healy's text attends to the politics of identity formation associated with Ireland's various language systems, the novel couches this premise in the phonetic and literate elements of language. Rather than demonstrating marked differences in grammatical structures as exemplified in novels like Deane's *Reading in the Dark*, Healy appears to be invested in the particular sounds of language systems in Ireland. His work, therefore, often focuses on collecting phonetic and rhythmical distinctions that mark specific locales along the west coast of the

Republic or that mark distinctions in class in Northern Ireland, therefore assembling a collection of sounds to demonstrate the hybridity of Irish voices. While in Belfast, Jack's desk is filled "with nonsense rhymes of Belfast speech patterns he had written down as he heard them...a collection of voices and moods that had no relation to each other. Speech overheard in pubs, on the street, in the back gardens, by the docks" (Healy 1994, 301). Similarly, Sergeant Adams is put off by the "quaint phrasing" and the "soft vowels" of the Republic. Both characters listen in order to categorize and record, enabling Healy to place considerable emphasis on the phonetics of language systems in Ireland, rather than strident distinctions in grammar or vocabulary. Healy also negotiates meaning from such constructions, or lack thereof, depending on the character in question. According to McCarthy, "Ferris feels his mind and body become disconnected. He experiences this as a disconnection between words and the things he refers to; the de-centered self is a repetition of the de-centered sign" (McCarthy 2000, 137). Similarly, Adams believes the Irish language "was denying him entrance" to the South of Ireland broadly, and the Mullet most specifically. As Jack writes the Adams' narrative and Jonathan Adams writes, reads and speaks through the South, Healy crafts a restructuring of a national collective that dismantles traditional conceptions of Irish identity. The juxtaposition of Adams' speech patterns against those of *"the Irishman"* Ferris, characters on the Mullet and in Belfast, Healy crafts a medley of utterances that dispel the notion of a single Irish voice.

Much like in Deane's novel, Healy's meditation on language in *A Goat's Song* is introduced through silence. Early in the text, Jonathan Adams develops an almost compulsive relationship to language systems due to his own paralytic silence. Upon graduating from seminary school:

> His family helped the young student get his first living at Cullybackey in Co. Antrim. The apprentice minister was introduced to the elders in a low wooden church with a red galvanized roof. Only one Masonic banner hung from the wall. He had chosen as his homily the powerful line – *to give some form to that which cannot be uttered.* It proved an unfortunate choice. For the minute he started to preach that which he had feared happened – he was possessed of such a feeling of disorientation that his chin and wrists shook uncontrollably. The joy the congregation did not see stirred in his soul, but elation did not reach his lips.
>
> Words refused to come to him. Meaning departed. (Healy 1994, 99)

This moment not only serves as the pivotal beginning of Adams' obsession with language but also demonstrates a point of intersection between the character trajectories of both Adams and Ferris. In this instance the young preacher's introduction and catastrophic end of a fledgling career, pile miserably upon one another. But the nature of this failure enables Healy to negotiate the meeting point for his two central male characters. Just as Jack's heartbreak renders language useless, Adams' paralytic introduction to preaching is saturated in silence as "meaning departed." Speech reluctantly returns to both characters, however, through literacy. As Ferris and Adams catalog, record and mimic speech patterns, they cultivate their own voices and begin to exercise autonomy in personal relationships as well as in their interactions with the State. Through layman linguistic studies these characters measure the complexity of Irish experience, its varied history, enabling Healy to craft a multifarious fictional landscape that fundamentally restructures approaches to the Irish historical narrative.

Adams' obsession with language manifests itself in various ways throughout the novel from studies on the etymologies of specific vocabularies like "the terms of hell" when considering Matti Bonner's fate after his catastrophic suicide, to place names clumsily translated from Irish to English by Joe Love, "who would guess at their meanings" (Healy 1994, 92 & 164). Yet his focus on elocution and pronunciation of English, and later as he invites teachers into his home to assist his family in learning Irish, serve as profound markers in shifting Adams' perceptions of identity formation and his individual relationship with Ireland, North and South. Early in the text, following his introduction to preaching, Adams insists on better prospects for his young daughters.

> From the beginning he expected a policeman's daughters to be beyond reproach. He took them to school, to Sunday school, to services. One on either hand, he descended the barracks steps. He washed them in the bath together. He was an old man graced by the miracle of young daughters. And the first thing their father did when they had learned to speak was to send them to elocution and drama classes. They learned to balance the sound of a word on their palate before they spoke it. He did not want any child of his to find themselves before a congregation or audience stumbling over the meaning of that word "I". (Healy 1994, 112)

Adams equates a sense of self with a command of spoken language. As he trains his children to "balance the sound of a word on their palate before they spoke it," Adams strives to ensure his children will be able to speak with composure, confidence and precision. He tries to offer his children a skill-set to assert autonomy and individuality, so that they will never stumble over "the meaning of that word 'I'." He associates such confidence with Standardized English.

This tendency arises often in the text as Adams insists on the importance of language in individual growth and identity formation. Early in the text, Catherine complains that she is not yet ready to move back into her own bedroom. Still sensitive after witnessing Matti Bonner's suicide, she argues with Jonathan Adams that she cannot sleep alone.

"Daddy, I'm afeared."
"And what's there to be afeard of?"
"Matti Bonner"
"Go long."
"I am."
"That's enough out of ye, once is enough, Catherine, for to tell ye. Matti is in heaven."
"He's in hell."
"Stop it, Catherine. Tonight you'll hike yourself back to your room."
"But Daddy, he'll folly me."
"Foll-ow!" the Sergeant said correcting her.
"Follow," said Catherine, "he'll *follow* me."
"There's no one going to folly ye, daughter." He took her by the hand and the two stepped briskly along. (Healy 1994, 94)

Through Jack's attention to speech patterns in the re-writing of Catherine's life history, Healy offers glimpses of Adams' reactions to non-standard English speech patterns uttered by his carefully trained daughters. Catherine and Jonathan's exchange demonstrates a struggle between Jonathan's insistence on Standard English pronunciation for his daughter, while he succumbs to non-standard colloquial forms. In the opening lines Catherine uses the non-standard vocabulary of "afeard" instead of afraid to express her fear of Matti Bonner's spirit, and Jonathan echoes this use. But Catherine's use of "he'll folly me" brings Adams' tyrannical wrath. His response, "Foll-ow!" demands that Catherine correct herself. But the closing lines of the exchange demonstrate Adams falling back into non-standard pronunciation despite his efforts to ensure that his children will be able to "balance the sound of a word on the palate before they spoke it" (Healy 1994, 112). Catherine's "folly me," and Jonathan's "There's no one going to folly ye daughter," illustrates a certain comfort with a specific speech pattern that is certainly not that associated with Received Pronunciation of English. Only when consciously attempting to standardize their speech do Catherine and Jonathan lengthen the second vowel with an emphatic "Foll-ow!" Neither conversant pause at Jonathan's use of "ye" to signify the singular "you," which is evident in a variety of non-standard dialects in Ireland from Irish-English to Southern Ulster English to Ulster Scots. The terms "ye" and "afeared," it would seem, are less egregious than the use of the shortened ending vowel of "folly."

Healy's work catalogs varied voices that demonstrate a rich milieu of sounds that distinguish the multiple speech patterns of modern Ireland. From Lizzie Summers' "Sure yon fellow...he only has it for to stir his tay," to the ladies on the train to Belfast who say, "I was talking tay Alice yesterday. I wouldn't be capable taking on wha' she did," *A Goat's Song* portrays a collection of language systems that demonstrate the range of Irish-English phonetics and syntax that crystallizes the multifarious nature of language in Ireland. But the politics of language become most readily apparent in Healy's representations of Irish in the novel. Adams' motivation to enter Irish culture through language is received differently by each of his visiting teachers:

> the inclination of Master Adams towards Irish and Irishness became contemptible in MacDonagh's eyes. What was driving the old bollacks? It derived from guilt over violence done. He had probably taken part in some vile deed in the past. His wish was not reconciliation, but to disguise himself in another culture. There was no other explanation. (Healy 1994, 170)

MacDonagh's evangelism in revitalizing the language brings him originally to Adams' door. But his growing contempt is nurtured as he slowly deciphers Adams' involvement in the Northern-Irish conflict. Adams seeks admission to a national narrative, a mythic pastoral though his language training but MacDonagh is reluctant to grant such access. As he interprets Adams' motivation to learn Irish as a wish "to disguise himself in another culture," instead of seeking reconciliation, MacDonagh rescinds his obligation as instructor.

In contrast to MacDonagh's attempt to control the dissemination of Irish, O'Muichin offers a mystical, sentimental approach to language.

A language is for thinking in, O'Muichin explained over supper. He grew verbose and animated. The original images are sometimes in Irish, he said, and the English occurs only by way of explanation. Sometimes, with concepts, the opposite is true. The new language is merely the learning of an old and well-tried discipline, he said, for which our senses – tired of the language we usually express ourselves in – cry out. A language will return to its source, even in a stranger's head. The great joy is selecting from various languages what best expresses content of the mind. (Healy 1994, 178)

O'Muichin's philosophy focuses on the freedom of thought and expression afforded the individual privileged enough to gain access to multiple language systems. His mystical descriptions of these systems, "for thinking in," dispel notions of essential characteristics of one language versus another. In his approach, O'Muichin advocates the interchangeable need for one language over another, depending on the circumstances an individual may face. He claims "images are sometimes in Irish ... and the English occurs only by way of explanation. Sometimes, with concepts, the opposite is true." As he parses out the convenience of utilizing languages depending on the necessary mode of digesting, investigating or expressing a given problem or solution, O'Muichin demonstrates how languages enable an individual to approach a material reality from various standpoints. Unlike McDonagh, who wishes to grudgingly deny Adams access to an Irish collective, O'Muichin's approach suggests a multifaceted sense of self – Adams' "I" – through the varied experience of multiple linguistic systems.

Unlike Deane's attention to Irish in *Reading in the Dark*, which avoids direct presentation of the language, Healy's work offers a few key moments where Irish is represented through phonetic means. When the Adams' first move to the Mullet they are quickly introduced to Irish:

"And there's a *gaeltacht* down the road," added the neighbor.
The Adamses went quiet.
Eventually Catherine said: "I'm sure they won't mind us."
"Why should they? They don't mind people that speak English. As a matter of fact they speak a little English themselves."
"They do?" said Jonathan Adams, astounded.
"They only speak the Irish among themselves." The neighbor smiled.
   "And in time you might pick up a word or two."
"Say something in Irish," asked Catherine.
"*Taim go math*," said the woman.

"*Taw im guh my,*" repeated Catherine, "What does it mean?"
"I am good," she replied.
"Not an appropriate beginning in a new language for you, Miss" said her father. (Healy 1994, 138)

This initial encounter betrays the Adams' sensitivity to their minority status on the Mullet. As they go "quiet" at the mention of the gaeltacht "down the road," and Catherine innocently says, "I'm sure they won't mind us," Healy demonstrates a redistribution of power. Had Matti Bonner spoken Irish in the house next door to the Adams' home in Fermanagh would they have hoped to not offend him? Healy's mapping of the Adams' reluctance to offend their new neighbors, matched with a genuine curiosity of the unknown, offers reprieve from the often stifling conditions of affiliation with Unionism and Nationalism. Sergeant Adams' astonishment that the gaeltacht dwellers "don't mind people that speak English," begins his long process of dismantling well nurtured prejudices of his Catholic, Free-State neighbors. And Catherine's ironic introduction to the language, with a clumsily rendered "Ta im guh my," enables Healy to phonetically represent the Adams' first contact with Ireland's native tongue. Catherine's mimic of the neighbor's, "Taim go maith," rewrites the annals of history, centuries later, as the settler population revisits the customs of their fourteenth-century predecessors who embraced Irish language and customs rather than attempting to destroy them like their sixteenth century counterparts.

In the novel, Sergeant Adams' affinity to Irish marked the end of a "persecution." He would not go "back to being a Loyalist again," as his daughters feared.

He had passed on into the role of elder from which the word Presbyter takes its name. They heard him, as they passed his door, reading out loud what they first took to be ancient Greek. *Vee shay, vee may, vee tu; vee shiv, vee ameed, vee adder. Cod taw harlaw? Cod ay sin? Kay will asti?* All day it went on. Questions. Exclamations. Entreaties.

In 1710 the first Presbyterian preachers, hounded by the High Church, began translating the Bible into Irish. True to that ecclesiastical republicanism which let the individual form his own government, Jonathan Adams had set up his own private republic.

In The Dwellings he began his first translations into Irish with the help of schoolbooks loaned by Joe Love's children. He began at the beginning. *He was, I was, you were. We were. They were. We all were. What happened? What is that? Who is within?* (Healy 1994, 166)

Through Ferris' reconstruction of Catherine's familial history, Healy again touches on the link between language and political autonomy. With the oral exposition of language, the verbose "vee shay," "vee may," "He was," "I was," Healy allows Adams' transformation to reverberate from the page. With each sounding, Adams builds "up his own private republic." He slowly emerges from the binary Nationalist / Unionist bind through emersion in both cultures, pairing his own evangelical compulsions with the "help of schoolbooks loaned by Joe Love's children." The conflation of his "role of elder" while starting "at the beginning," children's school books in hand, mirrors Healy's form. At once at the end and the beginning, Adams' proximity and distance suggests freedom and autonomy where there is seemingly none. As Adams resists his Loyalist tendencies, embracing the language and culture he fears, he rediscovers himself. And while he cannot escape the crowded proximity between languages, cultures and histories, in contemporary Ireland, his relationship to language allows him to renegotiate his own position. Although "Irish myths and antiquities had led him back inexorably, even contemptuously, to events in contemporary Ireland, a place where he did not want to be at all, having had his fair share of it in previous lives," Adams' journey though the repetitions of *"Ta may," "Cod ay sin?" "Who is within?,"* reposition relationships between individuals and an imagined collective, in the contemporary Irish state (Healy 1994, 174 & 166).

Although Deane claims, "Nothing is more monotonous or despairing than the search for the essence which defines a nation," *Reading in the Dark* and *A Goat's Song* suggest that each Irish man and woman may "build his (her) own private republic." Through the metaphors of language, Deane and Healy's novels pave an imagined road to individual autonomy, which may serve as the means for developing legitimate democracy in Ireland. While "the search for the essence which defines a nation" may in fact be an elusive, "monotonous" endeavor, Deane's and Healy's novels suggest that the answer to Adams' repetitious "Kay will asti?" may actually be outside. If the self defines the other, how can we learn the self without embracing our other?

3
Writing Republicanism: A Betrayal of Entrenched Tribalism in Belfast's Own Vernacular

It is a basic precept of modern democracy that politics should cater to the common good. What that precept means is that a democratic state is supposed to serve not a majority but the totality of its population. A democratic state is a community of privilege, not the privilege of a partial, majoritarian interest.

(Richard Bourke, " 'Imperialism' and 'Democracy' in Modern Ireland, 1898–2002")

I

Since the complete disbandment of the Provisional IRA in September of 2006, withdrawal of all British military presence in the region in accordance with the Good Friday Peace Agreement and the erection of a power-sharing government in Northern Ireland in May of 2007, the region's populations now share the challenge of reconciliation after decades of bloodshed and isolation. The journey to this pivotal crossroads has certainly been marked with serious challenges of failed ceasefires, multiple breakdowns in cross-communal talks and very slow economic growth in the late decades of the twentieth century but the region's political structure is slowly developing into a legitimate democracy. Today's Northern Ireland continues to distance itself from its historical precedent of a state built on Protestant privilege in the early decades of the twentieth century. If, as Bourke claims, it is a basic precept of modern democracy that "politics should cater to the common good...that a democratic state is supposed to serve not a majority but the totality of its population," how then can power-sharing in Northern Ireland fare in a society so heavily steeped in colonial traditions of privilege for the few at the expense of the masses and zealot nationalism to counter such traditions?

While concessions have certainly been made by all players in this conflict from the British and Republic of Ireland governments to the constituencies who support the Democratic Unionist Party, Sinn Fein and the Social Democratic Labour Party, amongst others, some very interesting changes have been underfoot in Northern Ireland's Republican communities since the early nineteen-eighties. Desperate to develop and assert electoral and cultural agency in a historically skewed political system and to distance their community from negative media portrayals throughout "The Troubles," writers, politicians and various community leaders have turned to cultural venues since the late nineteen-eighties to begin to articulate Republican communities' plights within a "Protestant state for a Protestant people." While these efforts have certainly been underway in communities across the region for decades now, this study will focus on Belfast.

In 1992 Gerry Adams released *The Street*, a collection of vignettes set in his own neighborhood of West Belfast. Adams claimed the endeavor was:

> A celebration of the people and the place it is about. Because everybody knows the other side of the killings and about the destruction and about the tragedy of this place and I wouldn't try and disguise any of that. People here survive these difficulties with a certain dignity and good humor, and if there is a sort of political sub-text to "The Street," it is a celebration of the people I refer to. (Jackson 1993, 2)

In an interview with *Sunday Age* reporter Andra Jackson, Adams went on to claim "I have tried to write in a very bare way and I wouldn't argue that this is great literature. I think it is certainly working-class literature and I consciously tried to use dialogue as much as possible." Unlike J.M. Synge's efforts to "speak" for the "country people of Ireland" in his turn of the twentieth century plays, Irish Republican writers of the late twentieth century, like Adams, turned to fiction and theater to speak as part of a minority population that they perceived as silent, amidst the bedlam of pulp fiction and media coverage of three decades of Northern Irish conflict. Throughout this period Republican communities in the North of Ireland were often characterized by rioting, record high levels of unemployment and a seemingly endless chain of conflict and violence with Protestant paramilitaries, police forces and the British military. Glimpses of life outside of these chief characteristics were usually unavailable to anyone living outside of the province. Although news reporters and government officials alike dutifully informed domestic and international audiences of the most recent party talks, bombings and sectarian killings, only sparse coverage gave any indication of the everyday existence of Northern Ireland's various and often isolated communities.[1]

Adams' efforts in publishing *The Street* as a "celebration of the people" of West Belfast marked a conscious effort to rewrite his community's public narrative. As he employed "dialogue as much as possible," Adams sought to legitimize his depiction of the community with a language system he seemed to assume as particular to this region of Northern Ireland and possibly to his specific enclave of Belfast. In this, Adams could craft a voice that literally came from the "people and the place that it is about" to mark the authenticity of his effort, to speak not for but as a member of this community. This proved a particularly potent political action in the early nineteen-nineties as Sinn Fein's popularity gradually grew and Adams slowly distanced the party from the day-to-day activity of the IRA. As Adams asserted a Republican parliamentary voice as a Sinn Fein MP and a cultural articulation of his working-class constituency's life experience in their own vernacular in *The Street*, Adams insisted on Republican participation in the region's historically skewed political system and deeply fragmented cultural terrain. But Adams' focus on representations of "dialogue as much as possible," an element shared by many though not all Republican writers of the period, not only came to mark the specific linguistic system of his community in Belfast but all of the communities in the area who share the particular language system of Belfast English. As Adams ensured his minority community a voice amidst Protestant populations accustomed to such privilege in the Northern Irish state, he, and writers like him, actually highlighted a shared cultural strand that inextricably links historically disparate Catholic and Protestant populations across the war-torn city.

Aside from the perpetual onslaught of media coverage of "The Troubles," fiction writing attending to the conflict in Northern Ireland saw a relative explosion between 1969 and the mid nineteen-nineties as more than 700 texts were published.[2] Initially penned by international writers whose research never mandated a life-threatening trip inside the war torn province, outsiders fed hungry imaginations with fictional details to fill gaps in the otherwise saturated media market. But such fiction writing often fueled already virulent propaganda wars as truth was spun to directly and indirectly propagate various and contesting political agendas. According to critics like Republican Patrick Magee:

> After a wide reading of this type of fiction for a doctoral thesis, the composite Irish republican to materialize was of a Mother Ireland-fixated psycho-killer, aka a Provo Godfather, readily discernible with recourse to an indentikit indebted to Tenniel's "Irish Frankenstein" and other images from *Punch* redolent of Victorian racism. Various permutations of the formula reveal a blarney-spouting thug with a "ferrety look" and halitosis, or, as a recent novel puts it, "the Fenian world of rotten teeth and puffy blotched skin." Obscured in this murky understanding, the violence attributed to republicans results from an ingrained bloodlust and is not the effect or symptom of a deeper political malaise. And when romantic nationalism, via Pearse's putative call for "blood sacrifice," doesn't provide the motivation for violence, then personal aggrandizement and enrichment, often through drug trafficking is frequently the slander of next resort. (Magee 2002, 2)

Drawing from the long history of Fenianism and Republicanism in Ireland's historic conflict with Britain and its settler population in the Unionists of Northern Ireland, writers could choose from a variety of Irish types to assemble their newest IRA villain with interspersed details from contemporary tragedies. Sensational anti-colonial rhetoric like that employed by Pearse in the late days of his militarism before the Easter siege of the General Post Office, enabled a link of one generation of Irish madness and compulsion towards violence to the most recent chapter of Ireland's struggle. According to Danny Morrison's reading of Magee's work,

> Pat's forensic analyses of the texts under review (a representative 150 out of some 700 published since 1969) reveals that in the use of language, staple plots, the stereotypical depictions of the various protagonists (IRA baddies / SAS goodies), most of the authors are actually witting or unwitting "players" in the propaganda war. Pulp fiction PROs for the British establishment or – as he ingeniously puts it, they represent "the paramilitary wing of Brit propaganda." (Magee 2002, v)

Despite the fact that many international writers may have "wittingly" or "unwittingly" been absorbed in such propaganda wars, the stakes began to change in the late nineteen-eighties and the early nineteen-nineties in a period where Republican writers decided to write their own community's story, contributing an assembly of voices conspicuously absent before this period. The notion of members of the Republican community re-writing their public narrative dramatically changed the dynamics of "Troubles Fiction" from a source of entertainment loosely connected to propaganda wars to a central battle ground for disseminating public images of their community in Northern Ireland's decades long tragedy.

In 1987 American journalist John Conroy released *Belfast Diary: War as a Way of Life*, a narrative offering intermittent glimpses of West Belfast's working-class neighborhoods. Residing predominantly in the Catholic district of Clonard, Conroy found himself lured again and again to the familiarity, and therefore relative security, of its ghettoized streets. Although his initial efforts were to report on Unionist and Nationalist communities, his repeated stays throughout the early nineteen-eighties in this predominantly Republican district offered a compelling picture of the particular challenges that this community faced from the eyes of an outsider:

> My neighbors are haunted by the living, haunted by the dead, haunted by myths and legends and history. The conflict defines their lives. Men and women say they are Catholic, describing not their churchgoing habits but their political beliefs: they are Irish, not British. And their lot grows worse each year. More go to jail. More are killed or maimed, and others are ruined by alcohol, unemployment, and despair. Yet many believe they are winning, that they are far closer now to a united Ireland than they were when the latest round of fighting began eighteen years ago. "The contest on our side is not one of rivalry or vengeance, but of endurance," said Terrence McSwiney, an IRA man who died on hunger strike in 1920. "It is not those who can inflict the most, but those who can suffer the most who will conquer."
>
> And in suffering, my neighbors have had a lot of practice. (Conroy 1987, 3)

While suffering was certainly a chief element of everyday life in Catholic working-class West Belfast, many in the district had reasons to "believe they are winning, that they are far closer now to a united Ireland than they were when the latest round of fighting began eighteen years ago." Despite unemployment levels as high as 86 percent by 1988, alcoholism, incarceration, poverty and bloodletting on almost every street corner, the "conflict" that had come to define Conroy's neighbors' lives was certainly at a turning point by the early nineteen-eighties.[3] A conflict steeped in the rhetoric of "suffering," propagated by early twentieth-century martyrs like McSwiney and the recent legacy of the Long Kesh Hunger Strikes in 1981, had slowly morphed from myths of blood sacrifice to a rudimentary though savvy political machine. By 1983 Republican West Belfast had a parliamentary voice in Gerry Adams (though quieted by absentionism), and by the late nineteen-eighties the political campaign for Republican representation was carefully negotiating its fragile and complex relationship with IRA violence. Although Conroy's recount of suffering amongst his Clonard neighbors offered a non-fiction, non-partisan depiction of a West Belfast Republican community, Adams' "celebration" of the intimate details of West Belfast's Republican community in dialogue centered prose in *The Street*, and Jake MacSiacáis, Danny Morrison, Brenda Murphy and Christine Poland's collaborative play "Binlids," were just two of several new literary works offering voice to an often silenced population that by the late nineteen-eighties was poised and ready to rewrite its own narrative.

II

Unlike writers like Healy and Deane, or Lady Gregory, Synge and Joyce, Republican writers of the late nineteen-eighties often wrote from positions of defense, attempting to fill a seemingly infinite void with the echoes of their first literary efforts. Work like Danny Morrison's *West Belfast* and *The Wrong Man* and Brenda Murphy's "Curse" sought to humanize and politicize IRA volunteers amidst unrelenting criticism and criminalization of actions associated with the organization's propagation of violence. These works in particular offered perspectives on some of the most tortured elements of the conflict so engrained in civil injustice, lack of political agency, police brutality, and rationales for the seemingly callous, unimaginable acts of violence characteristic of the IRA's campaigns. While such writing certainly changed the dynamics of "Troubles Fiction" with the toxicity of perceived authenticity, the focus still remained on Northern Ireland's violent streets and deeply entrenched divides that continued to appear irreconcilable. As Republican writers depicted fictional renditions of the unfamiliar or less publicized elements of their communities, however, their representations of wit, generosity and goodwill had the potential to dramatically change perceptions of these "terrorist neighborhoods."[4]

Although lines of sectarian and political division arguably ran deepest on the streets of Belfast where Peacelines separated (and continue to separate) neighboring communities for decades on end, both sides of the divide share a common and particular Belfast English vernacular. According to Alison Henry:

> One of the interesting characteristics of Belfast English is that, although Belfast is known to be in many ways a divided society, with often little contact between Protestant and Catholic communities, Belfast English is not distinguished, either phonologically or grammatically, along religious lines. All of the constructions discussed in this book are used by both communities, and where there is any distinction in usage, it is between working and middle-class speakers or older and younger speakers, rather than along religious lines. It is simply not possible to tell to which community persons belong by how they speak English. Belfast English is thus very much something which the communities have in common, something which tends not to be noticed because of two factors: First, the fact that the allegiance of one community to England (and Standard English), or sometimes to the rural Ulster Scots dialect with its clear Scottish roots, and the other to Ireland (and Irish) means that the local variety of speech is championed by no one. Second, and perhaps more important, this is a variety of English which has little status and which is not officially recognized. Schools, both Protestant and Catholic, devote a great deal of time to the teaching of "correct" (=standard) English, and the ability to use standard syntax is considered to be a mark of education; conversely the use of local syntax is considered a badge of the lack of education. (Henry 1995, 8)

Henry's articulate description of the linguistic landscape of contemporary Belfast exemplifies the deep connections between language use and identity formation in Ireland. According to Henry, Belfast English is "not distinguished either phonologically or grammatically, along religious lines." In fact, continual cultural and social disaffiliation from the "local variety of speech" that "is championed by no one," offers indication of political affiliations that are linked to Belfast English's parental language systems. Like representations of the heteroglossia of Irish-English discussed in Synge's, Joyce's, Deane's and Healy's work, Belfast's vernacular betrays the Northern Irish province's history of plantation and eventual colonization that led to the hybrid language system of Belfast English. Henry briefly delineates this progression in an effort to frame her analysis of the local, contemporary variety of Belfast English.

The irony of Belfast's divided communities sharing a particular strain of Irish-English points to inextricable historical links that undermine rhetoric of cultural, social or ethnic purity on either side of the sectarian line. According to Henry, Belfast's linguistic history is indebted to continued interaction between the region's native Irish populations and the Scottish and English settlers who arrived in the seventeenth century.

> English speakers in Belfast are largely monolingual, and there is no community of native Irish speakers in the area, although there is a small but growing number of Irish-medium schools for children whose parents wish them to be educated in Irish. For most Belfast English speakers Irish is a subject learned at secondary school if at all; there are few bilingual speakers, and thus any influence from Irish almost certainly derives from historical rather than contemporary, contact between the two languages.
>
> The English spoken in this area of Ireland descends largely from that introduced by the plantations of Ireland, when English and Scottish settlers came to Ireland in the seventeenth century, bringing their language with them. The local population at that time was Irish-speaking, and indeed quite a few of the settlers learned Irish. The use of Irish in the Belfast area had however died out by the end of the nineteenth century.
>
> The plantation took place on an extremely large scale; the census returns from 1658/9 show that of a total population of 31,221 in Antrim and Down, the counties which border Belfast, 13,614 were of English or Scottish descent. Although many of the settlers learned Irish, the introduction of such a large number of English speakers, who held the economic and political power, marked the beginning of the decline in the use of Irish in this area. (Henry 1995, 7)

Although many argue that history overshadows contemporary relations in Northern Ireland, deepening divides centuries in the making with the thumping of drums in Orange Order parades or the waving of green flags emblazoned with golden harps in Republican neighborhoods, Henry's delineation of the region's linguistic history is informed by continued interactions between these artificially separated communities. While Antrim's and Down's plantation was certainly a violent, unjust period marking a particularly tangible British presence in Ireland that led to a redistribution of political and cultural sway, irony lies in the contemporary adoption of vestiges of particular cultural and social trends of this period. In an effort to analyze the significance of Belfast's particular strain of English, Henry laments each community's seeming disregard for the local vernacular. She claims, "this is a variety of English which has little status and which is not officially recognized. Schools, both Protestant and Catholic, devote a great deal of time to the teaching of 'correct' (=standard) English, and the ability to use standard syntax is considered to be a mark of education; conversely the use of local syntax is considered a badge of the lack of education" (8). Despite political or religious affiliation, Standard English continues to serve as a language associated with power, capital, respect and class mobility in Northern Ireland. As the local vernacular is continually denigrated as "a badge of the lack of education" the standardized language of the colonial force continues to yield power over a population well into the twenty-first century.

As Standard English pronunciation, grammar and syntax are instituted as the norm in Belfast education on both sides of the sectarian divide, regardless of "the allegiance of one community to England (and Standard English), or sometimes to the rural Ulster Scots dialect with its clear Scottish roots, and the other to Ireland (and Irish)," it would seem any effort to catalog, analyze or highlight the vernacular form could be read as a challenge to the existing political, social and cultural trends in the region. In the course of Northern Irish history since the erection of the partitioned state in 1920:

> The Protestant interest in the province was identified by its government as a privileged portion within the democracy, against which the Catholic minority became *imperium in imperio* – or, in strictly modern parlance, a democracy within the democracy. That arrangement defined the existing situation quite precisely as an undemocratic state: Northern Ireland was not the common concern of a united population, but instead it became the particular privilege of a portion of its people.
>
> Curiously, the absence of a comprehensive democracy became a point of Protestant pride in the first phase of the Troubles: Stormont, at that time, was happily extolled as a "Protestant parliament" servicing a "Protestant state." In the presence of a system of majority government, this arrangement was allowed to masquerade as a point of democratic principle. In an organ of loyalist propaganda, the *People's Press*, published in August 1969, a motto was emblazoned

on the front page: "The People Chose Britain – We Are the People." Yet throughout the annals of democratic thinking, it has been an affront to the principle of democratic unity to convert a "majority" into a "people" by a spurious sleight of hand. Democracy, in fact, has always been defined by the principle of unanimity: *everybody* counts in a real democracy, although only a portion rules. (Bourke 2004, 115)

Northern Ireland's conflict, which erupted into violence after initial peaceful protest of Protestant privilege in the province's "democracy within the democracy," displayed all the characteristics of a militaristic quagmire by the mid-nineteen-eighties. The disbandment of Stormont more than a decade before hand, continued British occupation for almost two decades and escalating violence by 1988 with the Gibraltar killings, Protestant paramilitary attacks in Milltown Cemetery and the vicious murder of two off-duty British officers while cameras from various news agencies continued to roll in Catholic West Belfast, demonstrated that political rather than militaristic solutions were needed to resolve the region's conflict.

Contributing to the need for such social and cultural change were political gestures in the form of cross-party talks. Initially forged between the Social Democratic Labour Party leader John Hume and Sinn Fein's Gerry Adams, such interactions began to set the stage for some rudimentary changes in Northern Ireland's political landscape as parties on either side of the sectarian divide began to converse, laying the groundwork for eventual cross-sectarian interaction in the mid to late nineteen-nineties. Such efforts marked substantial challenges to the cultural normalcy of Protestant privilege in Northern Ireland's then virtually bankrupt democratic society and a very slow, incremental distancing from violence. Hume's and Adams' efforts demonstrated a Catholic insistence on the development of a true democracy, as Bourke defines, a political system defined by "the principle of unanimity: *everybody* counts in a real democracy, although only a portion rules." In order for such a principle to serve as the overriding spirit for the development of democracy in the Northern Irish province, significant cultural shifts in both Nationalist/Unionist and Catholic/Protestant communities would need to be well established before substantial support could be garnered for Northern Ireland's emerging changes in relations between communities scarred by decades of conflict. This is where the emergence of Republican writers in the late nineteen-eighties came to bear considerable significance in their own communities at first, and later in Northern Ireland at large.

Although Northern Ireland's democratic processes were guided by an allegiance to Protestant privilege entrenching centuries-long divides, Henry's investigation indicates that cities like Belfast exemplify a shared language system that deeply connects divided communities. As Belfast's Republican writers began to employ the local language system, shared by populations on either side of the Peacelines, as a mark of authentic representation of their particular community, they unwittingly highlighted a strand of commonality between their own communities and their Protestant/Unionist neighbors. This strand of a shared central component in each community's culture (even as Unionist populations may have theoretically strived towards mastery of Standard English and Nationalist communities sought training in Standard English and Irish) in Belfast English, also served as a mechanism for connecting communities based on class and levels of education attainment. As Republican writers like Adams have attended to their local communities, representing Belfast English speech patterns in prose where he "tried to use dialogue as much as possible," they solidify a literary connection between all of Belfast's communities who share this language system. Although their nationalist political end game differs greatly from their Unionist opponents, Republican writers' representations of everyday existence in Belfast's Catholic working-class districts from Clonard to the Falls to Ballymurphy probably *sound* remarkably familiar to their neighbors along the Shankill.

III

Gerry Adams' initial attempts to advertise *The Street* were greeted by stringent opposition in the Republic of Ireland as the national broadcaster RTE and the Independent Radio and Television Commission "rigidly interpreted government censorship laws denying airtime to Sinn Fein members in refusing to run an advertisement for the book that uses Adams' voice" (Jackson 1993, 1). Brandon Brooks, Adams' publisher, devised the script for the banned advertisements and later fought an unsuccessful battle in the High Court to overturn such censorship. Adams claimed "There is an on-going effort to marginalize and demonize Sinn Fein so the production of a book of fiction doesn't exactly fit into the type of image that the establishment is trying to project... the fact that RTE is making such a fuss about the whole thing is an indication of that." Although Adams' reaction was clearly biased, his reaction was not unfounded. Strong governmental efforts in Northern Ireland, Britain and the Republic of Ireland sought to marginalize

Sinn Fein's public voice through formal or informal censorship of various media outlets. From the late nineteen-eighties onward, elected officials in Northern Ireland whose parties were affiliated or in any way connected to proscribed paramilitary organizations were banned from radio and television airways throughout Britain, Northern Ireland and the Republic of Ireland. The bans were later extended to anyone who might support or advocate the work of such parties.

On 19 October 1988, Douglas Hurd announced "the most stringent controls imposed on the electronic media since the Second World War" in England (Maloney 1991, 3).

> Using powers under the BBC's Licence and Agreement and the 1981 Broadcasting Act which governs ITV companies, television and radio organizations were forbidden from carrying interviews or direct statements from proscribed paramilitary groups in NI, from representations of Sinn Féin, Republican Sinn Féin or the UDA and from those who "support or invite support for these organizations." (Maloney 1991, 3)

Although the government was instituting regulations widely used by media outlets like the BBC and ITV in regard to silencing paramilitary groups since the mid nineteen-seventies, the legislation's focus not only banned proscribed paramilitary groups in NI from the airwaves, but now reached to elected political officials in Sinn Fein, Republican Sinn Fein and the UDA, and most significantly to "those who 'support or invite support for these organizations.'" This reflected dramatic alterations to everyday practices in Britain's once free press. According to Maloney, Hurd's announcement marked

> a dramatic extension of censorship in Britain and NI, all the more so since the law had been explicitly employed to control what the public was able to listen to or view. Censorship had always existed in Britain but it was invariably a "nudge and wink" variety, arranged in the singular ways of the establishment or self-imposed by journalists, companies and regulatory bodies well aware of the limits to official tolerance. Having it formalized in a ministerial edict, written down in black and white was however an entirely different matter. It was redolent of the methods used in authoritarian antidemocratic states. As Kevin Boyle, director of the free speech group, Article 19, commented on the day the ban was announced: "Although the situation in South Africa is vastly different from the situation in Northern

Ireland, the means now being used by the British government to stifle debate – political censorship – is the same as the means used in South Africa." (Maloney 1991, 4)

The formalization of British regulation of media outlets' coverage of the conflict in Northern Ireland was certainly a symptom of continually escalating violence in the region by the spring of 1988, as well as British governmental frustration and despair at the growth of Sinn Fein's political popularity in Nationalist communities. By 1988, Gerry Adams was still the MP for West Belfast, but the party also boasted 55 councilor seats. Republican Sinn Fein had elected three councilors and the UDA had only attained one council seat. Hurd's announcement, therefore, had the most significant impact on Sinn Fein and its constituency as the British government sought to squeeze the life blood of Northern Ireland's most prolific paramilitary groups by any means necessary.

Hurd's announcement of stringent censorship of British media outlets was certainly no novel act in a long history of social and political control in Northern Ireland, however. According to Maloney:

> South Africa first introduced laws to control and limit freedom of expression in 1950. NI's own censorship regulations were thirty years older. They were contained in the 1922 Special Powers Act, a draconian law which empowered the Unionist Minister of Home Affairs to ban newspapers, films and books – as well as to intern without trial, ban political organizations, impose curfews and prohibit inquests. It was used from time to time to silence republican, nationalist and left-wing criticism of the government. In 1940, for instance, the *Derry Journal*, the nationalist newspaper of Derry, was banned, initially for six months, although it was lifted after a fortnight. (4)

Given the implementation of the Special Powers Act after the Civil Rights movement in late 1968 and well into the early 1970s in the forms of internment without trial, banning of political organizations, curfews and other sinister attempts to maintain a "Protestant state for a Protestant people," backed by a British military presence, Britain's new more stringent censorship bans on radio and television may have seemed par for the course. The Republic of Ireland's ban on advertising for Adams' work, while certainly disappointing to an individual whose political efforts focused primarily on reunification with the southern province, was certainly in keeping with that government's history of conservatism and censorship as well. But could these acts of censorship that attempted to limit public dissemination of Republican perspective on the conflict in Northern Ireland through radio and television outlets have directly or indirectly effected the small explosion of fiction texts released by Republican writers from the late nineteen-eighties through the nineteen-nineties? Was literature, no longer under the authoritarian thumb of the Northern Irish Special Powers Act, a venue for publicizing an alternative public narrative for the region's marginalized Republican communities? Or were these almost simultaneous circumstances mere historical coincidence?

Adams's advertisement was banned due to his direct affiliation with Sinn Fein. Although *The Street* was not a political organ for the controversial party, Adams' name (and voice, according to RTE) was so deeply intertwined with the organization that even a work of fiction brought forth the wrath of political censorship. While some references to Republican ideologies surface in this work that is a "celebration" of the largely Republican base in Catholic working-class West Belfast, the political potency of this work is actually in its focus on "dialogue." While Adams' self described "bare" style may or may not be considered "great literature," his focus on the language systems he clearly associates with "working-class literature" demonstrates an investment in the region's particular strain of Belfast English. This characteristic certainly challenges Henry's assertion that "this is a variety of English which has little status and which is not officially recognized," but it also challenges the value systems associated with a "Protestant State for a Protestant People" and the privileged status of Standardized English on either side of Belfast's sectarian divides. Although Adams' work was translated and published in Irish as well as English, and he employs Standard English as a mode of narration in several of the stories with interspersed token Irish phrases, the book largely catalogs Belfast English as the chief shared characteristic amongst the various characters inhabiting West Belfast's "streets." This emphasis on a local minority population, rather than an imagined Irish collective, marks considerable difference in Republican writers from most other contemporary Irish writers. If we consider the history of political suppression, class immobility, limited access to fair employment and sectarian discrimination in Northern Ireland's most impoverished Catholic districts, however, Republican writers' efforts to uplift their communities through literary representation come to symbolize an awakening of individual and communal participation in Northern Ireland's political and cultural forums that is arguably most profound in its complete disassociation from violence.

Adams' vignette, *She Says To Me*, crafts a glimpse of West Belfast's most virulent form of news dissemination aside from partisan newspapers: neighborhood gossip. Although Maisie and Aggie's interactions focus on oral exchange as the means for arriving at the truth of their mutual acquaintance Lily's fall from grace in their district, Adams' crafting of these characters' personalities relies exclusively on representation of dialogue. Unlike other stories in the collection, *She Says To Me* has no narrative framing. Lily's trajectory is conveyed entirely though Maisie and Aggie's exchange. And the details of Maisie's and Aggie's lives in Catholic West Belfast's working-class districts, the community's widespread economic struggles, societal plights like alcoholism and domestic violence and the overriding influence of the Catholic church, are all intertwined in the pair's seemingly mundane conversation over a "wee mouthful of tea" (Adams 1992, 23).

Instead of opening with a "blarney spouting thug" that Magee claims as characteristic of "Troubles Fiction" in the earlier decades of the conflict, *She Says To Me* begins with the rhythmic, compassionate voice of Maisie:

> "She never had her sorrows to seek. That's what I say. She always had it hard, so she did, even when others were getting it easy."
>
> "Ach, I wouldn't altogether agree with that, Maisie. Like, I'm the first to admit that she never got it aisy but then who did? Who around here did? Answer me that?"
>
> "Nobody did, but some got it harder than others and Lily was one of them, so she was. Sure you know that yourself, Aggie. You saw the way she was brought up. Her poor mother didn't get much help from oul' Davey."
>
> "She couldn't keep him out of the bloody pub!"
>
> "And was that her fault? Was it? Aggie, sometimes you get my wick! You'd think the rest of us married saints, so you would, to hear the way you talk. Let oul' Davey rest in peace. He did more harm to himself than he did to anybody else, and even if he did spend a lot of time in the pub we know that he wasn't on his own. There was always plenty there to keep him company, so there was. Drink was his problem all right, but one thing I'll say for him: drunk or sober he never lifted his hand to her or the children. How many could say that about their man these days?" (Adams 1992, 22)

In this initial exchange, evidence pertaining to Henry's claim of a shared linguistic system amongst all of Belfast's various populations is evident in the characteristics of Belfast English that Adams represents. Maisie's claim in defense of "oul' Davey" that "there was always plenty there to keep him company, so there was" demonstrates a disagreement in the subject-verb agreement that in Standardized English would be "there *were* always plenty there to keep him company" instead of the disagreement of "there *was* always plenty there." Henry describes this as a "singular concord," claiming:

> Singular concord is always optional; that is, it is always possible to have the plural form of the verb with a plural subject. As pointed out by Policansky (1976), it would therefore be more correct to use the term "variable concord;" However, it should be noted that the variability only exists for plural subjects; thus, while it is possible to use a singular verb when the subject is plural, as in (1) above [(1) These cars go / goes very fast.], it is not possible to use a plural verb with a singular subject.
>
> Singular concord is available for most speakers in all tenses of the verb which marks agreement: thus in addition to the present, it appears with the verb *be* in the past tense (*Be* is of course the only verb to show agreement in the past tense in English).
>
> [(6) The students was late]. (Henry 1995, 17–18)

In addition to the "singular concord" Henry cites as characteristic of Belfast English, there are phonetic elements like Aggie's pronunciation of *easy* as "aisy" and Maisie's repetition of assertions in the rhythmic "so she did" and "so there was." The exchange also displays elements often associated with Hiberno English. Although Henry claims "any influence from Irish almost certainly derives from historical, rather than contemporary, contact between the two languages" Adams' employment of "an unstressed syllable in initial position in conversational questions" as well as in answers to such lines of inquiry, demonstrate some vestigial influence from the parental Irish language system on contemporary Belfast English (Henry 1995, 7 & Todd 1989, 37). In Aggie's and Maisie's lines of questions, phrases such as, "Like, I'm the first to admit that she never got it aisy but then who did?" and "And was that her fault?" as well as "Sure you know that yourself, Aggie" demonstrate such characteristics. But the question then arises whether or not Adams has included such phrasing in an effort to authenticate an Irish social and cultural connection to differentiate his Catholic West Belfast characters from their sectarian or political counterparts, or if such representations of linguistic characteristics are merely efforts to faithfully "use dialogue as much as possible" to catalog a shared linguistic and political history that inevitably leads to a hybrid language system and society in Belfast?

Todd claims, "phonologically, Hiberno English speakers approximate to the Ulster Scots or Anglo-Irish norms of the area, but certain features of Gaelic are preserved" (36). This would seem to be the case with Adams' representation of Aggie and Maisie's speech patterns. In regard to speech patterns in Belfast in general, however, Todd claims "uneducated Belfast people often reveal their ethnic (and consequently their religious) affiliations in their preferred speech patterns...There is, however, a homogeneity about working-class Belfast speech which allows it to be instantly recognizable." The seeming contradictions of Henry's and Todd's work reflect the particular focus of their respective projects as Todd's relies primarily on a small sample of interviews and literary representations whereas Henry's is a comprehensive field study throughout Belfast's various districts across all class levels and ages. Their analyses, nonetheless, betray commonality in Belfast speech patterns in regard to class and educational attainment.

While Adams' work may represent some anomalies in Belfast's working-class language system to which Henry does not attend in her compartmentalized analyses of subject-verb agreement, overt-subject imperatives, *For-To* infinitives, inversion in embedded questions or subject contact relatives, Todd's and Henry's works do attend, respectively, to a shared linguistic system amongst Belfast's working class, which is consistent with work conducted by the Milroys. These elements of Hiberno-English, which Adams chooses to represent most likely mark historical vestiges from Gaelic in the region before the plantation of Ulster or they may reflect contact with outlying Gaeltachts throughout the region. Adams' representation of working-class speech patterns, in connection with the details of Aggie and Maggie's exchange, nonetheless, strategically place working-class Belfast as the focus for this vignette. This in turn triumphs the local working-class vernacular as a privileged language system, challenging the political and sectarian trends throughout Belfast that denigrate the local variation in favor of Standard English or Irish. This is not to say that Adams advocates the replacement of Irish or Standardized English with Belfast's vernacular. His work merely demonstrates that Belfast English is a predominant language system in the city, inscribing the system as integral to the local social, cultural and political fabric. Although Adams' efforts in this respect certainly bear characteristics of an early literary career in the levels of sophistication in the representation of such political subversion, Adams' efforts in *She Says To Me* are certainly some of the most striking and poignant in the entire collection.

Adams crafts a sense of a familiar story in Maisie's rendition of Lily's trajectory, a characteristic of the collection to which he hoped readers would respond, and that seemed all too familiar to the impatient Aggie.[5] In the cramped quarters of small row houses, stacked like cards throughout West Belfast, Lily's childhood is overshadowed by an alcoholic father, which, according to Maisie, was scandalous only in its lack of novelty in the district. Aggie accusingly claims Lily's mother was somewhat responsible since she couldn't "keep him out of the bloody pub!" But Maisie's emphatic response "And was it her fault? Was it?...There was always plenty there to keep him company, so there was" indicates the pervasive nature of alcoholism in one of the most impoverished communities in Western Europe. Lily's upbringing was clearly tarnished by poverty, alcoholism and the later revelation of an illegitimate son, but her father "never lifted his hand" to Lily's mother or her siblings. This is considered a rarity in Maisie's life experience. In these details of Aggie and Maisie's exchange, Adams reveals a central plot trajectory in Lily's story that seems to fall secondary to the characteristics of hardship in this impoverished, historically disenfranchised, underemployed and largely undereducated working-class community.

As Maisie praises Lily's father's refrain from lifting "his hand to her (Lily's mother) or the children," she then demands "How many could say that about their men these days?" Through Maisie's emphasis on Lily's father's saving grace in his ability to refrain from physically abusing his family, Adams' short story documents the proliferation of domestic violence in West Belfast. While his commentary could have focused on such societal trends in an environment of historical disenfranchisement and exposure to horrific violence for prolonged periods of time, he attends instead to female efforts to assert agency in such circumstances. Adams claims one charge he set for his collection was to "write women characters into the stories, consciously at the beginning, but then it became almost a matter of reflex...Most material you read, the characters are male and what I tried to do, to some extent, was to write women back in because women are the backbone of this community" (Jackson 1993, 2). This is evident in Maisie's emphatic tone and irresolute defense of the alcoholic and presumably unemployed "oul' Davey" who did "more harm to himself than he did to anybody else." Aggie's efforts to side with Lily's "poor mother" who "didn't get much help from oul' Davey," however, reflect an expected base level of human dignity where a man does not deserve praise or celebration just for never "lifting a hand" to harm his family.

Aside from alcoholism and domestic violence, Adams artfully reveals economic struggle in the district. In the course of their conversation Maisie states, "Here, take this cup off me. I'm scalded, so I am. There...That's better. Will you have a wee piece of cake? I've nothing in. You should have come next week. That's my pension week; this week is my bad week" (23). Adams demonstrates that Maisie is retired and dependent on a set income of limited means to cover the most basic of personal expenses. She is unflinchingly generous, however, offering Aggie a piece of cake though she has little else in the house. Tending to an emphasis on hospitality regardless of class, Adams' rendition of friendship and generosity in even the most impoverished of Northern Ireland's Catholic communities marks a certain dignity and pride denied to most Northern Irish Catholic working-class communities in other forms of public narrative.

Adams' work also documents significant blurring of lines between private and public spheres in Maisie's retelling of Lily's first illegitimate pregnancy:

"Is it true that her mother used to follow her about the place?"

"Aye, but only because she was worrying for her. Me mammy says Lily had a wee want in her, a wee weakness, and her mother knew this. I think it got worse after she lost the child. I remember hearing her mammy and ours talking one day and her mammy was saying that when you lose a child like that you have a wee craving inside you for another one. When I asked me Ma about it afterwards she told me I'd understand when I got older."

"Who's the father?"

"No one knows. Except for Lily, of course. I heard years later it was a married man from Leeson Street. Lily's mother always blamed poor Sean Dunne from one of the Rock streets. Sean was as innocent as a baby himself but Lily's mother gave him dog's abuse. She never gave him the light of day, shouting at him in the street and this, that and the other thing." (Adams 1992, 24)

In the cramped quarters of Adams' West Belfast "Street," a house's threshold does not necessarily mark the boundary between private and public spheres. Lily is not an independent being after departing from her family home as her "mother used to follow her about the place," publicly disgracing the young girl who had a "wee craving" for attention from men in the district. Just as she strives to protect Lily in the confines of her home from external influences of sexual relations, violence or any other lurking negative forces, Lily's mother attempts to expand her realm of protection, reaching beyond the privacy of the family home.

In the close confines of impoverished urban neighborhoods like that of West Belfast, the intimacy of crowded living quarters also blend public and private spheres of influence. Just as individual homes in West Belfast became public space throughout "The Troubles," susceptible to police and military raids and searches in the earliest hours of the morning that often led to destruction of property, harassment of inhabitants and sometimes violent conflict, the streets of these communities were privatized by inhabitants bursting out of their cramped homes but otherwise confined to their ghettoized streets. The street, therefore, becomes a region for social overspill for individual houses but the irony of this public space is the limited mobility of West Belfast's population outside of this tiny enclave. Lily's mother always blamed "poor Sean Dunne" who is instantly associated with his home on "one of the Rock streets" and Lily's rumored lover remains nameless but he is associated with Leeson Street. As Lily's mother spouts "dog's abuse," blaming Dunne for her daughter's illegitimate pregnancy, "shouting at him in the street and this, that and the other thing" Adams not only points to a mother's effort to protect a seemingly wayward child, but it also demonstrates one of many ways in which the public space of "the street" has been usurped for interactions that would be considered intensely private in middle-class society. While Lily's mother is scandalized for such behavior, even by the patient Maisie, the frequency of such occurrences seem to be as expected and almost characteristic of the district in the same vein as the predominance of an alcoholic father like "oul' Davey."

The scandal of Lily's second illegitimate pregnancy compounds the permeability of public and private space when Lily actually reveals the identity of her child's father. Amidst the sensation of this neighborhood melodrama, Adams focuses on gossip as a form of information dissemination.

> "Anyway, a year or so later Lily was pregnant again. Only this time she told everybody and her family and all of us helped her, so we did. The only thing was the fella she said was the one that done it: he said it wasn't him."
>
> "Typical! Was he married too?"
>
> "No, not at that time. I might as well tell you his name. It was big Sammy Mallon."

"Big Sammy? Nora McCluskey's man? Him?"

"Aye, he was a fly man in them days. All the girls were dying about him, so they were. Like, I don't know what they saw in him. It was said if you spat in the street you were bound to hit one of his children. But he denied making Lily pregnant."

"And did he?"

"Of course he did. Lily thought the sun rose and shone on him. She would have done anything to get him. Like I said before, she was a wee bit foolish that way. Sure he wasn't fit to clean her arse. He was the road to no-town. He actually came round to see me, so he did; he was never short on cheek. He knew Lily and I were very close. He swore to me it wasn't his child, that he hadn't been seeing Lily for over four months. I told him that I had seen the two of them together on Halloween, which is the night she conceived, and he got all flustered." (Adams 1992, 25)

As Maisie reveals the past injustices and troubles Lily faced as a young woman, she attempts to correct the false information disseminated through the informal channels of gossip. Although "Big Sammy" denied his connection to his child indefinitely, Maisie claims authority on the subject assuredly answering Aggie's "And did he?" with an emphatic "Of course he did." Ironically, Maisie corrects Lily's public legacy in the privacy of her own home with Aggie where neighborhood gossip has almost been transformed into urban legend in this story telling session with the significant distance of time.

Adams' insistence on the importance of oral exchange within his community, however, again challenges the public dissemination of information in Belfast on either side of the sectarian divides. Maisie attempts to salvage Lily's reputation by disseminating the *true* narrative of Lily's hardships in her conversation with Aggie. And in this process Adams again introduces elements of Belfast English with the non-standard construction of "them days" instead of Standard English *those days*, as well as Maisie's habitual and rhythmic reassertion of claims with "and all of us helped her, so we did" and "He actually came round to see me, so he did." Additionally, Maisie's revelation relies heavily on judgments delivered in metaphors like "he was the road to no-town" and particularly crass phrasing in statements like "It was said if you spat in the street you were bound to hit one of his children." In combination with the grammatical constructions that mark Belfast English as a non-standard vernacular, these statements can be associated with a Belfast working-class culture. Maisie's metaphor for Sammy as "the road to no-town" demonstrates how profoundly a woman's affiliation with a particular man would define her life-trajectory in this community in this period: "No-town" marking a future of despair and waywardness that she seems to wish on no one. And her crass repetition of Sammy's reputation as a particularly virulent and irresponsible father to many children in the district criminalizes his behavior that brought such hardship on Lily. As he compiles multiple factors to identify particular characteristics of Catholic working-class Belfast that is evident in Maisie and Aggie's dialogue, Adams challenges the linguistic and political privilege of Standard English in the region.

Unlike other vignettes collected in *The Street*, *She Says To Me* makes no reference to the political or violent legacies of "The Troubles" in Catholic West Belfast. It is a seemingly ordinary story where a young woman is subjected to neighborhood scrutiny and judgment for promiscuity, where her parish priest "did everything but call her a hoor." But in Maisie's estimation it is also a story of redemption. The story ends with the tender notion of Lily finally finding "a bit of love and affection and dignity." As Aggie asks "How would she get that now, Maisie?" Maisie replies with the seemingly obvious "From her grandson, Aggie, from her grandson. Everybody loves a granny, Aggie. Don't they?" (Adams 1992, 27). And in these final phrases, Adams points to the heart of a domestic, intensely private sphere of influence in West Belfast that has not previously been penetrated for public scrutiny. While homes and streets were infiltrated by political and social struggle, Adams' story demonstrates an effort to preserve and highlight whatever is left of familial intimacy. Although Lily's trajectory does not coincide with traditional familial values in Catholic Ireland as she raises her fatherless son and remains unmarried, she nonetheless finds some peace in the family unit that seems unscathed by Belfast's war-torn contemporary. While Adams' work refuses to romanticize his community's economic and social depravities, stories like *She Says To Me* mark admiration and pride in the local language and value system of resilience and generosity.

Adams' work may not advocate a triumph of Belfast English over the parental languages of the region in Standardized English and Irish, but his catalog of the region's vernacular system that he associates most particularly with his community unwittingly connects a ghettoized population to all of Belfast society. It is difficult to determine how conscious such elements are in Adams' work. Clearly, the dialogue is used as a tool to identify his particular, historically silenced community. But to what degree can Adams acknowledge Belfast's shared vernacular without undermining the nationalist premise of enabling his community to speak through the veil of fiction?

The strength of Adams' collection is in his effort to highlight characteristics of his West Belfast community that were simply omitted, ignored or silenced in the decades of "The Troubles." Vignettes like *She Says To Me*, *A Safe Bet*, *Phases* and *Just A Game* illustrate that everyday life can and does continue in the shadows of war and violence, humanizing a community often ostracized in public forums. Adams' involvement in the various political, social and cultural permutations of Catholic activism during "The Troubles," however, infiltrates several other stories, precariously compromising the artistic integrity of each of the works. In *Belfast Diary*, Conroy claims:

> While the British call the Provos thugs, criminals, mindless psychopaths, the unemployed and the unemployable, and Protestants see them as sectarian assassins, Catholics see the IRA as something else entirely. To a Catholic, an IRA man is not some outsider causing violence and death, but Sean down the street, or Mickey, whose father was interned, or Mrs Sands' son Bobby. There is a definite ambivalence in the Catholic community; most Catholics support the IRA's goal of a united Ireland, but condemn the IRA's means.
>
> The only evaluation of the IRA by disinterested observers, based on statistics and hard data, that I am familiar with can be found in the book *Ten Years on in Northern Ireland*, a 1980 report written by three academics, published by the Cobden Trust, a London-based civil liberties foundation. The authors – Kevin Boyle, Tom Hadden, and Paddy Hillyard – analyzed 300 terrorist trials and concluded that "the bulk of Republican offenders are young men and women without criminal records in the ordinary sense." The authors went on to say that those Catholic men and women who were tried of terrorist offenses were "reasonably representative of the working class community of which they form a substantial part...They do not fit the stereotype of criminality which the authorities have from time to time attempted to attach them...The pattern of recruitment demonstrates the essentially communal nature of the movement and its close relationship to the political aspirations of the Catholic community and the continuing deprivation and discrimination which it experiences." (54)

Adams' work in *The Street* that directly attends to the violence and political strife of "The Troubles," marks an effort to echo Conroy's findings and those of the *Ten Years on in Northern Ireland* study that he cites. In vignettes like *The Rebel, Civil War, Shane,* and *Granny Harbinson* Adams demonstrates that the IRA was an assembly of volunteers locally known as "Sean down the street, or Mickey, whose father was interned." Adams represents such intimacy through the particular language system of Belfast English throughout the collection, interspersing his presentations of everyday life amidst "The Troubles" by activists and "ambivalent" Catholic supporters in the community. His work also demonstrates the difficulty for many individuals in the community to demonize or ostracize such individuals based on their involvement during "The Troubles" after sharing the same "street" for generations. In the "absence of a comprehensive democracy" that had become a "point of Protestant pride in the first phase of the Troubles," Adams' work points to the profoundly tight-knit community of a working-class Catholic population that was well practiced in historically quiet "suffering" and isolation with no one to turn to but one another.

As Adams and other Republican writers of the late nineteen-eighties and the early nineteen-nineties have attempted to illustrate the complex loyalties and dignities of their own communities, they have often sought to humanize and valorize those who have supported the goal of a united Ireland as the means for legitimate democratic representation after decades of disenfranchisement under a Protestant majority in Northern Ireland. But according to Magee:

> Republicans generally are perhaps still too close to events which for them represent an ongoing, continuous traumatic stream. This is reflected in the quite narrow concentration of issues and themes in the fiction written by republicans: security; the experience of interrogation, imprisonment, the dislocation of family and relationships. Another common factor is the focus on events from the earlier years of the contemporary conflict, partly explainable because some of the novels have an autobiographical dimension, being influenced by personal involvement and a continuing political commitment. Typically, the narratives are set in the 1970s or 1980s, when authors were active and before imprisonment. The experience of conflict was still too raw for these authors who in common took part in the struggle. (2002, 201)

As Magee states, this has also led to a relative narrowing in the scope of content for the first generation of Republican writers emerging from "The Troubles." Such characteristics are strikingly apparent, however, in

Adams' vignette *The Mountains of Mourne*. The premise for the story is certainly interesting and demonstrates some potential, but Adams' close proximity to the Republican movement and the seeming biographical content for the story leads to a predictable and fairly lifeless delivery in comparison to stories like *She Says To Me*.

The Mountains of Mourne represents an effort to depict cross-communal and cross-sectarian interaction between the Protestant Geordie Mayne and his young Catholic counterpart operating under the false name of Joe Moody. Staged in the early nineteen-seventies, Adams' story serves as something of a superficial list of commonalities between the disparate communities that suffer from decades of estrangement. Although Geordie from the Shankill and Joe from the Falls would seem to have little in common, their shared employment delivering spirits throughout the Northern province not only forces each to frequent the other's ghettoized community but most of the story focuses on neutral territories from the Belfast city center to the Mourne Mountains that are available for any population to explore. Throughout the story, however, Geordie's lack of texture and depth as a character demonstrate that after decades of violent struggle, Adams can depict precious little in the way of a detailed character sketch of his Protestant, working-class counterpart. Strangely, Adams does not represent Belfast English in dialogue for either Joe or Geordie throughout the story aside from a few catch phrases tossed in intermittently. While their conversations are in a vernacular form, there are few characteristics in their dialogue that would actually mark the language system as particular to Belfast. In juxtaposition to this Adams does use the symbolism of language systems to mark Irish and British contingents in the story, though they are not necessarily integral to the plot line.

After a visit to Geordie's house, which "was no different from ours. A two bedroomed house with a toilet in the backyard and a modernized scullery. Only for the picture of the British Queen, I could have been in my own street," Joe then "walked down to the corner and gazed along the desolation of Cupar Street up towards what remained of Bombay Street. A British soldier in a sandbagged emplacement greeted me in a John Lennon accent. "Lo, moite. How's about you?" (Adams 1992, 45). Registering a phonetic system that is seemingly foreign for both Joe and Geordie, the British soldier's voice marks an outside presence in an enclave of Belfast familiar to Joe only from the neighboring Catholic side. Although Adams does not represent Belfast's shared non-standard language system in this story, the lack of this presentation marks a level of commonality between Joe and Geordie. The British soldier's

"John Lennon" accent is affiliated with an external culture and political system that has imposed on the "bleak pitifulness" of a domestic conflict, further complicating an already bankrupt political system. Geordie distances himself from the destruction along Bombay Street and Cupar Street in the region between Clonard and the Shankill, where Catholic homes were burned out by Protestant mobs in the early years of the troubles. When Joe climbs back into their delivery van Geordie says,

> "By the way," he said, "I wasn't there that night."
> There was just a hint of an edge in his voice.
> "I'm sorry! I'm not blaming you," I replied. "It's not your fault."
> "I know," he told me firmly. (2002, 45)

Although British soldiers were initially deployed to protect all of Northern Ireland's citizens, extensive reports claim the military did not attempt to intervene in these acts (Conroy 1987). Geordie's claim, "I wasn't there that night" demonstrates an effort to distance himself as an individual from mob acts attributed to all working-class Protestants in Belfast. Joe's reply, "I'm not blaming you" demonstrates an effort to see Geordie as an individual despite cultural and social pressure to comply with well nurtured prejudices. But Geordie's emphatic "I know" may also demonstrate his own discomfort with the escalation of hatred in Belfast fueled further by such widespread destruction.

Adams' stiff depiction of the fairly contrived conversations between Joe and Geordie is consistent with discomfort demonstrated earlier in the vignette. As soon as Adams decides to step out of the comfort zone of his Catholic community where he can confidently speak with and for those silenced in his community in stories like *She Says To Me*, the wear of the conflict becomes readily apparent. In the opening of *The Mountains of Mourne*, Adams' indulgent narrative in Joe's voice demonstrates a use of Standardized English consistent with other narrative sections in the collection, which may betray an assumed connection between authority and this language system as has been documented in Henry's work. The content, more so than the representation of a language system in this case, however, seems to almost bewitch Adams as writer into Adams as politician and member of the Catholic working-class Falls community. These passages demonstrate a seeming inability to imagine or create a complex vision of his local Belfast "other."

> Often bemused by expressions such as Catholic street and Protestant area, I find myself nonetheless using the very same expressions. How

could a house be Catholic or Protestant? Yet when it comes to writing about the reality it's hard to find other words. Though loath to do so, I use the terms Catholic and Protestant here to encompass the various elements who make up the Unionist and non-Unionist citizens of this state.

It wasn't my intention to tell you all this. I could write a book about the *craic* I had as a child making my way in and out of all those wee streets on the way back and forth to school or the Boys Confraternity in Clonard or even down at the Springfield Road dam fishing for spricks, but that's not what I set out to tell you about. I set out to tell you about Geordie Mayne of Urney Street. Geordie was an Orangeman, nominally at least. He never talked about it to me except on the occasion when he told me that he was one. His lodge was The Pride of the Shankill Loyal Orange Lodge, I think, though it's hard to be sure after all this time.

I only knew Geordie for a couple of weeks, but even though that may seem too short a time to make a judgment I could never imagine him as a zealot or a bigot. You get so you can tell, and by my reckoning Geordie wasn't the worst. (Adams 1992, 40)

Adams as Moody demonstrates a certain level of resignation, a compliance with a local vocabulary (rather than a linguistic system) that has been shaped and institutionalized after decades of Northern Irish conflict. Much like Adams' lack of representation of Belfast's local language system throughout *The Mountains of Mourne* that fails to document the specific characteristics of a shared vernacular system between Joe and Geordie, Adams' rendition of Joe's introduction to his story about an Orangeman, in name only, depicts a similar fatigue in resisting stereotypical language to identify Belfast's disparate factions of the community. Joe claims that he is often "bemused by expressions such as Catholic street and Protestant area" but he justifies their use because "it's hard to find other words." While of course it is challenging to develop a particularized vocabulary that has the potential to undermine the proliferation of language that contributes to rather than detracts from Northern Ireland's conflict, Adams' Moody fails miserably to even attempt such subversive efforts. In this Adams too falls short of his own charge to "celebrate" the people of his district.

While it is difficult to identify the chief factors in Adams' stage-like sketching of Geordie, it seems Adams' work in this story exemplifies Magee's assertion that "Republicans generally are perhaps still too close to events which for them represent an ongoing, continuous traumatic stream." While Adams' efforts to depict cross-communal dialogue are important in their symbolic resonance and in the potential for other writers to build upon and fully exploit such trajectories, his efforts in *The Mountains of Mourne* are uncharacteristically clumsy in comparison to some of the other vignettes. Perhaps this betrays the long term effects of Adams' community's isolation. It is safer to imagine the Orangeman who may not actually be a bigot than to engage with him to find a way to share more than just a language system.

As Geordie and Joe approach the Mountains of Mourne in their wintertime adventure between deliveries, they happen upon Paddy O'Brien who is in need of a "lift" from a rural pub to his substantially more rural home town on Christmas Eve. In Paddy, Adams interjects substantial representations of Northern Irish bilingualism that rivals the symbolic significance of the "Lennon" accented British soldier. This comes to serve as the pivotal exchange in Joe's and Geordie's interactions and interestingly serves as only one of few moments where Joe and Geordie exhibit any characteristics of the local Belfast vernacular in any of their dialogical exchanges.

> There's only one thing you can't see from Donard, and many people can't see it anyway although it's the talk of the whole place, and even if it jumped up and bit you it's not to be seen from up there among all the sights. Do yous know what I'm getting at, boys? It's the cause of all our cursed troubles, and if you were twice as high as Donard you couldn't see it. Do yous know what it is?
> We both waited expectantly, I with a little trepidation, for him to enlighten us. "The bloody border," he announced eventually. "You can't see that awful bloody imaginary line that they pretend can divide the air and the mountain ranges and the rivers, and all it really divides is the people. You can see everything from Donard, but isn't it funny you can't see that bloody border?" I could see Geordie's hands tighten slightly on the steering wheel. He continued smiling all the same.
> "And there's something else," Paddy continued. "Listen to all the names: Slieve Donard, or Bearnagh or Meelbag or Meelmore – all in our own language. For all their efforts they've never killed that either. Even most of the wee Orange holes: what are they called? Irish names. From Ballymena to Ahoghill to the Shankill, Sughrim, Derry and the Boyne. The next time yous boys get talking to some of them Belfast Orangemen you should tell them that."

"I'm a Belfast Orangeman," Geordie told him before I could say a word. I nearly died, but Paddy laughed uproariously. I said nothing. I could see that Geordie was starting to take the needle. We passed through Kilkeel with only Paddy's chortling breaking the silence.

"You're the quare *craic*," he laughed. "I've really enjoyed this wee trip. Yous are two decent men. *Tá mise go han buiock daoibh, a chaired.* I'm grateful to you indeed."

"*Tá failte romhart,*" I said, glad in a way that we were near his journey's end.

"Oh, *maith an fear,*" he replied. "*Tabhair dom do lámh.*"

We shook hands.

"What d'fuck's yous two on about?" Geordie interrupted angrily.

"He's only thanking us and I'm telling him he's welcome," I explained quickly. "Shake hands with him!"

Geordie did so grudgingly as the old man directed him to stop by the side of the road…

"*Go n'éirigh an bother libh,*" he said. "May the road rise to meet you."

"And you," I shouted, pulling closed the van door as Geordie drove off quickly and Paddy and his box vanished into the shadows.

"Why don't yous talk bloody English," Geordie snarled savagely at me as he slammed through the gears and catapulted the van forward. (Adams 1992, 52)

Although Joe claims that Geordie is not a bigot or a zealot, Adams demonstrates the potential toxicity of sectarian and political affiliation in the symbolism of language in this passage. As aforementioned, language plays little role in this vignette until this moment where Adams places elements of Hiberno-English, Irish and only token elements of Belfast English in juxtaposition in to one another (Standardized English is employed only as a narrative system). Nothing remarkable is presented in this exchange, however. It only offers glimpses of anger and frustration as each participant attempts to assert his identity.

Paddy's dismay about the symbolic resonance of an arbitrary border that is invisible but all-pervasive in Northern Irish relations makes Geordie predictably uncomfortable. It is presumed in much Unionist and Orange Order lore that the border serves as a measure of protection for the region's Protestant minority. It is a boundary sanctioned by the British government that signifies Protestant dominance in a Northern Irish province, secure from the Republic's Catholic majority. Nationalist and Unionist affiliations become polarized, however, once Paddy opens remarks on his understanding of the resilience of the Gaelic parental language system in Northern Ireland that continues to exude its influence even in the "Orange holes." As he states "Listen to all the names: Slieve Donard, or Bearnagh or Meelbag or Meelmore – all in our own language," Adams fashions a mouthpiece of almost mythic Gaelic revivalist sentiments that eventually provoke Geordie. Paddy then launches into a flood of Irish pleasantries to which Joe dutifully responds in Irish, characteristic of Republican Irish language revivalism and preservation during "The Troubles." While this shared language system comes to serve as a bonding element between Joe and Paddy, Geordie is estranged. His response, "What d'fuck's yous two on about?" that is followed up by the slightly angrier and possibly desperate, "Why don't yous talk bloody English" mark some of the only elements of Belfast English that appear throughout the story. Geordie's use of "yous" demonstrates a plural construction particular to Belfast English that often manifests as "ye" in Irish-English but would be the plural inflection of "you" in Standardized English.

Although such a representation would mark a common language system between Joe and Geordie, Joe seems to relish in the novelty of his Irish exchange with Paddy. Rather than offering any glimpse of social or political transgressions in this scenario, Adams' representation, like Joe's lament at the difficulty in finding "other words" to describe Northern Ireland's conflict, demonstrates resignation to "using the same expressions" or convenient stereotypical representations of a Catholic/Protestant or Nationalist/Unionist interaction that masquerades as a remarkable exchange only in each character's refrain from bigotry or violent extremism.

Adams' work in *The Street* and that of his fellow Republican writers is important to the development of a legitimate democracy in Northern Ireland in that it contributes to the cultural, social and political confidence of Catholic working-class communities throughout the region who suffered innumerable injustices in the state of Protestant privilege established with the Anglo-Irish treaty. Adams' work is particularly subversive in its challenge to the privileging of Irish or Standard English only in Catholic and Protestant, Unionist and Nationalist communities throughout Northern Ireland as his work demonstrates a living, politically significant language system in the local vernacular of Belfast English. Inconsistencies in the representation of such potentially revolutionary characteristics in his work may be influenced by Adams' relative inexperience as a fiction writer. Or, as Magee claims, they may be symptomatic of his proximity to Belfast's political, social and cultural strife, which could hinder his ability to imagine or represent caveats to the region's binaries of affiliation.

Much like the early "Troubles Fiction" writers who "wittingly or unwittingly" contributed to fervent propaganda wars, Adams work, like that of many Republican writers, ironically illustrate close links between Catholic working-class communities and their Protestant working-class neighbors. As these writers speak out for their communities, "celebrating" resilience in the face of economic depravity, violence and limited access to ample employment and education, they often touch on haunting commonalities amongst all of Belfast's working class that move far beyond a shared language system. Just as Joe discovers that Geordie's house was "no different from ours. A two bedroomed house with a toilet in the backyard and a modernized scullery. Only for the picture of the British Queen, I could have been in my own street," Adams' work, and that of other Republican writers, could potentially serve as a catalyst for political and social affiliation based on a shared working-class experience rather than the historically divisive binaries of sectarian and nationalist associations that continue to haunt the region.

IV

Although fiction certainly played a pivotal role in the re-writing of Belfast's Republican communities' public narratives, theater has also served as an influential venue for expression in Northern Ireland at large and Belfast specifically. In 1997 Jake MacSiacais, Danny Morrison, Brenda Murphy and Christine Poland's "Binlids" was first staged by Dubbeljoint Theater Co. under the direction of Pam Brighton. Like Adams' *The Street*, the collaborative work by four Republican activists from Belfast demonstrates an imagined chorus of voices attending to the enclaves' public narrative in the wake of saturated media coverage and pulp fiction. Its premier in 1997 marked a period of fatigue with violence, hope for peace and a particularly uncertain future for all players in Northern Ireland. But the play insists on a spirit of "celebration" that Adams articulates in regard to his work, in an effort to negotiate a platform for a population once silenced to finally tell their story.

The play's general emphasis on informal communication practices begins in its staging. Firstly, the audience is asked to stand up for the duration of the show unless individuals are too infirm, elderly, etc. to do so. Secondly:

> There is no stage to which one's focus is drawn; there are five stages spread about the auditorium. The "action" doesn't begin on any of them, but rather with actors milling among the standing audience in what becomes, in essence, a town square. They pass along news of the "internments" – pre-dawn raids in which British troops arrested and detained, without trial, hundreds of Catholics in West Belfast on "suspicions". (Gutman 1)

From the opening scene, the audience is not only asked to join in the production of "Binlids" in their participation in assembling a "town square" but they are actually embraced as part of the West Belfast community who have not yet learned the local history. The play's ambition is apparent, then, as the predominantly female characters disseminate the local version of the community's almost thirty year history during the course of "The Troubles" through intermittent conversations, gossip, family disputes and run-ins with the British military and the Northern Irish police forces. On a very basic level, the production is a democratizing mission in its effort to place the audience literally on equal footing with the actors but also in its effort to forge levels of intimacy in the traditionally public space of a theater. And the almost emphatic insistence on local social, political and cultural trends is evident in the writers' attention to detail in regard to speech patterns, vocabulary usage, and a feeling of almost claustrophobic intimacy in the district (and due to the configuration of the theater for this production) that enables considerable interdependence between individuals and families. This is crystallized in the audience's almost uncomfortable proximity to the "action" of the play but also signifies the community's isolation (just as the theater doors separate the audience from the world outside) amidst the violence of "The Troubles."

"Binlids'" careful staging, according to critics like Les Gutman, "is hardly comfortable, either physically or otherwise." As audience members are drawn into West Belfast's community, actors assume authority on a local narrative that is portrayed as inaccurate or incomplete without a local retelling or contribution. In response to the play, Adams claimed:

> It appears to me that part of the process of creating peace includes, and needs, people reclaiming their own stories and telling their own tales. This has to be a part of any healing process. Getting others to listen then becomes the other part. The sum total of all the parts – all the stories and the understanding of the stories in their totality – is

what peace and the makings of peace will be all about. (Gutman 1998, 2)

Under the direction of Pam Brighton, the collaborative writers of "Binlids" create a space in which an audience is compelled to "listen" to initial attempts for a community to "reclaim" their "own stories" and to tell their "own tales." Adams' vocabulary, laden with the detail of fiction in reference to "stories" and "tales," seems to indirectly attend to the subjective nature of such narratives in any "healing process." Yet he unflinchingly insists on the necessity of an opportunity for any population to articulate their grievances for peace to prevail. He does, however, insist on the need for audiences to then "listen." As he claims that "the sum total of all the parts – all the stories and the understanding of the stories in their totality – is what peace and the makings of peace will be all about," he demonstrates that plays like "Binlids" and many others in the political Northern Irish genre attending to the legacy of "The Troubles" really only mark a first stage in this historical, cultural and political process of peace and reconciliation.

The role of "truth telling" and the "reclamation of stories" in post-conflict societies is a complicated subject to which literary representations thereof can only attend in a limited manner.[6] In the context of "Binlids," the authors' primary focus on female narratives in West Belfast during "The Troubles" attends to a little told history. With the historical framing of a working-class Catholic population emerging from the political and cultural dominance of a "Protestant state for a Protestant people," the premise for such a population to tell "their own tale" assumes that the majority population has not only usurped the political and social infrastructure but has also determined which population can and will tell their respective histories. This would certainly be in keeping with the trajectory of censorship, incarceration, militaristic occupation and draconian police measures in working-class Catholic districts throughout Northern Ireland but how were such measures executed in working-class Protestant districts following the banishment of Stormont as the province fell under direct British rule for decades? The historical record demonstrates that police brutality, military raids, incarceration, unemployment and all of the other plights of "The Troubles" certainly impacted Catholic populations with considerably more fervor than their still somewhat privileged Protestant counterparts but how do representations of "truth-telling" like "Binlids" begin to address the complicated political, cultural and social terrain in Belfast as the region teetered on the brink of what came to be an enduring peace?

One of the most striking elements of "Binlids" is the authors' emphasis on the role of women in Republican communities throughout "The Troubles." As hundreds and later thousands of Catholic men and a small number of women were incarcerated for "suspicious" activity (though some were arrested for considerably more egregious violent acts), women were compelled to ensure the community would not fall apart. This is emphasized in many instances throughout the play but the scene, "Duck Patrols are Born," demonstrates events that led to the play's namesake. As women in the community despair as males are strategically rounded up in the first wave of internment in August of 1971, Sue asks Niamh, "But isn't there something we could do to stop them getting lifted?" (MacSaicáis et al. 21). The conversation that ensues illustrates the idea of using bin lids, banged on street pavement, to serve as a warning signal that British military infantry or RUC officers are in the vicinity and that raids, searches or arrests are probable. This development was significant as it gave women a non-violent venue for resisting such governmental efforts to control the enraged working-class Catholic population but the manner in which the playwrights present such developments again betray Magee's warning that some Republican writers may still be too close to the "continuous traumatic stream" that often was "The Troubles."

In the depiction of "Duck Squads," "Binlids'" writers offer representations of Belfast English that serve as examples of the population telling their own "tale" of experience during "The Troubles."

PATRICIA: I am starving.
VERA: I know. Mary, who is on the next shift?
SUSIE: My feet is killing me, Patricia.
Mary takes a book out and shines her flashlight on it.
MARY: Hold on girls, you still have another hour to go yet.
VERA: Sure by the time we get the next lot up out of bed our hour will be up.
Everyone laughs.
MARY: Right, you and Vera go and get a cup of tea and toast and me and Susie will keep watch until yous are finished. Ten minutes girls, no more, do you hear me!
VERA: No problem, Mary. Who's house is it anyway tonight?
MARY: Ma Kelly's
SUSIE: Hold on a minute girls. Hush, hush...
PATRICIA: What is it?
MARY: A radio. Quick girls, hit the dirt. (MacSiacáis et al. 22)

"Binlids" depiction of the "Duck Patrols" demonstrates a local effort to assert agency in an environment where power was all but denied to Catholic West Belfast except for that slowly garnered by the menacing presence of the IRA. As homes were searched, men and women were interned and local individuals lived in constant fear of brutality from British military or RUC personnel, the Duck Patrols illustrate an effort to spy on the occupying forces to ensure the community would not be caught unaware. The representation of this development also depicts one of many ways in which communal organization was established by small contributions from several community members, in this case all women. Mary's consultation of a book, which presumably lists the respective shifts for each patrol unit, signifies considerable participation in the community. Additionally, Ma Kelly's house seems to serve as that night's convening point or safe house where the "starving" Patricia can freshen up with some "tea and toast" and Susie's ailing feet may find some rest for "ten minutes." Aside from such characteristics, the playwrights also ensure that Belfast's particular vernacular is evident in some characteristics of the women's speech patterns. Vera's complaint that "my feet is killing me," demonstrates a characteristic of Belfast English Henry identifies as a singular-concord. In opposition to a Standard English construction of "my feet *are* killing me," the playwrights represent the local vernacular in such a subject-verb disagreement. Similarly, a non-standard form of the plural "you" in Standard English is offered in Mary's reference "keep watch until yous are finished" marks a particular construction of Belfast English.

In keeping with a spirit of depicting the West Belfast Republican community as an assembly of individuals whose voices, political and cultural contributions vary considerably, the writers of "Binlids" do make some attempts to imagine the individual beings who comprise the forces that confront their own community. Although Orangemen like Geordie do not appear in the play, Northern Irish and British governmental officials do appear spouting rhetoric that often denigrates the population. Many depictions of the RUC and British infantry also lack depth, like Adams' representation of the Lennon-accented British soldier in *The Mountains of Mourne*. But in the scene, "Isolated Soldier," the premise of a shared working-class experience becomes a focus as the ladies comprising a Duck Patrol interrogate a soldier separated from his foot patrol. Although the scene is significant as the playwrights attempt to represent distinctions between individuals and their public, communal representation, "Isolated Soldier," is a strange scene that demonstrates the long term effects of Republican isolation and denigration throughout "The Troubles." When the women of the Duck Patrol surround the soldier, he panics:

> SUSIE: Are you going to shoot us?
> SOLDIER: If you don't shut up I will shoot you.
> PATRICIA: What age are you?
> SOLDIER: Eighteen.
> SOLDIER: Get back, get back or I'll open fire.
> SUSIE: What's that accent? It's not English.
> SOLDIER: I'm Welsh.
> PATRICIA: Jesus, Wales. Abervan, I remember, we collected money here for all those poor kids.
> MARY: Aye, so do I.
> PATRICIA: Sure, you'd be too young to remember that.
> SOLDIER: I don't believe yous, you wouldn't do that – yous are all animals.
> PATRICIA: Where did you get that stuff about us being animals?
> SOLDIER: That's what we've been told. That's why we're here. To stop you animals from killing each other.
> PATRICIA: If you say that again, I'll fuckin' kill you.
> SUSIE: Now, don't scare the lad, he's shaking.
> VERA: Is that a miraculous medal around your neck there?
> SOLDIER: Aye, me Mammy brought it for me. I never go out without it on me.
> MARY: So you're a Catholic like us?
> SOLDIER: I'm a Catholic.
> VERA: Well now, we've a lot in common, you're a Celt so are we, you're a Catholic like us.
> SOLDIER: But you're not Catholics – you're Fenian scum. It's not the Catholics or the Protestants that cause the problems, it's ye Fenians.
> PATRICIA: Ya what? You wee Welsh fucking eejit...
> SUSIE: What's a wee lad like you doing in the Army son? The British are despised the world over, so they are.
> VERA: Aye son, look how scared you are, you're nothing but cannon fodder for them.
> MARY: Is your Da a miner, so? What's your name?
> SOLDIER: It's David, after my father and his father. No, he's not a miner, he was in the Welsh Guards, so he was, like me now.

PATRICIA: Is that right? A Welsh man in the British Army, not very Welsh of you, is it? The English don't like the Scots, the Irish or the Welsh, you wee fuckin' moron.
SOLDIER: The mines are closing and it's a living, you can get fed and waged and you get to see the world.
PATRICIA: You'll get to see the next world son, that's what you'll get.
SOLDIER: It's just a job to me, Mam.
MAIREAD: No son, a brick layer, a plumber, that's a job. Soldiering for wage, killing on another man's orders, that's not just a job. (MacSiacáis et al. 25–7)

As "Isolated Soldier" demonstrates an effort to depict an individual within the British occupying force that was rhetorically blamed for considerable Catholic working-class suffering in the course of "The Troubles" it also betrays the writers' discomfort in representing their political and cultural other. Few Northern Irish Protestants grace the "town square" stages of "Binlids" though British soldiers are numerous. The lengthiest representation of dialogue from such a character is given to not an English soldier but a Welsh, working-class soldier who serves in the British military because "it's just a job" where you can "get fed and waged and you get to see the world." Vera's and Mary's inquiries through the course of the conversation with David illustrate failed efforts to find some strand of commonality between the community he perceives as "animals" and "Fenian scum." Although "Binlids'" playwrights represent a shared class experience in working-class districts amidst rampant unemployment, and distinct non-standard speech patterns in the characters' use of Belfast English and Welsh English, respectively, in addition to a shared Catholic religion, David and the women of the Duck Patrol are inextricably estranged based on their Unionist/non-Unionist political affiliations.

In this depiction and others throughout the play, "Binlids'" strength is in its representation of the "story" telling Adams claims as crucial to lasting peace in a post-conflict society. The play serves as a rudimentary symbolic exercise of democratic activism in which a population once silenced is finally given opportunity to engage in the region's political and cultural dialogue. But the work still exhibits characteristics of isolation as it seems the play, in the company of other Republican writing of the period, circulates primarily in a community that has already lived the "stories" these authors tell.

In one of the final scenes of the play, "Newspapers Reaction to Corporal Killings," the collaborative authors set the women of Republican West Belfast in direct dialogue with Irish, Northern Irish and British print media coverage of the atrocities in the spring of 1988. The symbolic resonance of this juxtaposition, a thematic strand throughout the play, is crystallized in an exchange that is delivered in Standardized English:

> In every country where a television service operates, millions of people saw the real face of provisional involvement – a compound of hate, ferocity and animality, which removes its members almost from the human race. If this is the face of Nationalism then let us forget about Nationalism. It changes humans into animals. The provisions have caused many here to ask themselves if they would agree to accept the North back if it were offered to them and come up with a definite answer, then NO.
> *Irish Independent*
>
> WOMEN: That's not us. That's not us. That's not us.
>
> The modern day equivalent was allowed to butcher two young men and there was no one there to prevent them. The streets were not policed, the army were powerless to stop an act of savagery that stunned our nation. The sad fact is that West Belfast has been allowed to fall into the hands of our enemy.
> *Daily Star*
>
> WOMEN: That's not us. That's not us. That's not us...
>
> Are there no depths to which these people will not sink?
> (Margaret Thatcher)
>
> BRIDIE: This is not my people you speak of. My people went out to bury their dead with the respect they commanded on a day gone by. My people were murdered as they went out to whisper prayers over graves. We were hurt by an outside force who feared the strength within us. That attack was deliberate, our response was spontaneous, an act of defense. My people have survived despite all the lies, the heartbreak, the brutality. We will survive with dignity, courage and ingenuity that we have shown in the past. These are my people that I speak of. (MacSiacáis et al. 78–9)

Just as the murder of two British Corporals was a public act of raw violence, the female characters of "Binlids" attempt to publicly complete the historic record of this particularly horrific incident. Their repetitive denial, "That's not us" not only reflects the shame of bearing witness to several months of particularly chilling violence in the enclave but also demonstrates frustration with the limited portrayal of the events leading to these particularly grim months in the spring of 1988. In responding to the Standardized English associated with newspapers and English governmental officials, Bridie responds in Standardized English rather than the local vernacular of Belfast English that is represented in dialogue between members of the Catholic West Belfast community in various other scenes.

The assumption of this seemingly official language, that Henry identifies as a symbol of education and authority on both sides of Belfast's sectarian divide, demonstrates an effort on behalf of Republican women to speak and to in turn be heard in the neutrality of a common (and historically authoritative) language system. In regard to "Discourse in Poetry and Discourse in the Novel," Bakhtin claims:

> The word in living conversation is directly, blatantly, oriented toward a future answer-word: it provokes an answer, anticipates it and structures itself in the answer's direction. Forming itself in an atmosphere of the already spoken, the word is at the same time determined by that which has not yet been said but which is needed and in fact anticipated by the answering word. Such is the situation in any living dialogue.
>
> All rhetorical forms, monologic in their compositional structure, are oriented toward the listener and his answer. This orientation toward the listener is usually considered the basic constitutive feature of rhetorical discourse. It is highly significant for rhetoric that this relationship toward the concrete listener, taking him into account, is a relationship that enters into the very internal construction of rhetorical discourse. This orientation toward an answer is open, blatant and concrete...
>
> Linguistics and the philosophy of language acknowledge only a passive understanding of discourse, and moreover this takes place by and large on the level of common language, that is, it is an understanding of an utterance's *neutral signification* and not its *actual meaning*. (1981, 281)

In the newspapers and comments from Margaret Thatcher, the "conversation" has been initiated in response to events in Belfast. Bakhtin claims "living conversation" is "oriented toward a future answer-word: it provokes an answer, anticipates it and structures itself in the answer's direction." His observations on conversational exchange are useful here in regard to their emphasis on the process of exchange in dialogue and how such conversation can be represented in literature. If we are to apply Bakhtin's observations to the scenario depicted in "Binlids," newspapers' outcries against West Belfast violence and Margaret Thatcher's outrage at what she perceives as "the depths" to which "these people sink" seem to demonstrate a demand for an answer in regard to violence propagated on Belfast streets in the murder of off-duty British Corporals Derek Wood and David Howes. But are such utterances publicized in an effort to extort an answer from the West Belfast Republican community or are these statements merely rhetorical performance, a public form of chiding to convince that community to listen to the authoritative voices that surround them, to listen in order to learn to be civilized, to engage in less "animalistic" behavior? Bakhtin's effort to demonstrate the distinctions between conversation, that is always oriented towards an anticipated answer, in comparison to rhetoric, which is oriented towards a concrete listener offers a vocabulary for identifying some of the political tension evident in the seeming "conversation" between Republican West Belfast women and their counterparts in the region's print media outlets and governmental leaders like Prime Minister Thatcher in this play.

The collaborative authors of "Binlids" attempt to construct a representation of active discourse between the Republican women of West Belfast and the public narrative attributed to their community in the rhetorical outpouring evident in the collage of newspaper articles and comments from Margaret Thatcher. They have "listened" to the description of their community's brutal savagery and "animalistic" tendencies but they have chosen instead to offer an answer to these rhetorical efforts from years previous, in a belated attempt to initiate discourse. As they repeatedly swear "That's not us. That's not us," the writers gently remind their audience that these populations were historically silenced in the same outlets that decried their actions. And Bridie's assertion, "This is not my people you speak of. My people went out to bury their dead with the respect they commanded on a day gone by," opens the discourse beyond the newspapers' and Thatcher's focus solely on the brutal murder of the off duty Corporals to the historical context that led to such an outpouring of hatred and violence. In the wake of the Milltown Cemetery attacks by Protestant vigilantes only days before, West Belfast turned to the streets to bury one of the victims murdered in the grenade and gunfire attack. In an effort to avoid further clashes British military and RUC personnel avoided involvement in the funeral processions. In the course of the procession a Volkswagen driven by the plain clothed and off duty Corporals Howes and Wood approached the cortège and panic ensued. Mourners anticipated another attack like that experienced only days before at Milltown Cemetery. No questions were asked. The Corporals were dragged from the car and beaten and later publicly assassinated by the IRA.

Bridie's speech demonstrates an effort to answer a question that was rarely, if ever asked. As the women chant, "That's not us" they inherently beg anyone to please ask them just "who" they are instead. Bridie's assertion attempts to reclaim her community's dignity in public forums, it is an attempt to open discourse in a political venue where Republican participation in dialogue – political or cultural – was simply omitted, initially in the Protestant state and thereafter in British efforts to censor elected officials who represented the population. Bridie does not dismiss the violence of the events but she asks for a generosity of understanding not willingly offered to members of her district. As she claims, "that attack was deliberate our response was spontaneous, an act of defense," the play falls into the trend of Republican writers' efforts to justify "defensive" actions taken on behalf of the West Belfast working-class Catholic community. The question then becomes whether such utterances, even when articulated in the common language of Standardized English, can leverage "actual meaning" in discourse with English and Northern Irish players more accustomed to speaking to rather than sharing conversation with the population Bridie represents.

Over a decade has passed since the Good Friday Peace Agreement yet the role that Republican writing may play in Northern Ireland's political and cultural spheres remains to be seen. Belfast is in the midst of raising its first generation of citizens for whom "The Troubles" are merely part of recent history rather than the lived experience of only a generation before. And it is still unclear if this generation will ever share anything more than a non-standard vernacular of Belfast English as post-conflict resolution in the region is slow to develop after decades of bloodshed. As Northern Ireland's economy slowly grows, unemployment in Catholic and Protestant working-class districts has slowly abated though economic depravity remains a crucial concern. But the historically bifurcated politics of identity-formation in the region have become radically fragmented in recent years as record numbers of Eastern European, Asian and African immigrants now seek to make Ireland (North and South) their new home in a European Union. Hybridity in the region can no longer be defined by historical means so how will the minority population, so diligently represented by Republican writers like Adams, MacSiacáis, Morrison, Murphy and Poland, respond when they no longer constitute the region's minority in the wake of globalization? Martin McGuinness and Ian Paisley have considerable work in the coming years as they slowly guide the region through the development of legitimate democratic processes. We can only hope the forced silence that blanketed the region for generations will no longer prevail as the next generation addresses the political challenges of their day.

4
The Misfit Chorus Line: Ireland from the Margins in Patrick McCabe's *Call Me the Breeze*

> When you're small you're like a piece of white paper with nothing written on it. My father writes down his name in Irish and my mother writes down her name in German and there's a black space left over for all the people outside who speak English...
>
> (Hugo Hamilton, *The Speckled People*)

I

The resounding acclaim and success Patrick McCabe may have enjoyed with two novels listed as Booker Prize finalists certainly escaped his efforts in *Call Me the Breeze*. "Beware of a story that comes bearing many type faces," Lizzy Skurnick warns in "On the Borderline." "While an aggressive use of italics and exclamation points is the intrepid writer's prerogative... these graphical distractions, along with a jumble of increasingly unreadable fonts, serve only to partition what would otherwise remain an undifferentiated mash."[1] Journalists and mainstream media reviews were luke-warm in their reception of McCabe's endeavor. And while some reviews were certainly more forgiving than others, like David Crane's "A Refusal to Join the Ghosts" where he claims, "McCabe's method does work, and the gradual move from chaos and randomness to pattern and form, the slow teasing of plot and meaning out of Joey's incoherent junkie ramblings, cleverly mirror the central theme of the novel," the resounding response to the ambitious work was certainly mixed at best.[2] But was the novel anything more than a self-indulgent "writerly" text depicting a grown-up, less charming Francie Brady? Or had McCabe's work aggravated a sensitive national and international response to his tender though unabashed portrayal of provincial Ireland waking up from decades of cultural and economic isolation?

Hamilton's "black space left over for all the people outside who speak English" is relentlessly explored in McCabe's Ireland where Gaelic has been banished to nothing more than a faint memory, echoed in the occasional reference to a *craic*. In this novel, language reigns supreme as McCabe's work gestures towards the genius of Joyce's *Ulysses* in Tallon as a haphazard Bloom, untrained in the Enlightenment English or reason that his cosmopolitan predecessor displays. *Call Me the Breeze* has little of the flat, parodic journalese of McCabe's 2006 novel *Winterwood*, and it serves as a significantly more sophisticated study of language than *The Butcher Boy* in its ambitious interweaving of literary and vernacular influences. At once demonstrating a linguistic history particular to rural border villages like the fictive Scotsfield and documenting Ireland's susceptibility to external political and cultural influence (whether welcomed or not), Joey Tallon's wanderings offer glimpses of a community's effort to come to terms with a rapidly changing Irish society where only the region's historic "troubles" with violence, skewed democratic processes and its particular speech patterns seem to stay the same.

Like Joyce's relentless focus on Ireland's paralytic culture and political system under British rule, McCabe's rendition of contemporary Ireland depicts a nation embodying the seemingly tired koan of T.S. Eliot's "Little Gidding": "The End...is the beginning." As he opens the text with Tallon's colloquial rendition of Eliot's triumphant work, McCabe's novel nods to Joyce's precedent. In an interview with Christopher FitzSimon in the *Irish University Review*, McCabe acknowledges Joyce's influence on his work:

> I remember picking up a copy of *Dubliners* out there and thinking "this could have been written yesterday...just the sheer brilliance, the art of Joyce made it seem so contemporary, it was absolutely mindblowing. And not only that, was kind of going through a Dylan Thomas type thing between just music and rhythm and language. I didn't want it to be – bubbly, bubbly, kind of fishing-boat-bobbing – Irish lilt stuff either. I wanted to get the intellectual Joyce, the sheer vision of it, and combine that with the humanity and language. That's something I'd like to do. I've never really managed it but it was a good start, reading Jamser." (FitzSimon 1998, 183)

While McCabe may be said to mimic Joyce in regard to the breadth of historic and literary influence in the novel, it would seem "the art of Joyce" that particularly sparkles in *Call Me the Breeze* is the "mindblowing...music and rhythm and language" that never dilutes to simple Irish "lilt." Reading the "Jamser" may have served as a prolific "good start" for McCabe but his accomplishments in this novel are singular to his style: a chorus of voices continuously contesting one another, forever fragmenting notions of a singular Irish psyche. McCabe's imprecisely criticized "undifferentiated mash" is actually nothing of the sort. His uncanny talent in capturing the sensibility of an assembly of Irish voices on the page is dizzying at times but nonetheless demonstrates an effort to depict contemporary Ireland in its tapestry of sound. The challenge lies in attempting to identify each strand in this elaborate interweaving – but maybe McCabe's endeavor is to dispel any notions of Irish cultural or linguistic origins in order to attend to more pressing questions of collectivity in the nation's contemporary moment.

The distinguishing characteristic of McCabe's work comes in the vernacular form adopted for his anti-heroes. From Francie Brady to Joey Tallon, to the host of characters that grace McCabe's stage, he continually insists on the centrality of characters that represent fringe elements of Ireland's societal fabric. Through his characters' voices McCabe writes a national vision that emulates the hybridity of Ireland's cultural reality. He reminds audiences of shared cultural elements that continue to grow, like the region's particular vernacular language systems, amidst the apparent cultural and societal change that seems all but inevitable in the wake of Ireland's rapid economic development. McCabe's narrative style, which incorporates the seemingly contradictory nature of Ireland's language systems depict some characteristics described in Bakhtin's work:

> Every concrete utterance of a speaking subject serves as a point where centrifugal as well as centripetal forces are brought to bear. The process of centralization and decentralization, of unification and disunification, intersect in the utterance; the utterance not only answers the requirement of its own language as an individualized embodiment of a speech act, but it answers the requirements of heteroglossia as well; it is in fact an active participant in such speech diversity. And this active participation of every utterance in living heteroglossia determines the linguistic profile and style of the utterance to no less a degree than its inclusion in any normative-centralizing system of a unitary language. (Bakhtin 1981, 272)

McCabe's style is encapsulated in the "utterance of a speaking subject" that is not reserved for character dialogue, but instead pervades each text. Bakhtin's description of the utterance of a speaking subject as an intersection of seemingly contradictory "centralization and decentralization, of unification and disunification" is useful in an attempt to itemize and identify the characteristics of McCabe's work. His representations of language that "intersect" in a multitude of utterances provide the momentum that drives the text's consideration of Ireland's cultural and political hybridity. This in turn dispels nationalist myths of a singular Irish essence from which the region has deviated, which is delivered in a particularly stinging manner throughout *Call Me the Breeze*. The seeming contradiction of such "unification and disunification" proves to be an artful mode of storytelling for McCabe as Joey Tallon comes to represent the political and linguistic fragmentation that has resulted from Ireland's partition and still resonant colonial past as the nation marches on to the twenty-first century.

Throughout *Call Me the Breeze* McCabe's focus on the margins of Irish society demand a focus on multiple facets of Ireland's social terrain by the close of the twentieth century. His depictions of Bonehead's speech impediment marked by elements of Irish-English are evident in his exasperated, "Jasus, Joesup, will you take it aisy! he says. Sure there's bound to be people that's alive can write pomes as good as him [Eliot]" (105). In his representations of Bonehead's non-standard English, McCabe gestures towards characteristics of Irish-English that register not only in the grammatical structure of the phrases but in its cadence and phonetic elements as well. The voiced ae sound in "Jasus" marks an Irish-English pronunciation of the vowel differentiating it from the e associated with a Standard English "Jesus." In this instance, McCabe also seems to draw on an Irish-English characteristic of "the frequent use of references to God and religion" (Todd 1989, 45). This phonetic representation is also evident in "aisy" instead of the e sound associated with Standard English "easy." McCabe's work also depicts the use of an unstressed word to begin a sentence, which often corresponds to the rhythm of Irish in "Sure, there's bound to be people that's alive can write pomes as good as him." In this sentence we also see the disagreement of subject and verb in the discord of "people that's alive" which betrays a non-standard English vernacular instead of the standardized "people who are alive" in addition to the pronunciation of "pomes" instead of "poems."

McCabe's focus on such details of fragmentation in various forms of English may have developed from his move to London, crystallizing the disparities in sounds between various vernacular systems. He states:

> Perhaps there is something about being in a strange place, or in an alien culture. To some extent and in many ways England isn't an alien culture at all. But in terms of the voice and the language it is. You know – "Thirty cigarettes." "What?" "Turty cigarettes." "What?" – all that kind of stuff, you know, it kind of focuses the thing and refines your ear. I spell it out to them. I actually spell it out...I think as well as that, definitely being in London where you're surrounded by every culture in the world, you start to realize just how rich language is. That was what *The Butcher Boy* was partly about. I wasn't trying too consciously to do it, but you see, the things that people say, ordinary exchange you know – "Not a bad day," "Tis surely"; "How's it goin?" All that type of stuff that you hear, the rhythm of it, it's actually quite fascinating I think really. It's only when you put it down in a context that you start to see it." (FitzSimon 1998, 186)

As he addresses the varied sounds of English in London, "thirty cigarettes," versus "turty," McCabe points to a characteristic in Hiberno English that uses "a dental pronunciation of 't' and 'd'. This means that the sounds are made with the tongue against the top teeth, rather than against the ridge above the top teeth" (Todd 1989, 37). This distinction in sound demands the repetition that ensues in the instance McCabe recalls as he tried to communicate "thirty" as "turty" on the streets of London. "I spell it out to them," he says of his work, in order to communicate the significant differences, "unification and disunification," in a seemingly shared spoken and written language of English in England and Ireland. McCabe's work itemizes such distinctions throughout *Call Me the Breeze*, and in other novels as well, celebrating the organic growth of Ireland's particular vernacular systems.

Such a dialogic representation of multifaceted language systems saturates McCabe's narratives. In the interview with McCabe, FitzSimon inquires:

> Well, when you're doing the dialogue, it's fair enough. You follow the ordinary speech patterns of the people, the people whose voices are going around in your head. But when you come to what we would call the prose passages, how is it that so many writers, living and writing in this country today, when they come to the descriptive

passages or the thoughtful passages and so on, it goes into a sort of scholastic prose and it's quite different from the dialogue? (FitzSimon 1998, 186)

McCabe's response is significant, considering the interview dates to 1998. Since that time, his work has been more deliberately linked to the reworking of specific language systems. But in regard to his early work, McCabe states:

That's what I was trying in a way. You've said it much more articulately. In *Carn*, I found you constantly describe and then suddenly you're back into God-mode, you know, the omnipotent narrator sort of stuff and you think, "Ah, this is wrong." To actually get into that and to reinvent the language, as it were, that's what I was describing with *The Butcher Boy*. And you really have to feel the white heat of it because any other way is wrong. You can't think yourself into a novel by saying, "Right, what'll I do today? I'll write a novel about a young fella that grows up in Ireland and slaughters a middle-aged woman. What about that?" No, it's just the sheer intensity of the feeling. And it also has to be linked in with your own life. I don't know, maybe if you haven't known disappointment, or if you haven't known exile, can you do any of these things? But there does certainly seem to be a sense where the scholastic, dispassionate prose has disconnected you, or you don't want to be connected with the real pain of life or the real joy of life. Somehow, it's a fingernail-paring kind of thing, and ultimately it's not rewarding really for reader or writer. (FitzSimon 1998, 186)

Relying heavily on metaphor to describe his writing, McCabe cites the reinvention of "language" as feeling "the white heat of it because any other way is wrong." Tapping into the energy emitted by such carefully crafted prose, McCabe addresses the need for content to be reflected by form. The shocking narrative of a "young fella that grows up in Ireland and slaughters a middle-aged woman" is not necessarily art. But a novel that can create empathy for such a child, an energy likened to that cast off by the "white heat" of powerful reinvented language that resists "dispassionate prose," may enable McCabe to rival "the intellectual Joyce" he so admires.

As he strategically resists "God mode" in Tallon's narration, McCabe fashions an egalitarian semblance of utterances whereby Joey joins a chorus of voices within the text rather than dominating and ordering dialogue between characters. And it is in this structural composition that McCabe's novel speaks to Bakhtin's definitions of "heteroglossia." As McCabe positions the "low genres" of Ireland's vernacular in conversation with the "accepted literary language" exemplified in multiple references to canonical giants like Eliot, McCabe fashions a dialogic exchange between representations of the vernacular language systems employed by individual Irish citizens and the "official languages" associated with literary figures like Eliot. Bakhtin claims:

> Heteroglossia, as organized in these low genres [referring to street songs, folksayings, etc.], was not merely heteroglossia vis-á-vis the accepted literary language (in all its various generic expressions), that is, vis-á-vis the linguistic center of the verbal-ideological life of the nation and the epoch, but was a heteroglossia consciously opposed to this literary language. It was parodic, and aimed sharply and polemically against the official languages of its given time. It was heteroglossia that had been dialogized. (Bakhtin 1981, 273)

McCabe's vernacular narrations cast in characters who have been tossed to the margins of Irish society, undermine notions of an Irish unitary language, culture or politic. Bakhtin demonstrates that "low genres" not only challenged unitary languages with heteroglossia of "the accepted literary language" but just as importantly with vernacular strains of Italian, English or French to compromise the political and cultural dominance of Latin in Western Europe. McCabe's narrators render Ireland's linguistic parents, Gaelic and Enlightenment English, faint memories in the contemporary imagination. Throughout the text, McCabe's only reference to Gaelic is in the word *craic* and his representations of Standardized English associated with colonial Britain are so deeply imbedded in Ireland's social and political culture, it becomes evident that McCabe's Ireland employs a seemingly "official" language of a shared heteroglossia. McCabe's interweaving of literary and oral genres, however, like the work of his twentieth-century predecessors, demonstrates vestiges of these tensions. The profundity of such a democratizing mission, inextricably linked to the "white heat" of language reinvention, illustrates the historical significance of these disparities. As McCabe undermines tension between literary and vernacular precedents in Irish culture in a text that triumphs speech patterns in literary form, *Call Me the Breeze* demonstrates that Ireland's multifaceted heteroglossia fundamentally challenges the mythic supremacy of the region's unitary languages of English and

Gaelic as his work insists on Ireland's cultural, social and political hybridity.

Relying heavily on its namesake, *Call Me the Breeze* is a meditation on the potential for peaceful stasis rather than stagnation on linguistic, cultural and political planes in Ireland. Tending to general themes of paralysis, disillusion and violence amidst considerable cultural and political change, McCabe draws on J.J. Cale's 1971 song, "Call Me the Breeze" as a hauntingly appropriate, though ironic, soundtrack for Joey Tallon's narrative. It is a short, simple song that celebrates transience, self-reliance and isolation, characteristics rendered completely bankrupt in Tallon's trajectory. These are all characteristics also celebrated in the early years of the Irish Republic where DeValera hoped to boost the region economically with booming agrarian output and to isolate the fledgling nation from international strife in the Second World War and the Cold War to ensure self-reliance in the aftermath of British occupation. But as McCabe explores the potential for contemporary Ireland (North and South) to emerge from thirty years of violence and rapid technological and economic advancement, in the wayward wanderings of his village idiot in Tallon, his novel suggests that "the breeze" may be a figure only fit for song.

In order to negotiate space and transience from Scotsfield, Tallon refashions himself as "the breeze," blowing to California – a late twentieth-century pastoral West. Rather than enabling Joey to emerge from the static hell of violence, political corruption and cultural stagnancy of Scotsfield however, McCabe pushes the figure into momentary fits of madness as he watches all potential routes of escape slowly close. In Tallon, McCabe calls attention to the Republic's rapid exchange of cultural stagnancy and provincialism for economic advancement. Like Joey's imaginary "Breeze," Ireland's invitation of foreign investment, primarily from the United States, seems an undeniable escape route from the nation's trajectory of cultural, political and social occupation. But like Joey's failed endeavor "She called me The Breeze, you see. That's what you'll never understand Bone... That's what you – or anyone else, by the looks of things – will never be able to understand," Ireland's seemingly newfound independence was "a lie, of course" (McCabe 2003, 247). Jacy never called Tallon the "Breeze," at least "not in the way" that he wanted her to. And McCabe's rendition of Ireland's awakening from decades of isolation and provincialism suggests that such an economic revolution may prove too costly an endeavor for the region's cultural and political sovereignty. Just as Joey's untenable image of transience and impermeability in the pastoral west of his imagined America proves an intoxicating though bankrupt dream, McCabe's novel suggests that Ireland, in the wake of its cultural, political and social occupation by Britain and its later economic dependence on foreign investment primarily from the United States, will be challenged to express its sovereignty in generations to come. And the core of such expression, it seems, will be provided in the region's ever changing though omnipresent configuration of multiple voices, demonstrated in McCabe's representation of a novel "written in Scotsfield vernacular" (McCabe 2003, 154).

II

As McCabe fashions Joey, the misanthrope writer as narrator, he identifies the pinpoint from which the organized chaos of this novel can oscillate. Marking the tension between oral and literary trajectories in a seeming simpleton like Tallon, McCabe crafts an intersection where the perceived high and low forms of art, history, culture and language in Ireland can coexist. In Tallon, McCabe presents a series of snap shots depicting carefully chosen moments in Irish history between the 1970s and the fledgling years of the twenty-first century that capture the almost inescapable pressure manifested in the region's long political and cultural relationship with Britain and its more recent flirtations with the United States. In the rhythmical language of a "Scotsfield vernacular" McCabe moves with ease from one historical period to another, continually interweaving high and low cultural influences on a multitude of seemingly ordinary Irish citizens through Tallon's social networks (McCabe 2003, 154). McCabe carefully documents Ireland's tenuous relationships with Britain and America by the end of the twentieth century. In Tallon, McCabe can depict Britain's centrality in much of Irish culture despite its truncated reign of political dominance in the Republic by the nineteen-twenties. Nonetheless, Tallon's first literary explorations were the iconic English texts, *Just William* and *Biggles*, his literary career is dependent on a London publisher and he blindly wanders into the most turbulent center of Ireland's and Britain's contemporary contentious relationship in his hapless involvement in "The Troubles."

McCabe fashions occasional breaks in such binary tensions through representations of Tallon's understanding of America. As he draws on popular symbols of America's late nineteen-sixties and early nineteen-seventies counter-culture, as exemplified in Cale's song, McCabe offers Tallon a vision of cultural and political freedom that is unavailable in

Ireland in the same period. McCabe situates Tallon in the midst of "The Troubles" to demonstrate the explosive combination of Ireland's historic relationship with Britain once again coming to a violent head. As Tallon and his Scotsfield community assert their individual relationships to such national trajectories, McCabe inscribes the emergence of America's international cultural influence to arm his characters with an alternative cultural association that has played a significant role in the region's mythmaking since the mid nineteenth-century. But this relationship is superficial, at best. Immigration is a non-issue in this text as McCabe's marginal characters have neither the means nor the strength to endure the cultural trauma of immigration. Instead, McCabe fashions a very limited space in which characters like Tallon, Boyle Henry, Jacy, Mangan and Bonehead can negotiate their identity in the newest chapter of their nation's history.

Tallon's affinity for American culture is not simplistic but it is certainly filled with disillusion. As Joey struggles to find his role in the Scotsfield community, and Ireland as a whole, his limited vision of America enables him to imagine that this is a culture that can accept his eccentricities. Tallon's vision of this culture depends predominantly on nineteen-seventies music produced by artists like J.J. Cale and Joni Mitchell and all that he reads on "the Good" Charlie Manson and Carlos Castaneda. This is a welcome alternative, however, to the cultural and political strife Tallon confronts on a daily basis as violence associated with "The Troubles" creeps into the local community. In Tallon, McCabe considers the role that popular culture plays in influencing individual relationships to the "official culture" often associated with the state. In his egalitarian approach to such work, placing Eliot's poetry in conversation with Cale's song lyrics, McCabe suggests that we must consider the multiple influences at work that enable an individual to negotiate his/her relationship to their community, their language and their nation. "The word 'art' meant nothing to me," McCabe claims in the FitzSimon interview. "They were inextricable, these things, whether it was Thackeray or Minnie the Minx; it was all part of the same thing" (177).

McCabe extends such sentiments in his crafting of Tallon. Attending to the significance of literacy in Ireland's cultural terrain, McCabe's depiction of Joey's trajectory demonstrates the region's susceptibility to continual international influence throughout the twentieth century:

"Did you ever read T.S. Eliot?" he said to me one day, and I had to admit that I hadn't. To be perfectly honest, up to that point I hadn't

> read much of anything. I'd read sweet fuck all, to tell you the God's honest truth. Not since *Just William*, *Biggles* and shit.
>
> I don't know why, for it certainly seems stupid now. A writer who doesn't read – sounds really impressive, all right. I think what had happened was I'd developed a kind of a block. "I don't give a shit about that intellectual stuff!" I used to say, but, almost at once, would feel kind of ashamed. (McCabe 2003, 3)

Tallon's whimsical leanings are evident throughout the text and this passage is no exception. Nonetheless, Tallon's "block," his compulsion not to "give a shit about that intellectual stuff" may emphasize an element of impatience with an "official" culture that has traditionally rejected figures like the informally educated Tallon and seems to be assembled of predominantly foreign Western influences. Tallon claims he hasn't read "fuck all" since *Just William* and *Biggles*, which depicts not only the early influence of English letters on his intellectual development but a possibly immature end to such training in literacy. McCabe's reference to children's books indicates a cross section of cultural and literary influence in Ireland from Tallon's earliest of days, but what could their significance actually be? Neither McCabe nor Tallon lament such an occurrence in nationalist rhetoric attempting to eradicate all English influence in modern Ireland. But Tallon, eccentric as he is, has abandoned literary culture altogether for a period in his life, relishing the image of a "writer who doesn't read." The writer "who doesn't read" confounds the official culture's investment in a literary language that may not be in keeping with a "novel in the Scotsfield vernacular." But Joey's shame, associated with his seemingly unabashed rejection of "that intellectual stuff" illustrates McCabe's careful consideration of the multiple cultural and political influences in continual contestation throughout Ireland's history. What has defined Ireland's official culture? To what degree have the nation's relationships with Britain and the United States, respectively, shaped the culture that Tallon seems to ashamedly reject but that also quarantines him and figures like the traveler, Mangan, to the margins of town and Irish society at large?

The Seeker's emphasis on Eliot serves as the zenith of McCabe's otherwise fairly scattered focus on the multiple contesting factors affecting identity formation in late twentieth-century Ireland. Eliot's lines from "Little Gidding," to which Tallon relentlessly returns as the worn out mantra of his life trajectory, enables McCabe to attend to the region's cultural contestation, political stagnation and conflicted relationships to literary and oral traditions.

His name is T.S. Eliot, and what that guy has got to say is – Fr Connolly will remember – *"We will not cease from exploration, and the end of all our exploring will be to arrive where we started and know the place for the first time!"* (294)

Eliot's reference to a cyclical journey, one in which the exploration of an origin yields nothing more than a return to the beginning to "know the place for the first time" is echoed in Cale's Breeze. Although this lack of escape contributes to Tallon's mania throughout the novel, it also enables McCabe to comment on Ireland's seeming political paralysis despite significant economic and cultural change by the late nineteen-nineties. Eliot also enables McCabe to attend to the juxtaposition of oral and literary influences in the region in Joey's initial rejection of what he perceives as "intellectual shit" that is associated with literary (and therefore official) culture. As The Seeker refers to Eliot, rather than Joyce, Hesse or various other writers of the period, McCabe cleverly captures a central question of national affiliation in the symbol of Eliot's own struggle with patriotic leanings.

Eliot's lines that precede the oft quoted passage in *Call Me the Breeze* bear considerable significance when considering Tallon's relationship to influential characters throughout the novel and particularly in his relationship to the Irish State. Eliot writes:

We are born with the dead:/See, they return, and bring us with them. / The moment of the rose and the moment of the yew-tree / Are of equal duration. A people without history / Is not redeemed from time, for history is a pattern / Of timeless moments. So, while the light fails / On a winter's afternoon, in a secluded chapel / History is now and England. (Eliot 1943, 58)

Tallon's troubled familial relationships and his existence on the margins of Irish society demonstrate McCabe's exploration of individual relationships to the contemporary Irish state. "We are born with the dead," Eliot writes "they return, and bring us with them." In nineteen-seventies Scotsfield, Joey Tallon is not only born with the dead in regard to the aborted child of his father's lover Mona but just as importantly, he is perpetually haunted by the walking dead of The Troubles. Tallon's familial history is rendered bankrupt once his father abandons the family and his mistress, fleeing from Ireland. But Tallon's relation to a national history is equally flawed by British colonialism and fervent Irish nationalism. If "history is now and England," Tallon's journey that "will be to arrive where we started / and know the place for the first time" may prove a futile endeavor. But if McCabe's Vician[3] narrative demonstrates that "A people without history / Is not redeemed from time, for history is a pattern / Of timeless moments," Tallon's challenge will arise in his attempts to access the pattern of his national history through foreign voices and letters.

As Tallon tirelessly searches for a sense of belonging, a home, McCabe's reliance on Eliot's work and reputation in juxtaposition to Tallon's "Scotsfield vernacular" comes to serve as the point of intersection for English and American spheres of influence in contemporary Ireland. American-born Eliot, who fashioned himself as a naturalized English citizen and practicing Anglican Catholic can claim "the intersection of the timeless moment is England and nowhere. Never and always" because in his biographical trajectory such a conflation proved not only logical but spiritually fulfilling (MacCabe 2003). In Joey's imagination however, England as the "intersection of the timeless moment" resonates with considerable difference. It is a reminder of cultural homelessness. Not only is Tallon tossed to the margins of his Scotsfield community by virtue of his family's failure to live up to the ideal familial unit imagined in DeValera's Catholic Ireland, the nation continues to struggle to assert independence in the cultural onslaught emanating from England and the United States, respectively, up until and through the nineteen-nineties. Joey struggles to find his role in his small border town in the midst of a struggle to understand his cultural affiliation to a nation that seems to mortgage its culture depending upon its most aggressive investor. Said claims:

> To be for and in culture is to be in and for a State in a compellingly loyal way. With this assimilation of culture to the authority and exterior framework of the State go as well such things as assurance, confidence, the majority sense, the entire matrix of meanings we associate with "home," belonging and community. Outside this range of meanings – for it is the outside that partially defines the inside in this case – stand anarchy, the culturally disfranchised, those elements opposed to culture and State: the homeless, in short. (Said 1999, 11)

In the Republic, like many postcolonial states, Ireland's political and social framework look suspiciously like its English neighbor despite valiant efforts to differentiate the fledgling nation from its historical oppressor. By the nineteen-seventies, cultural changes demanded some shifts in the nation's political conservatism in opposition to censorship, demanding equal rights for women and challenges to the supremacy of the Catholic church. Nonetheless, the majority of Irish citizens assimilated to the "authority and exterior framework of the State" in exchange for "assurance, confidence...belonging and community," which were certainly compromised in the "anarchy" associated with the Northern Irish state at the time. But how does Tallon ascribe to such stability? Despite his valiant efforts, he and figures like him from Mangan to Bonehead, are actually not welcome in the "the majority sense" because they represent value systems that do not necessarily coincide with the culture of the State. Cognizant of the precedent of embracing "anarchy, the culturally disfranchised, those elements opposed to culture and State" as a deeply rooted sense of patriotism throughout Irish history, McCabe's novel investigates how such notions of "home" in culture and politics are negotiated in the region's conflict and post-conflict eras. But in figures like Tallon, McCabe demands that such negotiations begin to include all participants in Ireland's collective rather than those who have constituted "the majority sense." Although Joey may not serve as the archetype of change and personal development throughout the novel, the seeming hailstorm of change that surrounds Tallon, Jacy and the multitude of McCabe's other figures, calls for continued inquiries on individual identity formation as the Northern and Republic Irish states attempt to define and practice a collective contemporary politic.

III

From the Campbell Morris incident and the Banbridge bombing to the Peace Rally and Jacy's kidnapping, sectarian and political acts of violence serve as catalysts in Tallon's trajectory, characterizing late twentieth-century culture as inextricably linked to nationalist and sectarian violence in Ireland. Opening the novel Tallon claims "you always felt that in a small border town like Scotsfield nothing serious would ever happen...but that was before the 'Campbell Morris Incident'," marking the precise moment he believes Ireland's national struggle suddenly became of local concern (2). In this segment McCabe not only introduces specific elements of historical circumstances along the Northern Irish border but also layers the details of Tallon's everyday existence as he navigates the intricacies of Scotsfield's violent underworld.

Campbell was a salesman who happened to drop by for the Lady of the Lake festival but ended up getting himself killed. It's impossible to say who started the rumors about him.

Either way it ended with him being pulled out of the reservoir and the cops going apeshit, raiding pubs.

It wasn't my business. I was too busy getting on with my life, pulling pints and thinking about Jacy. She was all I ever thought about in those days.

"He was a fucking spy! And that's it!" you'd hear them shouting late at night, full of guilt over what they had done. There had been six or seven of them involved, I think.

"How about we go out to the Ritzy?" they'd said, as the salesman drunkenly grinned. "You'll see things out there that you'd never come across in Dublin or London."

It was a ruse, to get him on his own. They used to show all these blue movies in a barn way out the country. They had dubbed it "The Ritzy" and for a tenner you could watch the films and drink all you wanted. There was talk of Boyle Henry and the Provos being involved in its operation, but you'd never say that openly. "I couldn't tell you anything about The Ritzy" was what you said if you were asked. "I know nothing at all about any of that" – that's what you were expected to say.

And did, if you had any sense.

The "blues," as they called them, were very popular. Bennett had always liked them. "The best of crack," he used to say. "I always make sure to go out every Saturday."

But not any more.

After the salesman's funeral, Bennett had driven out to the reservoir and sat there for a couple of hours thinking about it all, and his part in it, I guess. He was discovered there a few hours later, slumped over the dash and poisoned with carbon monoxide.

Whenever I heard things like that back in those days, my reaction would always be the same: finish up my work, head straight home to fall into Mona's arms. (McCabe 2003, 2–3)

In this passage McCabe crafts Scotsfield's initiation to "The Troubles" through Tallon's traipsing on the margins of the rural border town. At first Tallon is an observer, barely capable of processing the horror befalling his hometown: "It wasn't my business" Tallon claims, as he was "too busy getting on with life, pulling pints and thinking about Jacy." Seemingly aloof, "too busy" to be concerned with the business of folks like Bennett and Boyle Henry, Tallon seems to nonchalantly avoid this violent initiation. But as he "pulls pints" at Austie's there is little he can do to avoid overhearing dangerously specific details. The tone of the passage changes dramatically after the first few sentences. Dreamily, Tallon describes being lost in the busy world of fantasizing about Jacy and pulling pints at the pub. But the jarring and resolute, "He was a fucking spy! And that's it!" punctuates the end of such day-dreaming without repercussion. Thereafter, Tallon describes the events in striking detail as he is slowly and ever so carefully, folded into the events that come to characterize Scotsfield's fall into the shadows of "The Troubles." His involvement comes through overhearing "them shouting late at night, full of guilt over what they had done."

Resisting the "god-mode" of narration, McCabe crafts an unassuming Tallon as storyteller in the oral tradition to disseminate the tale of Scotsfield's initiation to "The Troubles." While this passage does not exemplify characteristics of Irish-English like that depicted in Bonehead's "Jasus, Joesup, will you take it aisy!" Tallon's narrative garners trust and seeming reliability offered in the first-hand account associated with an Irish oral tradition. As Tallon begins, "somehow you always felt that in a small border town like Scotsfield nothing serious would ever really happen," he simultaneously seems to mean that *he* never "felt that in a small border town like Scotsfield" anything even remotely serious of national or international consequence would happen but also that his "imagined community" had similar skepticism. Creating the illusion of semblance between he as storyteller and the community of Scotsfield, the initial sentences craft Tallon as an insider who heard and can now retell the oral history of Scotsfield's demise.

This is tempered slightly when Tallon claims, "it wasn't my business." But the flood gates seem to open when Joey simply becomes a vessel through which the story can be delivered. The quick move to dialogue within Joey's recollection, "He was a fucking spy!" renders the role of narrator almost invisible as Joey's voice slowly falls to the background. This makes way for the anonymous though well rehearsed repetition of "I couldn't tell you..." that could have come from any Scotsfield frequenter of the "blues." Then the specific voice of Bennett, who believed the Ritzy was "the best of crack," comes to serve the dual purpose of providing authenticity to Tallon's story as well as vocabulary specific to Ireland. Relying on slang like "crack" or the Irish "craic," known widely as a social gathering and a good time or more literally translated as a "chat," McCabe offers a small cultural marker to situate Tallon's story. The employment of the word, "tenner," referring to ten Pounds or Punts in the 1970s, however, betrays a shared Irish and English slang that enables McCabe to remind the audience that the two nations' histories are inextricably linked, economically and linguistically in Irish culture.

Violence that seems endemic to parts of Irish culture often manifests itself in the language of McCabe's work. Even in discussions on the prospect of peace in Ireland, verbal and physical violence seems to loom closely in the shadows. In a seemingly innocent exchange between Tallon and Austie, these opposing forces are brought into close proximity.

> I had seen them on the telly, talking about setting up a movement for peace after three innocent children got run over. "Maybe we could get Boo Boo and the boys to play at it," I said.
> "Like fuck we could," said Austie, rolling a keg along the floor in front of him. "Can't you read? The word's 'peace,' not fucking mayhem. Will you change that barrel there Joey and make yourself useful the fuck out of that!"
> *"Peace,"* I said and smiled, giving him the "V" sign just for a laugh. When I was changing the barrel, Hoss came in and I handed him the leaflet. He sneered, then rolled it up in a ball and tossed it on the floor. "Doddering old bollocks of a padre," he said.
> "Nothing better to do with his time than talk to these mad bitches."
> "I think it's a good idea," I said, although to tell the truth I didn't think any such thing. I wasn't thinking about it at all. I was thinking: *Soon it begins. T.O. Total Organization.*
> "Peace with justice – that's all we've ever wanted," Hoss said and flicked a flame from his lighter. "And we won't have that until those cunts are gone." (McCabe 2003, 24)

Almost childlike in his excitement about a peace pageant, Joey's suggestion, "Maybe we could get Boo Boo and the boys to play at it," not only marks his almost brotherly affection for Boo Boo and his band but even more so an eagerness to contribute to the Scotsfield community. Tallon introduces the context as seemingly commonplace: "I had seen them on the telly, talking about setting up a movement for peace after three innocent children got run over." In these sentences, McCabe offers light touches of non-standard English to demonstrate Tallon's and Austie's distance from an official literary culture. Joey's reference to the "telly," a colloquial reference to the television and his reference to "three innocent children got run over" instead of a Standardized English "three innocent children who were run over," each reflect a vernacular exchange that presses up against the literary endeavor that is McCabe's novel.

Tallon's voice, however, is tempered by Austie's harsh response. "Like fuck we could...Can't you read? The word is 'peace,' not fucking mayhem. Will you change that barrel there Joey and make yourself useful to fuck out of that!" While Austie's language may actually serve as just a colorful reminder of this character's no-nonsense attitude throughout the text, it would seem McCabe's representation of such language also marks an everyday pub proprietor's limited vocabulary that leads to reliance on swear words to signify an emotional response to what he perceives as a preposterous idea. Rather than simply stating "no," or any other negation of Joey's proposed plan, Austie's "like fuck we could" offers a violent edge that seems to truncate any further discussion. His then insensitive follow-up question of "can't you read," adds insult to injury, demeaning Tallon's suggestion while enabling McCabe to focus on Joey's contentious relationship to literary culture. Reminding Joey that Boo Boo's punk band is more associated with "mayhem" than the "word...peace," Austie then falls into a verb leading imperative that demands Tallon put himself to good use. Austie's "change that barrel there Joey and make yourself useful to fuck out of that!" betrays an Irish-English construction that places a request for action at the beginning of the command and the reason for such a request at the end. This enables McCabe to situate the exchange culturally in Ireland through such linguistic representation, which comes to bear considerable significance in the region's history of violence. Weary, though undaunted by Joey's silliness, Austie barks for order and focus.

Joey's playful *"Peace"* matched with the "'V' sign just for a laugh" demonstrates a tongue-in-cheek effort to keep the peace with Austie while nonetheless fanning the flames of his fury. But as the focus shifts to Hoss and his Republican rhetoric for an independent Ireland, the issue of a Peace People rally in Scotsfield jockeys between the local and national spheres. "Peace with justice – that's all we've ever wanted," Hoss explains, diligently toeing the party line. As he closes with, "And we won't have that until those cunts are gone," it is not quite clear if he is still swearing at the "mad bitches" who he claims constitute the Peace People or Britain. In either case, McCabe furnishes the would be "freedom fighter" with ornamental sexist rhetoric stereotypically affiliated with IRA male volunteers (see Magee 2002). Infuriating Hoss with a disingenuous claim that he "thinks it's a good idea," Tallon also betrays his instability as narrator – someone who will say one thing and mean another.

Joey's instability however, is not limited to narrating McCabe's novel or interacting with Austie and Hoss. And his life altering traumas began long before he started "pulling pints" for Austie or heard stories of the Campbell Morris affair. Like countless other male protagonists in Irish literature, Tallon's troubles began with a defunct familial unit. The twist, however, comes in Tallon's efforts to continually refashion his origins through imagined metaphorical and sexual rebirths and recreations with Mona and Jacy and cultural refashioning in his infatuation with America. Glimpses of such trajectories escape quite early in the text in passages like the following:

> But the fact that my mother had had a hard life (she was in Cavan General Hospital a while before being institutionalized totally – they wheeled her off gibbering about "Chinamen") kind of helped my situation, and when she passed away they offered me this rundown mobile home on the edge of a tinker camp just a mile outside of Scotsfield town.
>
> I tried the factory for a while after flunking out of school – I drank a bottle of whiskey before Latin class and when the president asked me how ashamed I was (they found me asleep in a pool of vomit) I replied, "No, baby, I ain't ashamed because when you ain't got nothin' you got nothin' to lose."
>
> Which of couse is a characteristically acerbic quote from Mr Robert Zimmerman, the defiant Jewish minstrel – not something that the president of the college was aware of, as I was to find out very shortly... (McCabe 2003, 4)

Demonstrating his familial disposition to madness, Tallon recaps his mother's rapid demise into "being institutionalized totally" as they "wheeled her off gibbering about 'Chinamen.'" All but orphaned by a philandering father and a mother slipping into fits of madness, Tallon's troubles are neatly disposed of on the margins of the margins. Conveniently imprisoned in a "rundown mobile home" on the "edge of a tinker camp just a mile outside of Scotsfield town," McCabe ensures that Tallon's relationship to the Irish state is as distant as can be imagined in the confines of such a tiny country. Tallon's trajectory, therefore, seems to emulate McCabe's bleak diagnosis of Ireland's recent social and cultural history and its prospects for the future. Tallon's defunct family unit demonstrates the unraveling of a myth. Not all Irish families inhabited warm glowing homesteads along the nation's rolling agrarian hills that DeValera envisioned for his budding country. And even those who did boast such picturesque living quarters were certainly haunted by a postcolonial legacy of cultural violence and political conservatism in the shadows of the Catholic church.

Residing in a mobile home that cannot move, stationed permanently in a transient camp a mile outside of town where the "settled" population lives, Tallon is cast off to ensure his familial madness will not contaminate the perceived purity of dominant Irish Catholic culture.[4] Although McCabe ensures his audience immediately recognizes the bankruptcy of any such notions of true Irish collectivity, even in the imagined Scotsfield, Tallon's isolation is nonetheless palpable. It is reinforced by representations of his neighbor Mangan's language system that reflects not only the dismal conditions of his existence in the content of his comments but a non-standard system reflecting severely limited education (if not illiteracy). Even Tallon responds to the perceived irregularity of Mangan's speech patterns, enabling McCabe to mark further distinctions in populations between the traveler Mangan and the "settled" (ironically rendered, of course) Tallon. As Mangan states, "You'll be sorra... If he hadna been chained up you'd never have hurted him," McCabe cites phonetic pronunciations in a speech pattern that deviates considerably from either Standardized English associated with official or literary culture and the Irish-English employed by figures like Austie. Tallon pauses in response to Mangan, not to consider his responsibility for harming the animal, but to reflect on the supposed strangeness of Mangan's speech – "the way he said it" – marking their shared distance from the Scotsfield community and the familial units associated with Ireland's "majority sense" (McCabe 2003, 89).

In the midst of Tallon's family's demise and his expulsion from secondary school he utters, "when you ain't got nothin' you got nothin' to lose," mimicking the prolific Bob Dylan. Employing rhetoric associated with nineteen-seventies America and its counter-culture from a pool of his own vomit, McCabe fashions Tallon's limited understanding of America as a cultural release from the confines of his own personal and national circumstances. Tallon's response to the school master's question of whether or not he is ashamed of himself, demonstrates the failure of his own language system to reply to such a question in the throes of his personal desperation. Tallon is in the midst of being cast aside by virtue of his family's failed endeavor to live up to standards associated with a "majority sense." The President of the school and the Scotsfield community at large would prefer to cast Joey to the outskirts of town, like the ostracized traveler communities, rather than consider such individuals' roles in the nation's composition. Tallon's fixation on American "minstrels" like the illustrious "Mr Robert Zimmerman" offer Joey a succinct, convenient vocabulary that can be grafted from American circumstances onto Irish sentiments of dejection and isolation. They are consumable products that provide momentary release from a bankrupt symbol of Mother Ireland depicted in Tallon's own mother's madness and a rudimentary state infrastructure unprepared to attend to its nation's cultural and societal plights. And when such language is extracted from its cultural and political significance in American history as Dylan's, Cale's and Mitchell's albums were disseminated worldwide, Tallon can conveniently usurp such language for the particular needs of his own situation with a level of anonymity unavailable in the official literary language that he contentiously avoids or the local vernacular that reminds him of his nation's cultural and social failure to meet his most basic needs.

IV

McCabe's assault on the detrimental effects of Irish Nationalism on the nation's contemporary history is evident in his portrayal of Tallon's interactions with Mona and Jacy, two contemporary faces of Yeats' Mother Ireland in "Cathleen ni Houlihan." Tallon's relationships with Mona (the real and the rubber instantiations) and Jacy (imagined and actual interactions) are continuously haunted by Eliot's lines from the final stanza of "Little Gidding": "We shall not cease from exploration / And the end of all our exploring / Will be to arrive where we started / And know the place for the first time." As he seeks rebirth in his interactions with Mona and a romantic relationship with Jacy, McCabe fashions Tallon in search of a substantial connection to a female figure. This is in keeping with nationalist rhetoric that fashions Ireland as a woman: a contradictory vision of a virgin goddess protector married to the land or a mother caring for the sons and daughters of her nation. Mona and Jacy represent McCabe's stinging criticism of such a vision, which proves completely bankrupt by the late twentieth century as the Republic teetered on the brink of financial ruin before the mid nineteen-nineties flurry of foreign investment and the Northern province's slide into decades of bloody, sectarian violence. Attending to Tallon's almost deranged obsession with both his father's mistress in Mona and a virtual stranger in Jacy, McCabe initiates an analysis of Irish heterosexuality in a virtual hall of mirrors, where the reader comes to learn that Tallon's sexual explorations result in nothing more than beginning and ending in Tallon's isolation. The monotony is not broken until the final acts of sexual violence and disgrace delivered by Boyle Henry that ultimately shatter Tallon's until then protected, though tragic, solitary existence (McCabe 2003, 321).

Tallon's troubling relationships with Mona and Jacy throughout the text rely heavily on the tired trope of Mother Ireland. In this figure, McCabe can fashion the complete expiration of a nationalist imperative from the turn of the twentieth century. In McCabe's Ireland, the mother-tongue has died out with all the dated nationalist rhetoric associated with Ireland's cultural purity. Its replacement, a hybrid language, culture and political system, reflecting the region's long association with England and its newfound partnership with American economic, cultural and linguistic investment, enable McCabe to carefully re-write a hollowed out Shan van Vocht in the failed maternal figure of Mona and the elusive empty goddess in Boyle's mistress, Jacy. McCabe's configurations of these figures is reminiscent of Michael Farrell's late 1970s "Madonna Irlanda" series subtitled "The Very First Real Irish Political Picture" that attends to cultural hybridity in Ireland in the wake of the region's trade of a nationalist imperative for participation in a global economy. And Tallon's voyeuristic fantasies do not seem to stray too far from the asexualized Paddies rendered paralyzed by the aloof Miss O'Murphy in later panels (Herr 1990). McCabe's striking fashioning of Mona as Tallon's rubber doll companion in the caravan banished to the margins of Scotsfield, however, is a poignant reminder of DeValera's flawed vision of domesticated Irish femininity.

> I didn't expect Mangan to understand the complexities of the relationship I had with Mona. Or to know what she meant by "that precious harbour." The place of dreams that her and my father never managed to reach. You'd hear mutterings in the town: "He bucked her crooked and then fucked off both her and the wife, without even bothering to look back once."
>
> But that wasn't how Mona saw it, and I knew that. She had told me all about it when I'd visit her after school every day. I'd just sit listening for hours.
>
> "I know he loved me, no matter what they say," she'd say. "And I'm sorry for the pain it caused your mother. But one day we'll reach the Place of Wonders, the wondrous place, they'll all have come right again. Because that's what it's like there, Joey. And he's waiting there,

your father Jamsey, for my boat to arrive. At night, perhaps, when those lovely golden lights are twinkling. And when it does –"

She paused before turning to me and saying: "Mona," he'll say. "*Mona!*"

Sometimes she'd whimper when she said it, or fiddle about with tissues.

"Don't think bad of me, son," she'd say. "I know what the rest of them are saying. Because of what I done to my baby."

"Don't worry, Mona," I'd reply and want to climb inside her stomach so that *I* could become her baby.

"It could be you," she said one day. "You could be born again! To me! *Then* everything might come right!" (McCabe 2003, 93)

Although Tallon's biological mother was eventually carted off to a mental institution babbling about "Chinamen" in the wake of his father's departure, Joey manages to find a maternal substitute in Mona before she eventually commits suicide at the reservoir. Tallon's relationship with Mona is initiated when he is still a child, hearing almost occult stories of his father's relationship with a mistress. According to Mona, their love was a complex and fragile relationship that she believed would culminate in "that precious harbour," which she also refers to as "the place of dreams." While Mona and Tallon's father never reach such a figurative port, where their love could presumably flourish without the persecution that greeted them in Scotsfield, it can be assumed that their affair was consummated physically. Considering the town gossip that claimed he "bucked her crooked and then fucked off both her and the wife, without even bothering to look back," in addition to Mona's decision to abort Joey's father's child, Mona's "precious harbour" was certainly not her female anatomy.

As she is emptied of her perceived female virtue through her affair with Joey's father and hollowed out reproductively through her decision to abort the senior Tallon's unborn child, McCabe fashions Mona as the shell of a mythical Irish female icon, who *Shivers* in an intoxicated haze until she finally takes her own life. Analogous to Herr's analysis of Farrell's first *Madonna Irlanda* (1977), Mona's slow demise reflects McCabe's methodical gouging of the Mother Ireland symbol. For McCabe, Mother Ireland has become as silent, static figure. Stripped of the mother tongue of Irish, she stands blank eyed and lifeless, inflated with empty nationalist rhetoric delivered predominantly in Standardized English, like Tallon's rubber doll rendition of Mona. In regard to Farrell's work Herr writes:

Farrell pictorially exploits this elegant point to insist on O'Murphy's *motionlessness*. Held in place by a halo on the left and burning buttocks on the right, slowly turning from living flesh (Boucher was famous for his flesh tones, his rosy knees and buttocks) to statuary marble, she is cut free from the rococo world of pleasant motion and hooked into a profound stasis produced from ambivalence about the female body, about the body in general as eternal threat to the other half of the Cartesian scale. (1990, 13)

As Miss O'Murphy is suspended, *motionlessness* in the simultaneous contradiction of angelic virtue in the symbol of the "halo" and the worldly flesh of her "burning buttocks," Farrell fixes this abject Mother Ireland as she turns "from living flesh...to statuary marble" suggesting that *Madonna Irlanda* is similarly stuck in Irish psyches. Unable to furnish relief from English colonialism or globalization or to even serve as a symbol of a mythic Irish pastoral, Farrell's Miss O'Murphy is rendered omnipresent yet utterly useless. Likewise, Mona cannot possibly serve as an ample substitute for Joey's absent father or his mad mother.

Mona's role as McCabe's bankrupt symbol of Irish nationalist mythology becomes apparent in its least sinister formulation in the final section of the above cited passage. As she states, "Don't think bad of me, son...I know what the rest of them are saying. Because of what I done to my baby," Mona becomes the opposite of Mother Ireland. She is not revived by the spilt blood of another Irish man by the hand of an enemy; she single handedly refuses to perpetuate such cycles through an abortion. Conscious of perceived repercussions locally and nationally of such action she is soothed by Tallon's, "'Don't worry, Mona,' I'd reply and want to climb inside her stomach so that *I* could become her baby." As she responds, "It could be you...You could be born again! To me! *Then* everything might come right," Mona indicates a chilling understanding of an Irish intolerance for challenging even mythological traditions, never mind Catholic and Irish legislative objections to abortion. While she is trapped in the repercussions of her actions – the subject of callous gossip, "bucked crooked" by Tallon's father and dubbed *Shivers* after an alcohol induced mental breakdown – she asserts agency through suicide. But much like Farrell's Miss O'Murphy, Mona is condemned to a static purgatorial existence. In the scandal of her life and death she remains a socially bankrupt figure in the minds of small town Scotsfield and Tallon's fantastic representation of Mona in the rubber doll that Mangan sees through the filthy curtains of the caravan, proves equally damning.

Even on the margins of society, Tallon's "explorations" of and with Mona seem scandalous. After finding his dog wounded after one of Tallon's acid induced rages, Mangan threatens to uncover Joey's secret "affair" with the bankrupt maternal figure of Mona. Mangan states:

> "You'll pay for what you done, Joey Tallon! Now the whole town will know! I seen you all right! I seen you – *with her!*"
> He glared at me.
> "Pulling at yourself and talking in women's voices! A long black wig – I seen it!"
> "*Shut up!*" I said. "You don't know anything, Mangan! You don't know what you're talking about!"
> He squared up to me, quivering.
> "I do!" he snapped. "I know everything that goes on. You think I've been here in this camp for close on thirty year and not know what goes on? I know all right, and I know you hurt...you hurt my little – !"
> "He's not fucking little!" I spat. "He's not fucking little!"
> "He just wouldn't stop!" I tried my best to explain, but Mangan was already on his way out. He turned as he crossed the grass and raised his fist.
> "I seen you and don't think I didn't!" he called. "Through yon window, I seen what you be doing! Calling out her name! *Mona! Mona!* I know who you're talking about, sure enough! I seen her about the town, years ago, same black hair and all! Yes! That's what youse be at, you and her! You and your Mrs... *Mona!* Oh aye, Mona Galligan that fired herself into the reservoir! Aye! Riding the dead! Riding the dead – that's your game and don't tell me any different! For these eyes don't lie – dressing her up and talking to her! Lying there raving without a stitch on you, full to the gills with drink! Do you hear me, do you rav –"
> "Shut your mouth, Mangan! Get in there, I said! Get in there to fuck and shut your mouth! Who's going to believe the like of you, a halfwit old tinker!" (McCabe 2003, 89)

In Mangan's rant in the wake of his dog's injury, McCabe depicts a combination of tensions present in contemporary Ireland that cannot be eradicated by economic advancement or escape routes offered through fantasies of America. Instead, Joey and Mangan's exchange displays significant challenges to mainstream Irish culture associated with conservative nationalist rhetoric of the early twentieth century.

The tear-streaked Mangan, wearing an "old Faire Isle jumper with tea stains all down its front," paints a sad picture of an elderly traveler distraught over an injured dog. His confrontation with Joey, however, measures the disparate conditions even within the margins of Scotsfield's untouchable population. Mangan threatens to expose Joey's secret with the litany of his observations – "I seen you – *with her!*... Pulling at yourself and talking in women's voices!" As he reveals all that he has "seen" of Joey's affair with the rubber Mona, Mangan's accusations shake Joey. The moral conservatism associated with the Catholic church, which instigates shame in masturbation, never mind consummation with a rubber doll, seems to darken Joey's reaction to Mangan's threat to reveal all that he has "seen." Although Joey and Mangan both live in the camper grounds on the outskirts of town, McCabe's depictions of Mangan and Bonehead throughout the text candidly portray the traveler populations' subjugation in Irish history. Sporting a tea stained jumper, Mangan is a continual mess and the irony of his plight is he is a traveler that no longer travels. His language reflects a lack of education in Standardized English evident in his employment of "I seen you" instead of the standardized past tense *saw*. Additionally, McCabe employs elements of language associated with Irish-English in Mangan's use of "Through yon window" instead of through *that* window and the use of "youse" to signify the singular *you* of Standardized English but these would probably have entered traveler populations' speech patterns due to proximity to Irish-English speaking populations rather than a history of the use of Gaelic. The significance of this representation of language, however, demonstrates distances between Joey and Tallon based on their respective ethnic associations, despite the fact that both individuals inhabit similar social and economic rungs in the Scotsfield cultural hierarchy.

McCabe's use of these non-standardized vernacular markers suggests Mangan's disassociation from the majority of Scotsfield's citizenry, more so than assimilation to the speech patterns associated with the Irish-English of such a population. Joey's reply to Mangan's threat reveals disparities in their rank of affiliation with the community: "Get in there to fuck and shut your mouth! Who's going to believe the like of you, a halfwit old tinker!" Although he is shaken by the prospect of public shame associated with Mangan revealing his secret affair with Mona, Tallon seems fairly confident that his word can override the "halfwit old tinker." While he justifies his actions by claiming that he "didn't expect Mangan to understand the complexities of the relationship I had with Mona," Tallon seems just fearful enough to bully the old man with the callous derogatory name of "halfwit tinker." In this phrase, Irish prejudice against the region's traveler population is clearly evident, feeding into McCabe's criticism of a nationalist, majority sense. While McCabe's reaction to fixation on the static dual figure of Mother Ireland – the bloodthirsty hag/youthful goddess – is certainly analogous to Herr's reading of Farrell's *Madonna Irlanda*, his novel at large may also betray a similar reaction to stagnation and immobility in Irish culture. Herr writes:

> To say that the Catholic church (in complicity with English Victorian mores) *produced* this aspect of Irishness, as most historical analysts of Irish censorship have is to miss the main event: a reflexive and widespread resistance to *seeing* movement, to recognizing its necessity, and ultimately to sanctioning radical changes of posture. Similarly, one way to read the famous ambiguity and obliquity of English-as-it-is-spoken-in-Ireland involves noticing the protective coloration involved; the discourse swims with possibilities while bodies are imaged as changeless – inert, Finn MacCoolian masses on the verge of reabsorption into the landscape. (1990, 14)

As McCabe fashions Mona's trajectory from a shell of an Irish woman, wracked by romantic abandonment, abortion and alcoholism, to her transformation into a rubber doll in Tallon's isolated world, Ireland's "movement" from the 1970s to the early twenty-first century is all the more apparent in comparison to Mona's fixed representation. While McCabe's rendition of "English-as-it-is-spoken-in-Ireland" is the most pervasive characteristic of the novel to ensure that "coloration" can be recognized in more than the fleshy bottom of Irish culture (unlike Farrell's static representation of Miss Murphy *swimming* as *Madonna Irlanda*) Tallon's perceived madness is a continual reminder that as "discourse swims" the manner in which "bodies" can move and change does not necessarily mean that they can be controlled. As McCabe documents considerable cultural and political change in Ireland in the thirty years referred to in *Call Me the Breeze*, his rendition of a "Real Irish Political Picture" is no less chilling than Farrell's 1977 representation. This becomes abundantly evident in Tallon's desperate interactions with the static, synthetic Mona where lines between maternal and romantic interactions are blurred to disturbing distortion.

> I was so dehydrated when I got back to the camp that I had to drink five glasses of water. "I'm fine now," I said to myself. But then I began

to sweat. However, not to worry, I reassured myself as I lay down on the bed. It was a new doll but the same Mona. She was wearing her black wig with the centre parting and her long floaty dress. The wig looked a little lopsided, so I did my best to fix it, trying to steady my hands as I did so. I didn't put any lipstick on her. On Mona. Except that it wasn't Mona. It wasn't Mona Galligan, was it? Never had been and never would be. But I laid my head on her breast anyway. I lay on her breast. No, I didn't. It was between her legs I lay. Between her legs, way in under that skirt. And do you know what else I did? I sucked my thumb. I sucked my thumb and lisped: *"Tssht!"*

And then it was like I'd never been in the pub or seen Boyle Henry at all, safe for ever with her in the cave of wishful dreams. (McCabe 2003, 215)

The comic novelty of rubber dolls in Ireland late in the twentieth century is quickly sobered in this scene. Mona as a hollow mother, "a new doll but the same Mona" initially serves as a constant in Tallon's existence. She is a maternal figure who can calm Joey after his repeated encounters with the ever-threatening Boyle Henry. Rather than providing any real comfort to Joey though, Mona becomes a silent witness, observing Tallon's slip into ever deepening madness.

As Tallon states "I'm fine now," to himself, McCabe breaks the monotony of Tallon's role as narrator through a representation of dialogue. The uttered phrase suggests that Joey will engage in dialogue but the speechless "new doll" is unable to reciprocate Tallon's effort. The unnerving switch in perspective between Tallon as narrator to Tallon as character hones in on his solitary existence and the contradiction of his utterance that only results in talking to himself. Role transitions continue throughout the passage as Mona quickly slips from her role as mother to lover to mother again in almost blinding rapidity. Tallon claims, "she was wearing her black wig...and her long floaty dress" as though she blew herself up that morning and carefully fixed her synthetic hair and slipped into her favorite frock. This feigned normalcy is quickly tempered with "the wig looked a little lopsided, so I did my best to fix it" and in Joey's admission that he "didn't put any lipstick on her." In this turn the complicated nature of Tallon's relationship with Mona is clearly more than Mangan might be able to glean from peeking through the camper windows but this is also a moment in which Tallon finally begins to question his own behavior. After mentioning that he did not apply her lipstick that day, he identifies the "she" to whom he refers with the curt "On Mona." But this is tempered by the dialogic interruption of "except that it wasn't Mona" and the interrogative "it wasn't Mona Galligan, was it?" Slowly interweaving a dialogic exchange between Tallon as character and Tallon as narrator, McCabe depicts Tallon as continually under threat. But if his criticism of Mona as Mother Ireland renders Tallon virtually paralyzed in his efforts to assert autonomy and self-possession, what lessons might McCabe's anti-hero offer Irish citizens of the contemporary historical moment? As he states that the new doll "never had been and never would be" Mona, it seems some shard of reality seems to enter this dark, desperate scene. But if Ireland never was the old bloodthirsty hag or virtuous goddess of Irish nationalist myth, what then might represent an Irish collective? If the region's mother tongue is only a relic of a historical age, what can serve as the region's defining characteristic? Is anything definitively Irish in McCabe's twenty-first century vision?

When Joey states "but I laid my head on her breast anyway," McCabe's crafting of the scene suggests that this could be Tallon's desperate attempt to satisfy a need for maternal soothing or comfort. But with the interjection of "no, I didn't. It was between her legs I lay. Between her legs, way in under that skirt," the action seems charged with sexual exploration given the design function of a rubber doll. But much like the frequent changes in perspective between Tallon as narrator and Tallon as character in the stylization of language throughout the passage, Tallon again slips into a childlike posture to return Mona to her maternal station. "And do you know what else I did?" he asks his literary audience as narrator, "I sucked my thumb and lisped: '*Tssht!*'"

Relegated to infancy between the rubber legs of an imagined Mona, Tallon finds momentary safety from Boyle Henry "with her in the cave of wishful dreams." The steep cost for such comfort, however, is Mona's imprisonment in the trope of Mother Ireland. Silent, lifeless, subject to the whims of a deranged heterosexual male, she is defined by her son and lover depending on his ever fluctuating needs and moods. Like the figure of Mother Ireland, a relic of nationalist rhetoric, Mona serves as a pacifier for the infantile Tallon. The maternal symbol continues to provide comfort even when emptied of all her original substance.

As Tallon's need for companionship develops from seeking maternal to romantic comfort, his infatuation with Jacy rapidly escalates.

> Sinking her hands into the pocket of her Levis and fingering that lovely bead necklace, one exactly like you'd expect Joni to wear. You could tell straight away that she played the guitar. I could just

> imagine her, in a log cabin somewhere with the firelight flickering on her face as she looked into my eyes and strummed. I just stood there watching as she talked to her friend about Iowa, which is a state in America, of course, apart from that I knew nothing about it. Maybe they were going on holiday there or something because you could see a travel guide with this coloured cover sticking out of her bag with a great blue sky and waving golden corn and just that one word – *Iowa*. I even loved the way it formed on her lips. I would call her *"My Lady."*
>
> "A pint of Guinness," she said, and it was like I was kind of swaying in space. (McCabe 2003, 8)

While Joey's initial interactions with Jacy are tainted with seemingly innocent elements of romantic whimsy, his indulgent fantasy soon blooms into a dangerous obsession. "Sinking her hands into the pockets of her Levis and fingering that lovely bead necklace," Joey's fist impression of Jacy directly associates her with the late 1960s counter-cultural revolution in the United States. Jacy's beaded necklace is immediately associated with (the ironically, Canadian born) Joni Mitchell and her bleached blond hair only contributes to such a misidentification as Tallon claims "you could tell straight away that she played guitar." While it is difficult not to hear echoes of the first bars from Mitchell's 1971 *Blue* in Tallon's description of Jacy, her simple request for "a pint of Guinness" enables McCabe to ground her in the ordinary details of Scotsfield. Removing her from the "log cabin" and potential escape in "a great blue sky and waving golden corn" in the Iowa of Tallon's imagination, she is positioned in the ever narrowing social scene of small town Ireland, epitomized in a pint.

Although Tallon is safe to assume Jacy is a stranger to Scotsfield, his illusion of her association with America betrays an investment in cultural release associated with Irish nationalism.

> I wondered what The Jace – I felt I knew her so well now that it was OK to call her that – made of all that stuff, the killing and bombing, I mean. It was a long way from California, that was for sure. I had a fair idea she didn't give a fuck. "If that's how they want to live their lives, well, that's fine. All I can say is, include me out." The unblemished sands of Big Sur stretching out for miles behind her and the Pacific surf crashing. I couldn't stop thinking about things turning out differently for Charlie if he'd gone down the road of Carlos Castaneda and stuff and not got stuck with violent revolution and shit – just how great it all could have been. (McCabe 2003, 16)

Jacy as Joni surfaces in this passage again but the implications for such association escalate with each reference. Although McCabe attempts to temper Joey's imagined association between Joni Mitchell and Jacy in her simple and seemingly native request for "A pint of Guinness," that sends Tallon "swaying in space," this passage confirms Tallon's nurtured obsession for Boyle Henry's lover. Drawing on the lyrics of Joni Mitchell's *California* to fill biographical gaps in The Jace that Joey knows "so well now," McCabe is able to conflate Joey's bifurcated romantic obsessions. Abandoning a tired Mother Ireland and all she fails to deliver in her nationalistic glory, Tallon substitutes Jacy and American culture for everything that has failed him in his inescapable Irish experience. Unable to explore American culture through mediums other than literature and song, McCabe's rendition of Tallon's infatuation with America draws from Mitchell's lyrics and Carlos Castaneda's novels resulting in the frighteningly narrow fantasy that is The Jace.

Tallon's musing on Jacy's imagined reactions to Scotsfield's introduction to "The Troubles" reflects his effort to analyze Ireland's violently political stalemate from an alternative perspective. Yearning for release from Ireland's paralytic binary, Tallon relies on the convenient vocabulary of Joni Mitchell's song lyrics to ground his wishful escape. Seemingly referring to *California*, in which Mitchell catalogs a homeward journey, Tallon imagines that Jacy would probably "not give a fuck" about the "killing and bombing" though she would feel "It was a long way from California, that was for sure." Similarly, Joey's references to Big Sur "stretching out for miles behind her and the Pacific surf crashing" are no more formulated than his understanding of "Iowa...which is a state in America, of course" (McCabe 2003, 8). But his disillusioned understanding of Jacy escalates at the Peace Rally when

> he almost swooned as he saw her emerging in the light. She was dressed in white and wearing her steward's armband, with her long blonde hair tied back. Obviously she wouldn't be attired in denims at a somber function like this. But he hadn't expected her to look quite so beautiful – and pure. It was again a testimony to her respect for other traditions that she had deferred to local practice and worn just a white blouse and white skirt, which swept dreamily about her knees. (McCabe 2003, 180)

Susceptible to mythmaking akin to that propagated by Celtic Twilight renditions of pure Irish culture nestled in rural pockets of the West, Tallon's visions of Jacy and her American affiliation fall into feigned anthropological modes of analysis by this section. Tallon's claim that "It was again a testimony to her respect for other traditions" and her decision to "defer to local practice" demonstrate any effort on Tallon's behalf to distance himself from the Scotsfield community. His claims that Jacy has somehow "deferred" to local custom by virtue of her outfit, reflect Tallon's levels of desperation to craft some level of mediation between his romantic obsession, his community and its introduction to violence associated with "The Troubles." Like his crafting of Mona as an abject Mother Ireland, McCabe's rendition of Tallon's goddess of the West indicates a complete destruction of this symbol. Jacy comes to serve as both the icon and the passageway for Tallon's escape through the convenient vocabulary of America's 1960s and 1970s counter culture. Tallon's interactions with the bankrupt goddess of Ireland, however, result in his incarceration and permanent disassociation from Scotsfield's "majority sense," rather than inclusion in a mythic Irish collective.

Unlike Tallon's infatuation with Mona, which slowly fizzled with his growing interest in Jacy, Joey's fantasies of romantic involvement with Jacy prove toxic. Mona's suicide and subsequent resurrection as a novelty sex toy enable Tallon to exist in a solitary fashion, relegated to the fringes of society. But his obsession with Jacy leads to stalking, kidnapping and finally degradation in sexual humiliation at the hands of Hoss and Boyle Henry, which enables McCabe to document Tallon's final descent into madness. As reality creeps into Tallon's isolated fantasy world, Joey's experiences on the streets of Scotsfield become incrementally more precarious. Tallon's dream sequence with Jacy, following his release from Mountjoy jail, introduces the crumbling of a fantasy.

> Hoss appeared then, directing the men who were carrying the cross. I can still feel the pin of the nails as they went in. But it was nothing compared to the shame when Jacy approached me on the cross and started tugging at the strip of cloth they'd tied around my groin. She chuckled into her hand and then turned to the mourners, going – not in a Californian accent now but in a really drab country Irish one, from around County Wicklow or thereabouts it sounded – "Did you see the little yoke the fucker has in there? Tsk! Tsk!"
>
> I died then and they all went back down to Austie's. I can still hear her saying that, and the more I try to block it out the louder it seems to get. (McCabe 2003, 104)

While the dream sequence is not presented as a relived event, it ironically betrays a reality Tallon refuses to recognize. Relying heavily on symbols of Christ's crucifixion, McCabe crafts Tallon's childlike innocence as that which is martyred in his interactions with Jacy, Henry, Hoss, et al. Again demeaning the seemingly sacred with sexual overtones, McCabe's rendition of Tallon's burning shame "when Jacy approached me on the cross and started tugging at the strip of cloth they'd tied around my groin," suggests the sacrilege of Henry, Hoss and Austie's corruption in theocratic Ireland. But the dream also indicates Tallon's disillusions of self-grandeur.

As Jacy "chuckled into her hand and then turned to the mourners, going – not in a Californian accent now but in a really drab country Irish one, from around County Wicklow or thereabouts it sounded" McCabe plunges Tallon and his crew into the inescapable ordinariness of rural Ireland. Tallon's vernacular is particularly prescient in this scene marked by the word use of "going" instead of "speaking" but most importantly in the shift of Jacy's speech pattern. As she speaks with a "really drab country Irish" accent and not speaking "in a Californian accent now," McCabe can place emphasis on "now" as a marking of an Irish-English grammatical formulation that betrays the influence of the substratum Irish forms for "to be." Tallon's dismay at Jacy's accent change in the dream catalogs reversion to patterns of Irish-English free from the convenient vocabulary of Tallon's America. As she moves from a Californian accent "now" to the "drab country" one, McCabe's construction of Tallon's recollection relies heavily on Irish formulations of the past habitual form of "tá" in "bhíodh" when she spoke with a Californian accent to the present habitual of "bíonn" as she is now "going...in a really drab country one, from around County Wicklow or thereabouts it sounded." Drawing on the seemingly "drab" cultural and political backwater of Wicklow "or thereabouts" to ground Jacy's origins that are inextricably linked to her speech, McCabe all but strips her of any sense of mystery or intrigue.

Despite the detrimental effects of the dream on Tallon's psyche, this sequence betrays a reality that haunts all of his previous interactions with Jacy. The final blow in her comment: "Did you see the little yoke the fucker has in there?" strips Tallon of any remaining shreds of masculinity (not unlike Farrell's later panels of *Madonna Irlanda*). Although this is a dream sequence, the nightmare of a localized Jacy seems to ring with authenticity conspicuously absent in Tallon's Joni Mitchell fantasies. Although gentler renditions appear in Joey's recollections of her kidnapping and later as Hoss and Henry strip him of any last shards of dignity, the image of Jacy as a crass, country girl who demeans Tallon's sexuality seems a chillingly authentic representation of McCabe's vision of Ireland.

V

While McCabe's dark, often paralytic representations of contemporary Ireland may be considered bleak, each text reflects an unflinching support for exploring Irish culture that all but ignores convenient release valves like immigration or consent to colonization. Tallon relies heavily on American fantasies to move through everyday Scotsfield, but by the story's end, McCabe ensures that his narrator is inextricably rooted in Ireland. Is this emulative of an Irish condition of purgatorial changelessness? Or does McCabe's works suggest that Ireland's collective depends on individual contributions to a national culture or politic regardless of the nation's susceptibility to foreign influences?

In the *British Writers Supplement* James P. Austin claims:

> In McCabe's work being Irish and being proud of it do not go together: The men and women in the pages of his novels want to slough off their rural Irish roots like a husk, to strip into something more glamorous, more promising, and less Irish, as being Irish is "associated irremediably with the local, the secondary, the menial." It is this desire, and the inevitable inability to consummate this desire, that drives the characters, tells their stories, and informs us just what it means to be born into the Ireland of Patrick McCabe. (Austin 2004, 127)

While McCabe's work indicates a refusal to romanticize Ireland it would seem his unyielding focus on "the local, the secondary, the menial" may not just be a catalog of Ireland's failure to consent to a "more glamorous, more promising, and less Irish" national identity but may be in fact an effort to showcase the everyday as somehow tragically beautiful. While Tallon serves as a chief example of a character attempting to "slough off" his "Irish roots like a husk" these efforts seem to be nothing more than momentary performance. Ranging from his "*Sure do!*" at the roadblock before the Banbridge bombing that the soldier describes as a "half American, like. Half Yankee" accent to his "private decision to tie my hair back in a ponytail so I'd look like one of these trendy New York businessmen you'd see going to work in Wall Street, swinging that old briefcase," Tallon's efforts are at best, superficial. But Austin's claim that McCabe's characters represent that "being Irish and being proud of it do not go together" may be to miss the point of his work entirely.

Like Joyce, McCabe refrains from romanticizing any element of Ireland's past or present. Nonetheless, his crafting of images that encapsulate painstakingly detailed visions of late twentieth-century Ireland in *Call Me the Breeze* exemplify a tragic though beautiful testament to a national culture. "After all of the negative convictions, to end up Lionized by London publishers, asked for my opinion on this, that and the other. Hailed as 'fresh and original,' not to mention as Mr Triumph of the fucking vernacular!" Tallon, as McCabe in this instance, reflects the particular potency of literary art (McCabe 2003, 244). McCabe can catalog the variety of voices that make up Ireland from the outskirts of the Tinker camp in Mangan and Bonehead to the theocratic center in Father Connolly, "rabbiting on" about "a sort of variety festival" (McCabe 2003, 121). From Austie's "Jasus, but you're the happy-looking boy!" to Bonehead's mock interviews, "So! Watcha tink, young fella? You're a Scotsfield man! Whaddya tink of the achievements of Joseph Tallon" to Johnson's "new mannerisms...That English sort of refinement," the voices of his novels consistently privilege the "local" and "the secondary." But in this venue they are not always considered menial. Rather than judging Irish identity domestically or internationally, McCabe studies it. He re-presents it for his audience to consider its significance, its beauty, its shortcomings. It is a more subtle endeavor than Tallon's "psychobilly," wherein the "effect that I hope to achieve is that, while we'll know it's the past, it will still hit us hard. We'll allude to each and every single tragedy. Within reason, of course!" But it shares his spirit as McCabe asks Ireland to question its past, present and future from its margins.

Just as Tallon relies on Eliot's "Little Gidding" to articulate his spiritual and intellectual explorations from early adulthood onwards, McCabe's novel is bolstered by the well rehearsed lines: "We shall not cease from exploration / And the end of all our exploring / Will be to arrive where we started / And know the place for the first time." Through the "triumph of vernacular," McCabe introduces Ireland through sight and sound, suggesting that identity-formation in this small nation will be in a constant state of flux, as he marks "unification and disunification" with each carefully crafted utterance. As the closing pages of the novel release Tallon from his duty as narrator and "god mode" is assumed by an omnipresent voice, McCabe's focus on Ireland ends with Tallon's visions of America. Mrs Tallon folds a blanket after the "Picnic of Dreams" where Tallon is conspicuously absent and the narrator then turns to our final glimpses of Joey.

Abandoning the premise of a novel written in the "Scotsfield vernacular," McCabe's closing depicts a bleak portrayal of Ireland in Tallon. The final image is of a nation transfixed by Americanization, tempted to abandon all for the fantasy of a cultural, social and political alternative. Confined to an Ireland that compromises his sanity, Tallon must continue to wrestle with his lot in life "because the truth was that Joey Tallon wasn't deranged. He was, in fact, as he insisted, simply in the wrong place" (McCabe 2003, 336). As McCabe places Tallon in the midst of "that huge but inconceivably easeful silence blowing as though before some ancient wind, the golden corn all about them swaying, as it might in a child's golden Paradise vision," he suggests that such a figure may need cultural and political escape or his fate in Ireland will be the purgatorial perch by the "harbour" where Mrs Tallon found Joey "each night" in the "wondrous place" (336–7). In this "easeful silence" of a "child's golden Paradise," the musicality of McCabe's Irish-English language systems in contention with the legacies of literary culture in Ireland, fall into the singular voice of a nameless narrator relating Joey's "tale" in Standardized English. And the final utterances from Scotsfield relate the sadness of Tallon's demise and the echoes of Joey's final "She'll be coming" (McCabe 2003, 336). While McCabe unabashedly comments on the triumphs and costs of Ireland's slow awakening from cultural and political provincialism in the late twentieth century to develop into a self-possessed participant in the European Union and global markets, Tallon's final scene in *Call Me the Breeze* may serve as a warning. If Ireland (North and South) remains culturally and politically for sale in the international marketplace, the musicality of its language may fall into the "easeful silence" of Tallon's America, rendered forever mute like the tragic Mona with the singular voice of an anonymous narrator.

5
Casting Cathleen: Femininity and Motherhood on the Contemporary Irish Stage

> Night and day
> Words fell on me.
> Seeds. Raindrops.
> Chips of Frost.
> From one of them
> I learned my name.
> I rose up. I remembered it.
> Now I could tell my story.
> It was different
> From the story told about me.
>
> (Eavan Boland, "Mother Ireland," *The Lost Land*)

I

On 3 December 1911, Lady Augusta Gregory informed *The New York Times Magazine* that she did not believe "Ireland has ever had a genius for the novel. Of course, there were plenty of Irish novels, but I don't think that was ever the natural means of expression for the Irish. What makes Ireland inclined toward the drama is that it's a great country for conversation. Oscar Wilde said: 'We are the best talkers since the Greeks'" (Mikhail 1977, 58). While her comments were polemic, according to Gregory an Irish gift for gab unquestionably yielded a national affinity to drama. But was this correlation simply a symptom of her investment in Yeats, Synge and the budding national theater or was there any substance in her claims? Gregory's statements pre-date Joyce's *Ulysses* and the relative flood of Irish novels of the late twentieth century but her advocacy of the notion of a gift for conversation as essentially Irish was certainly in keeping with her relationship to language systems as they were spoken in Ireland.

In the wake of protests in Dublin, Chicago and New York to the production of J.M. Synge's "The Playboy of the Western World," the playwright's "wonderful language that he uses in his verse plays" became a common topic of discussion as inextricable as references to public outbursts and the question of Irish sovereignty in discourse pertaining to the play (Mikhail 1977, 56). Serving as a representative of the Abbey Theater Co., Gregory spoke confidently of her assessment of the nation's artistic efforts, her comments much in keeping with Yeats' endeavor of this period to assemble and define the region's literary tradition. While acknowledging the integral role of language in Ireland in the region's literary endeavors, Gregory's comments also mark emphasis on the fusing of political and cultural aspirations for Irish sovereignty as she cites the "inspiration of the movement" in Parnell's death. "For twelve years before he died the whole imagination of Irishmen was taken up with the land war... And every one's eyes were drawn towards the English Parliament, and some patriots were dreaming of a nation once again; and there was no Irish literature written. There were a few novels by people of leisure, but they didn't express Ireland in any way" (56). Parnell's death was:

> Pretty much like the disbanding of an army. They had lost the keenness for the fight. The party broke up into two sections, and neither quite knew whom it was hitting at.
> And then the imagination of Irishmen, especially in Ireland, being set free, looked about for something to pitch on; and that imagination, at least among young Irishmen, turned to this dramatic form rather than to novels or poems. That, I think, is the origin of it.
> At the same time Dr Douglas Hyde formed his Gaelic League, for the purpose of reviving the Irish language; and although we don't use the Irish language in our plays, still the excitement caused by its revival, the discovery that there was a great deal of legend and culture and song-making still among the people, rather send writers back to the life of the country itself, instead of looking for an inspiration outside. (Mikhail 1977, 56)

Historically situating the move to drama, Gregory cites an inevitable link to the development of an experimental Irish Literary Theater (55). As she emphasizes the demise of a political anti-colonial movement with the passing of Parnell and the disbanding "of an army," in conjunction with a fledgling cultural resurgence in Hyde's Gaelic League, the circumstances all but begged the region's artists to respond. And the accessibility inherent in the medium of theater (to those literate or otherwise who could afford admission price for such a performance), would ensure the dissemination of a newly invented cultural vision for a prospective sovereign Ireland.

Although she demurely refers to her own work and cites Yeats' accomplishments in contributing to this virtual explosion of Anglo-Irish letters in this period, Gregory finds a chief example of Irish literary compulsion towards drama in Synge:

> It was so it happened with Mr Synge. He was living abroad, not doing anything of any value in literature; and then he came back, partly moved by this new excitement, and lived there in the extreme West for a part of every year, and wandered about, and there he got that wonderful language that he uses in his verse-plays, and also got his material.
>
> Of course the material is changed when it passes through an imaginative mind; it changes a little with the temperament of the writer. There is something of harshness and gloom in his writings, perhaps a slight morbidity, which casual critics put down to French influence, but which I think was due to the shadow of his early death. (Mikhail 1977, 57)

While Gregory's assessment of Synge's "slight morbidity" can be attributed to biographical details like his subjectivity to illness or casual critics' references to his French forays, Synge's work also betrayed a romantic picture of Irish cultural paralysis, the harshness of poverty and ignorance in rural pockets of the West and a commitment to hybrid language systems heavily impacted by the region's political and historical developments. Lady Gregory's deference to Synge as an Irish dramatist archetype not only supports her claim of an indigenous genius in drama, rather than the novel, but also enables her to tout an unflinching commitment to Yeats:

> "You spoke" said the reporter, "of Mr Synge's getting the language he uses from his observation of the people on the west coast. Surely they don't speak as poetically as he represents them?"
>
> "They do, yes," answered Lady Gregory. "Of course, he has heightened it a good deal, but they have a beautiful dialect, and they have

an extraordinary ear. The Gaelic language itself depends very much on ear and rhythm, and when those who are thinking in Gaelic speak in English they get the same rhythm.

"You may see it in my plays, where I have written in dialect, though much less than you will see it in Mr Synge's. They have also a repetition of phrase, which they use just as the Hebrew poets do.

"The Hebrew poet will say, 'The heavens declare the glory of God, the firmament showeth His handiwork.' You see the effect produced by the repetition of the idea in the second part of the sentence. So an Irish peasant will say, 'She is dead and she is not living, she is buried and gone to the grave.' For the sake of the sound the idea is emphasized and repeated.

"Of course Synge heightened it; one does in writing. It undergoes some change in passing through the mind of a writer. Synge made a study of it. I had used it before him, in my translation from the Irish epics – those epics which Mr Roosevelt has written about."

The reporter asked whether the original intention of the new Irish dramatists had been merely to express Irish life, or to establish a new school of writing.

"I don't think anybody sets out with a plan of that sort," said Lady Gregory. "All I wanted was to see Mr Yeats's beautiful verse-plays acted in Ireland and to hear his words spoken on the stage. Then I happened to write my comedies, not with any such purpose as you mention, but because it is necessary to have some comedies as a relief or change from listening to verse." (Mikhail 1977, 58)

Introducing elements of Synge's talent – his passion for the language of the "country people of Ireland," in his ready response to a cultural call for the depiction of domestic genius in "a beautiful dialect" of the "extreme West," Gregory hails his accomplishments, citing their almost ethereal origins in Synge's adventurous wanderings. As she compares his creations to the mythic verse of the Hebrew poets by delineating the similarities in phrasing between the rhythmic repetitions evident in "The heavens declare the glory of God, the firmament showeth his handiwork" and "She is dead and she is not living, she is buried and gone to the grave," she sets a foundation for the canon of Irish literature.

In the course of itemizing Synge's artistic development and the characteristics of his work, all the while providing a historical and cultural context to these progressions in Parnell's death, the upsurge of the Gaelic League and the formation and eventual development of a national theater company, Gregory's commentary indicates significant fragmentation of cultural, political and linguistic tension that flows underneath her explicit discussion of the Irish dramatic movement at the turn of the twentieth century. In Gregory, we hear the resounding voice of one of the most influential figures in modern Irish letters. Yet time and time again, she overshadows references to her own work as an Irish dramatist through deference to her male counterparts in Synge and Yeats. "You may see it in my plays, where I have written in dialect, though much less than you will see it in Mr Synge's," she remarks in praising Synge's work in "The Playboy of the Western World" and subsequent productions. And a mark of self-depreciation, perhaps in the name of humility or in line with appropriate social decorum emerges in her response to the reporter's inquiry as to whether the goals of "the new Irish dramatists had been merely to express Irish life, or to establish a new school of writing." Yeats publicized his efforts to "establish a new school of writing" in Ireland, to invent a tradition into which he could comfortably contribute his work as an Anglo-Irish artist.[1] Yet, Gregory's response is particularly humble: "All I wanted was to see Mr Yeats's beautiful verse-plays acted in Ireland and to hear his words spoken on the stage. Then I happened to write my comedies, not with any such purpose as you mention, but because it is necessary to have some comedies as a relief or change from listening to verse."

A revolutionary in her own right, Lady Gregory's role in the literary production and fiscal support of writers of the Celtic Twilight cannot be underestimated. Her ability to capture "peasant" dialects, which she admits to using "before" Synge "in my translation from the Irish epics – those epics which Mr Roosevelt has written about," demonstrates a precedent that certainly influenced Synge's later work. But her public deference to male counterparts in this movement, as demonstrated in her comments printed in *The New York Times Magazine*, has continued to influence the status of female playwrights and the depiction of women on the Irish stage throughout the twentieth century. Gregory's ability to recognize the conflation of Ireland's political and cultural movements in the wake of Parnell's death is particularly significant. As an Anglo-Irish female figure of status, Gregory yielded power unavailable to the peasantry she often profiled in her plays. Additionally, the socioeconomic and political influence garnered from her deceased husband offered power unavailable to the virtually impoverished Anglo-Irish males in Yeats and Synge. Gregory's repetitious public displays of deference to her male counterparts in Yeats, Synge, George Moore and Edward Martyn, however, depreciated the public capital of her work in her contemporary moment. Such a precedent for an Irish playwright in the early twentieth century, in addition to the Celtic Twilight's mythologizing the role of women in Ireland, yielded long term effects on the status of female playwrights and the portrayal of women on Irish stages for decades to come.

Lady Gregory offers a complex female precedent in Irish letters. Her work in developing the Abbey Theater Co., sponsoring Yeats', Synge's and other writers' development and production in the years of the Celtic Twilight, in addition to her own copious contributions to an Anglo-Irish tradition, are certainly staggering. But her work with Irish-English dialect and an almost innate consciousness of the political potency of codifying a symbol of Irish cultural particularity in the wake of anti-colonial turmoil in Parnell's death are particularly germane to recent developments in contemporary Irish theater demonstrated in the work of Christina Reid, Martin McDonagh and Pearse Elliott. Through the course of the early twentieth century, Gregory was precariously perched between her own work as a female revolutionary – writer, political activist, theatrical entrepreneur – and advocating Yeats' early visions of manufacturing a romanticized Irish cultural pastoral. His fashioning of Irish women, not as autonomous beings contributing to the development of a potentially sovereign nation as demonstrated by the privileged but grounded Lady Gregory, but instead as abstract symbols, goddesses and muses, relegated to supporting roles for Irish male genius had long standing cultural and political effects in the fledgling nation. Writing in regard to such precedents in Irish theater, Carla J. MacDonagh claims:

> When concentrating on a female character, moreover, male playwrights have tended to present them as symbolic representations of abstract ideas or as stereotypes. Yeats' work perhaps can serve as an arresting example of such unrealistic depictions. Writing to Katharine Tynan in 1889, Yeats admitted that his interest in a specific woman to whom Tynan had referred was "only as a myth and a symbol" (qtd. in Wade 117–18). Woman as myth and symbol is an apt description of women's positioning within his plays as well, particularly those that explore the (male) poet's relationship with his (female) muse, such as *A Full Moon in March, The Herne's Egg,* and *The Player Queen.* (Watt, Morgan, Mustafa 2000, 180)[2]

As figures like Yeats codified femininity as merely supporting or supplementing male action, inspiring the real work of man as an ethereal muse, what role were true women to play in the nation's negotiation of its sovereignty? How could artists like Gregory, who artfully depicted Irish rural communities in plays like "Spreading the News" and "The Gaol Gate," negotiate their contributions to the tradition of Anglo-Irish letters as women were pushed to the margins of society from the outset?

Gregory's comments in *The New York Times Magazine* in regard to Synge's "The Playboy of the Western World" demonstrate consciousness of the inextricable links between the politics of language (in Hyde's Gaelic revival and aesthetic representations of such tension in Gregory's early work and Synge's subsequent productions), a rapidly changing Irish relationship to Britain following Parnell's death and a burgeoning cultural movement propagated by artists like Yeats, Gregory, Moore, AE (the pen name of George William Russell) and others. These underlying developments can be traced in mythological plays like Yeats' iconic "Cathleen ni Houlihan" and Edward Martyn's "The Heather Field." But as female figures on the Irish stage continued to represent a mythically pure Irish nation in the figure of Mother Ireland or inspiring fantastical endeavors like pacifying and domesticating the wild heather fields of the west, was this feminine symbol also extended to representations of the region's contested language systems? Was the symbol of Ireland's faltering mother tongue yet another example of a mythic, abstract representation inspiring a flourishing dramatic movement that has continued to haunt Irish drama for decades thereafter?

II

In Christina Reid's 1989 play, "The Belle of the Belfast City," Janet laments "there are no women in Ireland. Only mothers and sisters and wives. I'm a sister and a wife. But I'll never be a mother" (Reid 1997, 210). From the mid nineteen-eighties to the late nineteen-nineties, Reid's plays considered the negotiation of individual identity and social participation in Northern Irish society in several plays ranging from "Tea in a China Cup" (1983), to "My Name, Shall I Tell You My Name" (1989), to "Joyriders" (1986) and its sequel, "Clowns" (1996). Reid's characters resist female stereotypes, characteristic of early Irish dramatic movements as she attends to rifts and divisions in explorations of female and male characters' interactions in Northern Ireland's deeply divided society. Like her predecessor, Lady Gregory, Reid's work depicts language systems particular to the communities she chooses to represent. Born into a working-class, Protestant and Unionist family in Ardoyne, Reid "considers herself Irish. 'We don't speak English the same way [as it is spoken in England],' she claims, 'our speech patterns are different, how we say things is different' " (Reid 1997, viii).

Considering questions of female identity formation amidst considerable Northern Irish violence in the nineteen-eighties and thereafter, Reid's plays question perceptions of solidarity in the region's sectarian communities. Her work demonstrates that:

> Schisms exist as much within communities as between them. *Tea in a China Cup, The Belle of the Belfast City* and *My Name, Shall I Tell You My Name?* all deal with the questioning of Protestant traditions by a younger generation of women who refuse to accept the intransigence and inflexibility of a particular masculine loyalist ideology which would dictate their behaviour. All these plays also link the construction of masculinity within the family to sectarian politics. Too often it is a destructive inflexible masculinity. All also draw sharp attention to the imposition of domestic roles on women by both Protestant and Catholic iconography. In Catholicism, we see woman as an angelic virgin figure reworked by the nationalist movement into Mother Ireland; in Protestantism, woman as loyal steadfast servicer and nurturer of men willing to die for Queen and Country. (Delgado 1997, xv)[3]

Janet's claim "I am a sister and a wife. But I will never be a mother" exemplifies just one of several moments in which Reid's work portrays resistance to "the intransigence and inflexibility of a particular masculine loyalist ideology." But her work also illustrates a variety of ways in which Irish men and women are continually challenged to negotiate and express autonomy and individuality in a society that is steeped in patriarchal and colonial traditions. Reid's representation of working-class Belfast speech patterns, in conversation with standardized English associated with political and religious rhetoric espoused by Northern Ireland's governmental and religious orders, offer a juxtaposition of varied cultural and political influences that continually impact the social formation of each of her characters.

> Constantly aware of the difficulties inherent in affirming a "female" identity, Reid's plays do deconstruct traditional dichotomies by concentrating on the plurality of women's experiences in Northern Ireland. Often this is articulated by the intersecting storylines merging past and present, dreams and memories, oral traditions and visual metaphors. Multiple tales are told in plays whose fluid structures

mark a healthy move away from the conventions of the classic realist text. (Delgado 1997, xviii)

Such characteristics are particularly evident in Reid's "The Belle of the Belfast City" (1989). Through the portrayal of multigenerational female interaction embodied in the Horner family, this play illustrates the complexity of familial and political affiliation and affinity in working-class Belfast. While Janet vows that she will never be a "mother," neither Mother Ireland nor the "servicer and nurturer of men willing to die for Queen and Country," Reid's careful depiction of a family's participation in a fervently loyalist community under the duress of "The Troubles" demonstrates a complex vision of women as opposed to the singular visions of "woman" depicted by Irish playwrights throughout the twentieth century. Her exploration of family demonstrates the varied roles of Irish women as "mothers and sisters and wives" as well as daughters, professionals, friends and protectors, continually interacting with and responding to their equally multifarious male counterparts.

Like Lady Gregory's and Synge's work at the turn of the twentieth century, Reid's work emerged amidst considerable political and cultural turmoil in Ireland, North and South. Attending to the negotiation of identity and autonomy amidst such societal unrest, her work demonstrates careful consideration of a nexus of political and cultural forces that inspired a considerable aesthetic response in Northern Irish theater of the period. Despite Reid's dynamic representations of female responses to such historical developments, her plays "have been deemed by one critic in an article about Irish 'political theater' [to] not be of political interest" (Shrank and Demastes 1997, 301).

> Reid herself would no doubt agree, in that she dislikes labels such as "political" playwright or "feminist" playwright, arguing that "I think labels diminish good art. I don't make political statements, I present words and images that are open to interpretation" (Campbell). However, it seems feasible for plays that straightforwardly examine the traditions, prejudices, and stereotypes that fuel political party lines to qualify for possible political interpretations. In this way, Reid's plays excel, offering insight into the everyday lives of the people of Belfast. She also offers the dramatic world a first-rate look into the lives of women and of the young – two groups often overlooked by male playwrights of greater fame. Reviewers of her plays tend to agree that her treatment of her characters is balanced and unsentimental. Wolfe

has even called *Tea* and *Joyriders* "two of the best Northern Irish plays of the Eighties." (Shrank and Demastes 1997, 302)

Much in keeping with Synge's rather benign response to riots following the initial staging of "The Playboy of the Western World," Reid's response to charges that her plays are not of "political interest" reflects an understanding of her work as an effort to produce art for "art's sake" or in Synge's rendition, "for the artist's sake." Although she states, "I think labels diminish good art. I don't make political statements, I present words and images that are open to interpretation," Reid asserts that her work resists convenient political or feminist rhetoric associated with a party or group. Instead, Reid's plays explore negotiations of individuality and autonomy amidst a particularly potent terrain of political affiliation and tribalism endemic to social and political existence in Northern Ireland. And wouldn't such art still bear considerable political significance in its effort to challenge "the traditions, prejudices and stereotypes" that have continually hindered autonomy in individual "everyday lives of the people of Belfast"? As Reid resists labels and statements, her work nonetheless illustrates particular social and political significance as she challenges the politics of her genre as a female playwright depicting multifaceted female figures on an Irish stage, while all the while considering the significance of "everyday lives" of the individuals of an urban Northern Irish community.

In "The Belle of the Belfast City" Reid's varied treatment of motherhood explodes traditional Catholic and Protestant portrayals of this female role in Irish society. Dolly Dunbar Horner, the matriarch of the family, explicitly grates against traditional notions of Protestant motherhood in Northern Ireland. The coquettish Dolly, aged seventy-seven in the context of the play, is a former vaudeville performer affectionately dubbed "The Belle of the Belfast City" from early fame as a child performer. She performs at all times, in public and private spheres alike, her songs and rhymes punctuating dialogue as the play develops. Although Dolly comfortably assumes the role of matriarch throughout the play, Reid reminds her audience that Dolly deeply challenges Protestant and Unionist values, which consistently enter the play through Jack's comments and interjections.

Although married before she turned nineteen, Dolly claims "I was never a housewife. My Joe never wanted that. He was a rare bird. An Ulsterman who could cook" (Reid 1997, 195). Unlike traditional portrayals of Irish marriage throughout the early twentieth century that demonstrate a match of economic or social convenience rather than love, Dolly and Joe's marriage is presented as a truly functional, warm, loving partnership. While this is demonstrated in Dolly's comments about her husband as "a rare bird," who never expected Dolly to conform to a traditional domestic role in their home, the considerable age difference between their two daughters contributes to the novelty of their match. Rose, born twenty years after Vi, serves as a scandal to the more conservative and proper Vi, but as a badge of marital authenticity and integrity to the very much still in love, Joe and Dolly. Dolly's maternal role is further explored in Reid's depiction of the Horner couple's adoption of Jack and Janet, Joe's brother's children who were orphaned in early childhood. Resisting traditional notions of Northern Irish Protestant motherhood by virtue of her progressive husband and a mixed family structure, Dolly repeatedly dismisses Northern Ireland's societal pressures on conceptions of femininity and motherhood with flippant comments or witty remarks: "She always calls me mother when she's bein' prim and proper" Dolly says of Vi. "She must of got that from your side of the family, Joe. But you see our Rose? She's like *my* ones. Fulla life an' rarin' to go" (181).

Although Vi is childless and single, through the course of the play she assumes a specific type of maternal role as she tends to Dolly in her old age and watches over the adult Rose and Janet as though they are her daughters, rather than her sister and cousin. Vi's role in the Horner family is connected to her parents' choices in raising the two girls that have vastly different effects on each of their daughters. From an early age Vi was incorporated into the Horner familial fabric as caretaker rather than child, well before Rose entered late in the Horners' lives. Vi recollects:

> I never remember a time when I was really young, the way children are. As soon as I was tall enough to see over the counter, Dolly kept me off school to work in the shop. I tell you, Davy can read and write better than I can. (Reid 1997, 216)

Dolly and Joe's decision to keep their daughter home from school in order to assist with the small family-run shop is certainly in keeping with working-class values in the early twentieth century. The family's communal economic subsistence was paramount to an individual child's education. This value of family well-being over individual autonomy and development is exacerbated in later years when Vi assumes the role of caregiver for Rose and Janet. Her interactions later in the play stem from her relationship with the women when they were children. In several passages it becomes evident that Vi assumes many of the day-to-day chores of raising Rose and Janet, just as she stood behind the family's shop counter from a very young age. This is evident in a brief exchange between Dolly and Janet when she was a child:

JANET (as a child): Auntie Dolly?
DOLLY: What, darlin'?
JANET: Can I stay off school and help in the shop?
DOLLY: Now you know what Vi's like about you wee ones missin' your schoolin' unless you're really sick. Not that she was ever all that keen on goin' to school when she was your age. Any excuse to get stayin' at home. (Reid 1997, 216)

As she defers maternal responsibilities to Vi, even after Joe's death, Dolly can ensure that she is never a "housewife"; she is never held solely accountable for either housekeeping or raising the children. But what effects have such decisions had on Vi's autonomy within Northern Ireland's deeply conservative society?

In this family structure Vi is given responsibility for most of the Horner family's domestic upkeep, ensuring an unconventional though apparently successful balance in the family home. But this is certainly not without its costs, as is evident in a heated exchange between Vi and Rose following a falling out with their cousin, Jack:

VI: ...You never could leave well alone, could you? You were an indulged brat when you were wee and you haven't changed one whit. Still stirrin' it. Always gettin' away with it. A pretty face. A clever tongue. Father always said you could charm the birds off the trees. "Look after Rose, Vi. She's our wee flower." He never had a pet name for me. Good old Vi. Martha to your Mary. Vi'll make the dinner while Rose is makin' daydreams. No matter what I did for him he always took it for granted. No more than was his due. God, he had it made. A wife to play-act for him. A little daughter to pet and indulge. And a dutiful dependable grown-up daughter to cook his meals and starch his shirts.
ROSE: Don't Vi. Don't. You always loved him so. He loved you.
VI: Aye. Because I deserved it. But he adored you regardless. *He* adored you. *Dolly* adored you. *Everybody* adored you. *(Pause: ROSE is very shaken that VI might be about to say she hated her. VI continues more quietly.)* I adored you. Silly oul maid. Pushing you round the park in that great Silver Cross pram they bought when you were born.

"Nothing's too good for our Rose." Strangers used to stop and compliment me on my beautiful baby. And I let them assume you were mine. I expect they also assumed you got your good looks from my husband. Not from a plain lump like me. I used to get into these terrible panics in case one of them would happen to come into the shop and discover that you were really my sister, and tell Dolly about my foolishness. And then she would have told father and they would have laughed together in that close way of theirs as if they were the only two people in the world. (Reid 1997, 230)

Registering elements of sibling rivalry and jealousies, Reid's depiction of Vi's exchange with Rose challenges notions of traditional family structures in working-class Protestant Belfast. Although the conversation begins with Vi venting pent up frustrations with the role she seems to have been assigned in the Horner family rather than chosen, Vi's anguish is a fairly predictable backlash against familial and societal pressures. Her affection for Rose and the rest of the Horner family, however, complicates Vi's lament. Not only does she love Rose as a sister, she envisions their relationship as a meta-connection lying between a sibling and a mother–child affection as she refers to herself as a "silly oul maid" who pretended the infant Rose was her own child. Vi's seeming partnership with Dolly in the Horner household, as Dolly performs the matriarchal role while Vi attends to various domestic responsibilities as a "grown-up daughter" who cooks her father's "meals and starch[es] his shirts," significantly compromises their mother–child relationship, evident in Vi's references to Dolly as "mother" only when she's being "prim an' proper" (Reid 1997, 181). Vi may then search for this connection in another manifestation as surrogate mother to Rose, since she is unfulfilled in her role as daughter to both Joe and Dolly. Rose and Janet respond accordingly, however, seeming to acknowledge both Dolly and Vi as the matriarchal heads of the Horner family.

Dolly's and Vi's conflation as maternal figures in the Horner family are not simply illustrated in their respective interactions with Rose, Janet, Jack and Rose's daughter Belle. In addition to Reid's depiction of their partnership in their respective and slowly morphing roles in the Horner household and business, Dolly and Vi share a specific language system particular to working-class Belfast. Unlike Rose and her daughter Belle, who are educated and living abroad in London, and Jack, who is associated with Protestant Unionist politics and religious fervor, that respectively employ Standardized English throughout the play, Dolly's and Vi's language often demonstrates a particular strain of Belfast-English that marks cultural and social hybridity even within the intimate circle of the Horner family. In addition to a shared role as maternal caretakers in the Horner family, Dolly and Vi seem to share an educational background. As a child performer in vaudeville in the 1920s, it is unlikely that Dolly attended school past the primary level. Similarly, Joe and Dolly's decision to keep Vi home from school in order to help with the family shop, ensured that Vi too would have limited education. She refers to this in regard to her reading and writing skill levels as on par or lower than the deaf-mute Davy who assists Vi at the shop. Unlike the politician Jack, who continually employs Standardized English in rhetorical outpourings associated with his conservative religious and political leanings and Rose's predominantly Standardized English associated with her educational attainment and a move to London as a very young woman, Vi's and Dolly's speech patterns repeatedly draw the audience into the intimacy and provincialism of working-class Belfast.

Disparities in Vi's and Rose's speech patterns are evident in the early lines of the play that introduce Dolly as The Belle of the Belfast City:

ROSE: My mother, the Belle of the Belfast City, happened to be performing in an Orange Hall in Belfast one night when my father Joe Horner was at a Lodge meeting in an upstairs room. They say he heard her singing and walked out of the meeting and into the concert like a man under a spell. And that was it. They eloped a fortnight later, and from then on she gave up the stage and did all her dressing-up and singing and dancing just for him.

VI: Our Rose is nuthin' if not romantic. The truth is that my mother's family were still dressin' her up as if she was thirteen instead of goin' on nineteen, an' trailin' her round draughty oul halls to sing to audiences of twenty or thirty. My father took her away from all that, and waited on her hand and foot for the rest of his life. Still, as they say, it's a poor family can't afford to support one lady.

DOLLY: An' a poor story that doesn't improve with the tellin'.

VI: When I was very small I used to lie in bed with my big sister Vi and listen to our parents gossiping and giggling like a couple of kids in the room next door. When the bed-springs started to creak, our Vi used to stuff cotton wool in my ears.

VI: Forty-one mother was when she had our Rose, and me already over the age of consent. It was the talk of the neighborhood.

ROSE: Bad enough to be still doing it at their age, but even worse to be enjoying it so much that she was careless enough to get caught.

Our Vi was that mortified that she wouldn't go out of the house. My mother and father were over the moon. (Reid 1997, 181)

In a shared telling of their parents' courtship, Vi's and Rose's contributions to the storyline exemplify a dialogic exchange that enables Reid to showcase a diversity of experience and association in two female subjects that inherently challenge notions of a singular understanding of Irish woman. By depicting an oral telling of the Horner's courtship and portraying a varied social network in the presentation of Northern Irish speech patterns under the Horner family's roof, Reid's work commands attention to the intricacies of everyday Belfast life emphasizing tension between literate and oral traditions (Milroy 1980). Details that are often absorbed into binaries associated with sectarian or political divides are highlighted in Reid's depiction of the Horner family's development, which are crystallized in presenting Rose's romantic version of the Horner's meeting in a neat, linear narrative. "They say he heard her singing and walked out of the meeting and into the concert like a man under a spell. And that was it," Rose claims in offering a synopsis of her parents' initial encounters. The fairytale-like rendition neatly extracts Joe and Dolly from the grittiness of early twentieth-century working-class Belfast, placing them in an idyllic pastoral registered in smooth and tempered Standardized English. Rose's language and sentence structure are varied in length and complication and paint a rosy, quaint story of a blossoming love between her parents that swiftly leads to marriage.

Unlike Rose's "nuthin'" if not romantic" telling of her parent's interactions, Vi's language is laden with non-standard pronunciation and grammatical structures that counteract her sister's gentle standardized language structure and pronunciation. The story too changes when delivered in this form. As opposed to a dreamlike trance capturing the young Joe Horner, bewitched by Dolly's voice, Vi's telling suggests an exploitative family parading their young, talented daughter from one Orange Order lodge to the next, masquerading a young woman of nineteen as a child of thirteen. Like the crude vision of a young woman fashioned as a child, who subsequently attracts Joe Horner, resulting in a marriage two weeks later, Vi's provincial language demythologizes Rose's romantic vision. Reid's phonetic differentiation between the sister's language in Vi's "nuthin" versus a standardized "nothing" and "oul" versus "old" are small simple markers that distinguish the particular sounds associated with sisters whose experiences are distanced by age, educational attainment and geographic location.

Although working-class Protestants would have even more limited exposure to the residuals of Irish Gaelic in the region than Catholic working-class nationalists (exemplified in Deane's, Adams' and Healy's respective works), Vi's reference to Rose's birth, "Forty-one mother was when she had our Rose, and me already over the age of consent," demonstrates a non-standard sentence structure in which the details of the mother's age precede the subject of the sentence and the scandal of this birth is not revealed until the final clause when Vi indicates she was "already over the age of consent" when her younger sister was born. While this structure may not necessarily be identified as particular to Belfast vernacular (as presented in Alison Henry's study), it nonetheless creates such an affect, signaling Vi, unlike Rose, does not communicate in grammatically or phonetically Standardized English. While this sentence cannot be classified with the "and + NP +V ing" associated with Hiberno-English structures, the delivery is similarly rendered in that Dolly's age of forty-one foregrounds the simultaneous detail of Vi's advanced age connoted in "and me already over the age of consent." This is registered in Hiberno-Irish sentences like "Terrible news that an' it at the mouth o' Christmas" which is akin to the Irish "Nuacht uafásach sin agus é i mbéal na Nodlag." But any such relationship between the sentence structures could only be explained through contact between Ireland's various language systems (Todd 1989, 44). While Vi of course has no Irish or proximity to the language, her sentence structures exemplify such linguistic contact, undermining notions of linguistic or cultural purity so heartily espoused and advocated by fervent politicians like Jack.

Serving as the matriarchal head of the Horner family, Dolly's speech patterns, like Vi's, hearken to working-class Belfast. Unlike her daughter Rose, her nephew Jack and her granddaughter, Belle, Dolly's dialogue serves as a detail in the play that reminds the audience of its specific locale. While the political stagnation associated with the region registers in Reid's depiction of Loyalist and Unionist characters, Dolly's speech patterns come to serve as that which is constant and simultaneously ever changing in the Horner's community. Although language is an unstable, ever-changing entity, Dolly's speech patterns are often juxtaposed with those of her children, her granddaughter and her nephew to suggest elements of continuity and stability associated with working-class Belfast in comparison to the geographical and socioeconomic moves associated with younger generations, which is further exacerbated in Belle. In addition to non-standard grammatical and phonetic markers, Dolly's speech rings of a particular type of dark Belfast humor, which is lost in

152 *Language, Identity and Liberation in Contemporary Irish Literature*

other characters' speech patterns. This is demonstrated in one of several instances very early in the play, in a brief encounter between Dolly and Jack:

> VI: Here's Jack to see you, mother.
> DOLLY: Jack who?
> VI: Our Jack.
> DOLLY: The one with the haircut that's never off the television?
> VI: You know right well who he is, now stop actin' the eejit.
> DOLLY *points out a photo to* JACK.
> DOLLY: That's you, with a face like a Lurgan spade as usual. An' that's me, and Rose and Vi and your wee sister Janet, God love her. My Joe took that photo the week after we brought the two of you here to live with us. (*Pause.*) Janet's stoppin' here again, ye know. Left her man. Don't know what's goin' on there at all. (*At* VI) Nobody every tells me nuthin' these days.
> JACK *sharply at* VI. VI *looks away.* DOLLY *reaches out as if to take off* JACK'S *glasses.* JACK *recoils.*
> DOLLY: I only wanted to have a look at your sore eye.
> JACK (Off guard): I haven't got a sore... (*He stops, realizing that* DOLLY *is making fun of him.*)
> VI: Mother! Behave yourself!
> JACK *walks angrily back to the shop.* VI *gives* DOLLY *an exasperated look.* DOLLY *smiles innocently.* VI *follows* JACK... (Reid 1997, 184)

Dolly's apparent dislike for Jack emanates from her impatience with conservative Christian ideologies associated with stringent Presbyterianism as well as the politics associated therewith in Northern Ireland. Vi opens the conversation with a reference to Dolly as "mother," indicating her heightened awareness and conformity to social formality in Jack's presence. Dolly blithely undermines such efforts, however, with her stinging yet playful question, "Jack who?" Vi's response that the visitor is "Our Jack," indicates a cross-class and cross-communal Northern Irish colloquialism that identifies an individual as belonging to a family or other communal circle with the endearment of "our." Dolly's response pushes against such tribalism, however, by mentioning the mediation of television as a means for distancing her nephew (and all he has come to represent in the public arena) from the intimacy of her predominantly female family.

Dolly slyly plays the role of matriarch and protector in her cagey exchange with Jack. Vi attempts to undermine her games with an all but hissing, "You know right well who he is, now stop actin' the eejit," reminding the audience of a particularly Irish rendition of "idiot" in "eejit." Other indications of Belfast English emerge in the non-standard use of "ye" as a plural form of a Standardized English plural form of "you" and the phonetic reference in "nuthin" versus a Standard English pronunciation of "nothing." Additionally, Dolly's reference to Jack's photo to open their exchange, brings forth a culturally specific phrase. "That's you, with a face like a Lurgan spade as usual," she says to Jack, meaning that the photo depicts a young Jack with a long, sorrowful face "as usual." Rather than comforting Jack in his everlasting sorrow and distaste for the world, Dolly combats him at every turn, seemingly in an effort of self-preservation in the face of all Jack and his political tribe may represent while simultaneously protecting her daughters and Jack's "wee" sister, Janet, "God love her." Dolly's references to Janet as "wee," to connote younger and a plea for her protection in "God love her," demonstrate "the frequent use of references to God and religion" and culturally specific vocabulary that enable Reid to set her play in the locale of working class Ireland (Todd 1989, 45). These markers, again, register in working-class Belfast speech patterns not necessarily due to continual exposure to Irish but most likely due to the historical contact between populations who conversed in Irish, English and Irish-English throughout the region. Nonetheless, Dolly's speech not only signifies cultural and social hybridity within the Horner's mixed family, but may also be associated with differences based on gender and political affiliations.

Dolly's tongue-in-cheek "I only wanted to have a look at your sore eye," much like her reference to Jack's face "like a Lurgan spade," challenge Jack's sober, often somber perspective on life. His harsh judgments and the power he yields by virtue of such conservatism continually threaten women, children and men who are not endowed with such sway in Belfast's conservative Unionist circles. By virtue of her age, her position of power in the Horner family and her resistance to such cultural and spiritual conservatism, however, Dolly pushes against Jack's compulsion to control and rule the women in his family. Dolly continually treats Jack as a child, evident in the tone of her voice and her effort to physically reach out towards the "sore eye" that she teases him about. Jack, however, seems unwilling or unable to combat the elderly Dolly any longer. His rhetorical response to Dolly's attack emerges in Vi's presence as he reacts to the news that Janet is "stoppin'" in the Horner household again. Dolly's "stoppin'" serves as a non-standardized vocabulary to signify that Janet is currently staying in the Horner house due to marital troubles at home. Dolly mentions this to Jack in an effort to spite him, to ensure that he understands that Janet turns to Dolly, Vi and the rest of the family rather than Jack when facing troubled times.

Jack is incensed, however, in his tirade of a conversation with Vi. As if he is his sister's keeper, he states:

> JACK: You should have phoned me immediately.
> VI: It wasn't my place.
> JACK: What's happened?
> VI: I don't know. She won't say.
> JACK: She'll say to me. Where is she?
> VI: She's out.
> JACK: You tell her I'll be back and I want to see her. Has *he* been here?
> VI: Just the once. Peter hasn't a lot of free time. The RUC are on full standby, what with one thing and another...
> JACK: I knew no good would come of that marriage. Sneaking off to a registry office instead of standing up and declaring themselves without shame in the eyes of the Lord. I suppose he's got himself another woman. Catholic licentiousness. It never leaves them.
> VI: Peter's a good man.
> JACK: A Catholic policeman! It's the like of him who've infiltrated the Royal Ulster Constabulary. Corrupted the force into fighting against us instead of standing alongside us as they've always done.
> DOLLY (*recites loudly*):
> Holy Mary Mother of God
> Pray for me and Tommy Todd
> For he's a Fenian and I'm a Prod
> Holy Mary Mother of God. (Reid 1997, 185)

Jack's demand, more so than an inquiry, in regard to Janet's circumstances reflect his effort to control his sister's actions. Vi attempts to mediate the situation by reminding Jack that it is neither his nor Vi's role to intercede in Janet's troubled marriage. Jack does not heed such warnings, however, which is clear in his ominous order "to tell her I'll be back and I want to see her..." As he continues the exchange with Vi, Jack reveals his prejudice against Belfast's Catholic population, in addition to his efforts to rule Janet's life. His comment that "no good would come of that marriage. Sneaking off to a registry office instead of standing up and declaring themselves without shame in the eyes of the Lord" indicate his religious fervor. His subsequent comments, however, enable Reid to present elements of Belfast's deep sectarian splits propagated by rhetoric and bigotry: "I suppose he's got himself another woman. Catholic licentiousness. It never leaves them." Ironically, Janet's frustration with Peter is based on their celibate marriage – a partnership that has never been consummated. Jack's judgment could not be further from the truth.

Jack's rant escalates in subsequent comments. His frustration with Peter stems not only from the manner in which he and Janet were married, but it is also integrally connected to Jack's political affiliation with staunch Unionism and sectarian bias. His disdain for Peter, "A Catholic Policeman!" (a rarity of course by 1986 when the play is set) surfaces in his claim that "It's the like of him who've infiltrated the Royal Ulster Constabulary. Corrupted the force into fighting against us instead of standing alongside us as they've always done." In these phrases Reid presents Jack's espousal of a "Protestant state for a Protestant people." While Vi does not necessarily agree with Jack's assessment of Peter personally, indicated in her timid though still present interjection that he is "a good man," she does not necessarily challenge the thrust of Jack's political rhetoric. Vi engages with Jack, quietly responding to his inquiries and demands. Dolly's voice and perspective enter the exchange, however, as Jack's anger escalates. Her poignant rhyme, playfully reminding audiences that not all of the Horner family or the working-class Protestant community would necessarily agree with Jack, pushes Jack to launch an attack on Dolly with the presumably acquiescent Vi.

It is not until Jack's attacks come back to the Horner family that Vi is finally pushed from the role of a passive figure to that of protector:

JACK: That old woman should be in a home!
VI: If that old woman hadn't taken you and Janet in when your mother died, that's where you'd have ended up, in a home! And don't you ever forget that, Jack!
JACK: I'm sorry if I offended you, Vi. I...
VI: You offended *her*. This family never badmouths its own.
JACK: I apologize. I said it without thinking. Not like me. One of the first things you learn in politics. Never speak without knowing exactly what you're going to say...I was angry with Janet. That marriage has always been a thorn in my side. (Reid 1997, 186)

Although Vi has been relegated to a fairly traditional domestic role in the Horner family since her youth, as she springs on Jack to defend her mother, Reid demonstrates that even figures like Vi, who appear sympathetic to Jack's political leanings are nonetheless complex beings. Vi is single and childless but she serves in a maternal capacity in the Horner family. She breaks from the expectations of maternal figures in Protestant/Unionist communities, however, whenever she perceives any threat to her family. Her resolute, "This family never badmouths its own," forces Jack to backpedal swiftly. In his effort to explain himself, he draws on his public role and experience claiming that he spoke "without thinking... one of the first things you learn in politics. Never speak without knowing exactly what you're going to say." Betrayed by his anger and bigotry, Vi's reaction to Jack shows that even seemingly passive figures can garner power in this community. Although Jack can exercise significant political and social power in the public realm, Reid reminds audiences that Vi and Dolly, and their female counterparts, command considerable respect and power in the domestic sphere. Jack's political training in rhetoric (and the power associated with such language systems) is all but useless in his repeated interactions with Vi and Dolly.

Reid's varied depictions of femininity and motherhood throughout "The Belle of the Belfast City," while critical of Northern Irish social and political compulsions to control female autonomy and expression of individuality, are certainly not pessimistic. In her treatment of Rose and her daughter Belle, Reid presents progressive, self-possessed figures who draw Belfast out of its provincialism into an international arena. Belle's introduction to Belfast enables Reid to depict several facets of Northern Irish culture at once, while simultaneously attending to rifts and divisions even within the Horner family structure. As Rose and Vi hug and kiss in their reunion at the family shop, Belle is briefly introduced to Jack. When she "half moves to shake his hand but doesn't as he just nods his head slightly to acknowledge the introduction," it becomes apparent that Jack's bigotry has infiltrated the Horner family in an unprecedented manner. Belle's African-American father and Protestant Northern Irish mother in Rose, are a fairly unique pairing to the xenophobic Jack. The novelty of Belle's dark skin, however, is more blatantly rendered in Davy's reaction to Belle.

> *She holds out her hand to* DAVY *who has been staring at her since she came in. He hesitantly touches her hand then shyly almost touches her face. Stops and signals to* VI.
> VI ((laughs): He's all of a dither because he's never seen nobody with dark skin before, except on the television.

BELLE: Is this a joke?
ROSE: There aren't many like you in Belfast, Belle. And those that are, are well-to-do. Restaurant owners, doctors, university lecturers, overseas students. They don't live round here.
BELLE: No working-class black ghettos?
ROSE: No.
BELLE (looking directly at JACK): No prejudice?
DAVY *signals to* VI *again.* VI *shakes her head at him and looks sideways at* BELLE, *who grins, and surprises* VI *by signaling to* DAVY.
BELLE: No Davy, I'm not from Africa. I'm from England. And my mother is from Belfast and my father is from America. I think that makes me an Anglo/Irish Yank. (Reid 1997, 192)

After undermining notions of a singular portrayal of Northern Irish motherhood, Reid's depiction of Ireland's next generation of daughters in Belle, serves as a sober reminder of Belfast's uncomfortable cultural, political and social straddling between old world provincialism and new world cosmopolitanism. In Belle, Reid can present a vision of cultural, racial and social hybridity that enables audiences to consider how gender, race, class and political agency are expressed and negotiated in a society plagued by violence, sectarian bias, bigotry and racial prejudice.

The aesthetic, social, linguistic and political profundity of Reid's play is encapsulated in Belle. As the only Horner heir, Dolly's matriarchal line continues in Belle, who is only tangentially affiliated with "the Belfast City." Although she serves as a figure of cultural tolerance, intellectual development, social mobility and transnationalism, how are we to interpret Reid's sole female heir in the Horner line? In Vi, Jack and Janet it would seem that new life cannot spring from the social, cultural and political constraints of late nineteen-eighties Belfast. Yet Belle returns to Belfast and immediately engages with all facets of its culture – the beautiful and whimsical, as personified in Dolly and the tragically ignorant and damaging, as exemplified in Jack. Reid's "daughter," nurtured by all the female Horners yet shunned by Jack, speaks to the resilience and complexity of femininity in Northern Ireland. In Belle, Reid suggests that Ireland's women cannot be defined by categories even as varied as "Anglo/Irish Yank." Instead, the region's female figures must be presented and attended to as individual, autonomous beings as varied and multidimensional as the region's history, landscape and language.

III

Reid's depiction of late twentieth-century Irish femininity certainly challenges the female characters that graced the Abbey Stage in the early decades of the century. Lady Gregory's influential work, however, continues to haunt contemporary Irish drama. In her attention to Ireland's language systems, depicted in her "dialect plays," Gregory introduced the manner in which theater serves as an adept medium for presenting Irish cultural and political particularity that differentiates the region from its colonial occupier. Reid adopts such elements in her own work in efforts to portray the complexity of Ireland's contemporary social, political and cultural terrain. Her interpretation of Northern Irish political and cultural tensions that are represented in negotiations of autonomy amidst linguistic, religious and cultural hybridity, as presented in "The Belle of the Belfast City," enable audiences to consider the historical precedents that have led to such circumstances as well as possible visions for emerging from these predicaments. Her portrayal of Belle Horner, specifically, offers a figure who embraces and simultaneously defies the contradictory nature of provincial and cosmopolitan Belfast. But Reid's work has not always been received warmly by her varied audiences. She has gained little of the public support or garnered the power enjoyed by a female playwright like the illustrious Lady Gregory of generations past.

Reid claims, "I have never had a major production of any of my plays in the South, though university students and fringe companies have produced them there in small venues. Some of them have been staged in the Lyric Theater Belfast. But so far, not in the Abbey or Gate Theaters in Dublin" (Kurdi 2004, 214).[4] Like other female playwrights throughout the twentieth century, Reid's work has not been embraced in Irish theater, despite her ability to present Ireland's gift for conversation and the complexity of culture and history inherently symbolized therein. Unlike Gregory, who enjoyed a position of power in the fledgling Abbey Theater Co. at the turn of the twentieth century, with the exception of Charabanc Theater Co. that folded in the late nineteen-nineties, Reid and fellow female playwrights have faced considerable resistance to staging their plays in the male-dominated Irish theater scene. According to MacDonagh,

> Marina Carr, Christina Reid, Anne Devlin and Marie Jones are currently familiar names on the theater scene. These women, however, are in the definite minority; there is a much longer list of well-known

male playwrights whose plays have been staged at prominent venues and who have received generous support for their failures as well as their successes. Why does it matter that plays by and about women rarely get staged? The answer is fairly obvious: The theater is a public realm where a people perform themselves to themselves, a part of cultural and national self-presentation; erasing the complexity of women's lives from this arena is, therefore, tantamount to erasing them from public life. In fact, the theater in many ways reflects how women's stories are often erased elsewhere in the public arena. (Watt, Morgan, Mustafa 2000, 181)

Do playwrights like Reid, Carr, Devlin and Jones meet resistance in Irish theater due to their insistence that the Irish stage reflect or portray "a people perform [ing] themselves" in all of their grandeur and shortcomings? Or do contemporary Irish audiences seek the erasure of "the complexity of women's lives from this arena" in keeping with traditional Nationalist visions of femininity confined to the homestead as espoused by DeValera in the mid twentieth century?

Despite the complex visions Reid presents of Northern Irish femininity and masculinity portrayed in "The Belle of the Belfast City," she endured considerable criticism in the period following the initial productions of the play in 1989.

KURDI: This female talent for storytelling and preserving the traditions through that is well reflected in your plays. However, the plays have received some criticism for creating rather one-dimensional male characters who are less interesting than the women.

REID: On the other hand, nobody criticizes plays because they are more about men than about women. This criticism of my plays is not even true. *Joyriders* (1986) has got two strong male characters in it. In *The Belle of the Belfast City* (1989) Jack is one of the most powerful roles in the play, actors liked to do it. Yet so many Irish plays are about men, and women are there only because they are somebody's mother, wife, sister, daughter or girlfriend, in other words, their part in the play is only to do with what is happening to the men that they are connected to. I have been criticized for my plays being labeled feminist by some people. And I have been criticized by feminists who found that my plays are too gentle. My reply to that is always that I hope I write about women as they are, not as feminism would want them to be, which would not be truthful. I find women easier to write about because the women in my background were entertaining, very funny, and very strong. While men made the big decisions about the country, the world and whatever, women were the ones who made families work, made life work. (Kurdi 2004, 208)

Reid's response to such criticism articulates her frustrations with standards applied to Irish female playwrights' work that do not necessarily arise for their male counterparts. She underpins such criticism, however, by immediately referring to her complex treatment of Northern Irish masculinity in regard to several male characters who appear in her late nineteen-eighties plays. Reid's reference to lack of criticism in regard to "plays because they are more about men, and women are there only because they are somebody's mother, wife, sister, daughter or girlfriend," hearkens back to Gregory's endorsement of such figures at the turn of the twentieth century and her deference to male playwrights responsible for propagating these tropes. In an effort to ensure that the Irish stage will not erase "the complexity of women's lives from this arena," Reid strives to depict "women as they are, not as feminism would want them to be, which would not be truthful." In this endeavor she challenges the precedents of her genre while inherently questioning the degrees to which an Irish stage can aptly serve as "a public realm where a people perform themselves to themselves, a part of cultural and national self-presentation" (Watt, Morgan, Mustafa 2000, 181).

Challenging notions of Irish male playwrights' representations of feminine singularity in contemporary Irish theater, Pearse Elliott's "A Mother's Heart" (1998) and Martin McDonagh's "The Beauty Queen of Leenane" (1996) consider portrayals of Irish femininity in plays that reflect Ireland's particular and often contesting language systems. Seeming to represent a compulsion towards drama as a medium for reflecting the region's reputation as "a great country for conversation," McDonagh's and Elliot's works attend to representations of relationships between mothers and daughters that are considerably darker although equally critical of Irish social, cultural and political parameters, as in Reid's earlier work. McDonagh's and Elliot's considerations of the factors that often limit female autonomy and the negotiation and expression of individuality in the late nineteen-eighties Republic of Ireland and the late nineteen-nineties Northern Ireland, respectively, are certainly more complex than earlier twentieth-century representations of femininity depicted by figures like Yeats, Synge or even Lady Gregory. But are these contemporary considerations of Ireland's women sufficiently representative of the region's multifarious, multifaceted female population? Or do male playwrights still fall prey to the region's cultural and political precedents of portraying women as supplemental figures in Ireland's political, social or cultural development?

The staging of these productions in vastly different venues – Dubbeljoint's humble venue at the Rock Theater on the Whiterock Road in West Belfast for Elliot's work versus the opening of the Druid Theater Co. / Royal Court Theater co-production at the Town Hall Theater in Galway for McDonagh's initial staging – illustrate a range of prospective production opportunities that may not be available to female playwrights in the region. Nonetheless, Elliot's and McDonagh's respective productions can serve as markers for the wide spectrum of opportunities for audiences to come in contact with the work produced by contemporary Irish playwrights lucky enough to see their plays produced on a domestic stage. While both plays certainly place Irish femininity as central to their exploration of Irish identity in the last decades of the twentieth century, both McDonagh's and Elliot's work offer staggeringly bleak portrayals of contemporary Irish culture. Unlike Reid's guarded optimism in the propagation of the Horner line in Belle, both "The Beauty Queen of Leenane" and "A Mother's Heart" depict bankrupt figures of Irish motherhood. Carefully rendered in a language system that immediately signifies a "strong North Antrim whistling dialect" in the case of Elliott and an almost staged Hiberno-English reminiscent of Synge's work to depict the rural West coast of Ireland in McDonagh's work, these male playwright challenge their predecessors' renditions of angelic, saintly visions of Irish femininity with their characters' negotiations of autonomy and expression of identity in a particularly hostile contemporary Ireland. Reaching audiences from a variety of class and educational backgrounds throughout Ireland, Elliot's and McDonagh's work made considerable impressions in the late nineteen-nineties in ways that Reid's work could not only a decade previous. But to what degree did their respective representations of Irish femininity build upon or derail complex, detail oriented visions of Irish women so carefully rendered by artist like Reid only a decade beforehand?

IV

While Elliot's and McDonagh's plays differ considerably from Reid's focus in "The Belle of the Belfast City," the playwrights' works exemplify shared attention to what Delgado cites as "the imposition of domestic roles on women by both Protestant and Catholic iconography. In Catholicism, we see women as an angelic virgin figure reworked by the nationalist movement into Mother Ireland; in Protestantism, woman as loyal steadfast servicer and nurturer of men willing to die for Queen and Country" (Reid 1997, xv). Unlike Reid's careful crafting of a variety of female characters who negotiate such cultural and political expectations in their contemporary culture in a variety of ways as depicted in characters like Dolly, Vi, Janet and Rose, McDonagh's and Elliot's response to the "imposition of domestic roles on women by both Protestant and Catholic iconography" involves a propagation of cultural and political violence ending in bankrupt symbols of maternal lines. Rather than staging a community of women who each respond differently to Ireland's cultural and social expectations, McDonagh's and Elliot's portrayals of mothers and daughters suggest that any resistance to such precedents can only result in violence, grief and the impossibility of reproduction. Their respective pessimistic outlook on contemporary culture suggests that Irish society cannot continue to propagate successfully without a fundamental revolution of the region's political, social and cultural norms.

First staged only a year after the historic Good Friday Peace Agreement of 1998, Pearse Elliott's "A Mother's Heart" opened amidst considerable controversy. Initially produced in the predominantly working-class Catholic neighborhood surrounding the Falls Road in West Belfast, the play's bi-partisan portrayal of familial loss in the violence of "The Troubles" was uneasily received by audiences on both sides of the region's sectarian divide. Elliot's chilling renditions of grief, fury and loss encapsulated in each of his "mothers," had a considerable impact on Northern Irish audiences that were still adjusting to the relative calm of a possible lasting peace. Unlike Reid's measured depiction of Protestant Unionism in "The Belle of the Belfast City," Elliot's rendition of Northern Irish Presbyterianism in Ruth truncates optimism affiliated with the newly brokered Peace Agreement. Instead, Elliot's work concentrates on periods of mourning, grief and indescribable human suffering endured when a mother loses her only child.

While Elliot's Ruth certainly challenges notions of traditional Anglo-Irish motherhood in "A Mother's Heart," she is not the charming, eccentric character Reid depicts in Dolly Horner or even the fairly conservative sketching of Vi. Instead, Ruth is a rural figure, heavily steeped in Biblical liturgy with low educational attainment and even more limited cultural exposure outside of her upbringing in North Antrim. Introduced as a woman "in her late forties although she looks older," Ruth wears glasses that are presented as "flamboyant for the rest of her attire, which is a bulky dress, with no flesh to be seen, a repressively black dress" (Elliot 1998, 1). Ruth's hair is "shoulder length and her features pinched and stern... nothing like the beautiful girl (Margaret) laughing on the wall." She was a reluctant mother, unexpectedly impregnated by the age of eighteen by a local Catholic boy, Colm O'Neil. Raised by a Bible-thumping Presbyterian father suspected of murdering her young lover, Ruth is portrayed as a woman thrust into a "domestic" role without guidance or training. She feeds the newborn Margaret "a bowl of porridge in the morn', milk when she wants and a bowl of stew at night," enabling Elliot to portray Ruth's role as mother a complete failure from the start (Elliot 1998, 5). Floundering in the absence of a mother of her own to educate her "in feedin' a child," the young Ruth seems doomed to imprisonment in her "imposition" in a domestic role, just as Margaret will be scarred by her mother's ill preparation and lack of education as she grows into young womanhood in later years (5).

Elliot's consideration of Northern Anglo-Irish motherhood opens with a reading from Ruth's "well-thumbed Bible," before she delivers a litany of questions directed at her daughter's unchanging face in a framed photo on the wall. From the opening lines Elliot intertwines threads of a "whistling Antrim dialect," attributed to a woman of limited education and life experience, with the rhetoric and vocabulary of religious fervor that Ruth has inherited from her overbearing and violent father and the political and social forces that he represents. In this configuration Elliot's Ruth seems to suggest a clashing of affiliation and association as she attempts to assert authority in conversation with her absent and silent child. Her demeanor changes with each shift in language use, however, oscillating from confidence and power that she repeatedly associates with passages from the Bible and rhetoric associated with "the good word" to pleading agony and vulnerability in her reflections on raising the young Margaret.

RUTH: "He who abides in God, abides in love"...
She allows what she's said to settle and looks to her daughter's photo.
RUTH: Why?! Did ye go there?... Inta' the, the dominion, amidst the damned? What black realm you chose to leave me for?... To... That sleek evil, ye always surrounded yourself with... Well it...
She returns to her black book, flicks though pages, settles, points condemning finger to little girl, reads out loud...
RUTH: "There is nothing that can be hid from God. Everything in all creation is exposed, and lies open before his eyes; and it is to him that we give all account of ourselves."
She looks up at the little girl.

RUTH: And there ye are Margaret...and there ye are...
The look changes on her face, she seems serene...serene by a memory.
RUTH: Why? Cudn't you've stayed like that my love?..."Sugar and spice and all things nice"...If you'd a' stayed like that?...If you'd a stayed like that? With them beautiful, beautiful eyes, as blue as sky...and that hair as gold as corn...
She gazes into the past.
RUTH: And that plait...I worked on that plait, likea', likea' sculptor worked on clay...
She begins to weave an imaginary plait.
RUTH: Every night before I put you to bed...and we'd sing our wee song
She begins to hum her wee song...
RUTH: Our God reigns...Our God reigns...
She still weaves an imaginary plait, then stops abruptly.
RUTH: But oh'no!...Ye had to grow up...corrupting yer' beautiful face with, with, that disgusting make-up! Prostituting yer' beautiful eyes...so ye resembled a, a, a doe!...A stupid doe deer! Wearing them obscene clothes!...Obscene shoes...whorish attire, not befittin' a God's child! Not God's one...not my child...and then yer', yer' beautiful plait...ye shorn it off! Ye' shorn my beautiful plait off...
She remembers...
RUTH: Polluted yer' hair...with those disgustin' colours, green! And then!...And then!...you mutilated your body!
She stares vitriolic and becomes Margaret aged 17.
RUTH: "It's a sign of my sexual identity"
She holds her head...
What have I reared!...What have I reared God in heaven? I tried God, I brought her on every Sabbath day...I sent her to scripture class...I read her the good book...(Elliot 1998, 1–2)

Ruth's combating personalities, reflected in switches of language employment, suggest grief that borders on madness. Her verbose delivery of passages from the Bible that illustrate an authoritative, Standardized English language system lend Ruth strength and vitality that is absent in passages that are delivered in non-standardized language that betray her fragility and grief. In both public and domestic spheres, Ruth's identity seems limited to her role as Margaret's mother. This singular existence is rendered completely bankrupt with her daughter's absence, leading to almost mad swings from one linguistic system to another as Ruth attempts to find a "voice" that can aptly articulate her rage at familial betrayal, significant bereavement and a feeling of general loss and isolation from the public and domestic realms she once knew.

Elliot's depiction of Ruth's raw emotion, evident in fluctuations in her speech patterns, is an interpretation of contemporary Irish femininity as continually under threat. Driven to the brink of virtual hysteria by legacies of cultural conservatism and violence in public and private realms, Elliot's portrayal of Ruth suggests that any resistance to these systems can only result in tragedy. After defying her father's warning that "Catholics were all the 'whore of Babylon'" in her brief affair with Colm, Ruth is rendered completely powerless under her father's violent reign in addition to the societal expectations for Anglo-Irish women to which Delgado refers (Elliot 1998, 7). Steeped in the rhetoric of Presbyterianism, she is taught that "Lucifer, if summoned, appeared as a handsome boy... and that Colm's real name was 'Asataroth'... and that he really was one of the demons but not to worry, as he had expelled him to the abyss." In this exchange Ruth not only receives tutorage from her father and his faith but she also learns that he is not to be "trusted with my Margaret," who will inevitably inherit the public and domestic expectations that have confronted Ruth since early adulthood (7). As she fluctuates between speech patterns in the opening passages of her monologue, her faltering sanity also suggests considerable efforts to negotiate assertion and independence in the wake of tragedy, which Elliot suggests is inevitable for women who have challenged the region's cultural and societal traditions.

In "The Belle of the Belfast City" Reid associates Northern Irish women's imposition to domestic roles with cultural and political conservatism associated with the region's various religious orders and political parties. This is often symbolized in Jack's Standardized English speech patterns that frequently emerge in his efforts to control Janet's behavior or to combat Dolly's resistance to such political, cultural and linguistic systems. In the case of Elliot's Ruth, however, the opening passages of her monologue suggest her efforts to adopt these language patterns result not only in her impending madness, as she attempts to negotiate some form of autonomy from the patriarchal system she associates with her father and her religion, but also an effort to assert some level of power or authority over her now absent daughter. Unlike Dolly, whose songs and non-standardized language patterns empower her in the domestic realm to at least confine Jack's influence on the women of the Horner family to the public sphere, Elliot's treatment of Ruth's negotiation renders her still completely powerless in all elements of Northern Irish society.

Ruth's fluctuations in the opening passages of her monologue reveal desperation in her efforts to come to grips with the memory of her now presumably lost child. Turning to Standardized English of the Bible's written word for strength and authority, Ruth attempts to channel the power she associates with religion and literacy as she communicates with her absent daughter. Pointing a "condemning finger to [the] little girl" in the frame she reads "there is nothing that can be hid from God. Everything in all creation is exposed, and lies open before his eyes...". The rhythm of these sentences, carefully constructed in uncompromising declarative forms are placed in contrast to Ruth's own language patterns that continually falter into repetitive utterances, beginning and ending with little adherence to grammatical or phonetic standards. Although Elliot depicts Ruth's speech patterns in sync with standardized pronunciation in passages that she reads, her own language betrays a disaffiliation from the authority and stringency that is associated with the written word when she speaks. The Standardized English "couldn't" is pronounced as "cud'nt," which according to Elliot's stage directions is to connote a dialect of English associated with North Antrim (Elliot 1998, 1 & 2). Similarly, the enjambment of the Standardized "like a" in Ruth's "likea', likea' sculptor" are characteristics of speech patterns that seem to be placed to register significant switches in Ruth's language patterns to highlight disparities in power associated with a male dominated Presbyterian cultural, social and political movement in Northern Ireland and their traditionally less powerful female counterparts in the community.

Aside from Elliot's focus on various speech patterns that identify the specific locale each of his mothers inhabit, the language of naming plays a crucial role in Ruth's and Margaret's trajectories in the play as well. Due to the illegitimacy of her birth, Ruth's father insists on calling Margaret by her presumed father's name.

> RUTH: ...Margaret, he called her, he called her "O'Neil"...God in Heaven...I wanted to call her our name "Calderwood"...but he wud'nt let me...said there wud' never...never be "Papish blood in the Calderwood line." (5)

Exerting his perceived paternal right, Ruth's father determines the name of his female grandchild in an effort to isolate her from the Calderwood line. By virtue of this naming ritual, Ruth's father attempts to undermine any effort Ruth may make in legitimizing what he perceives as her sinful behavior. By the end of Ruth's monologue, however, we learn the significance of such a name in Northern Ireland's sectarian culture amidst the violence of "The Troubles." After escaping the wrath of an overbearing mother in Ruth, who has assumed the language, posture and irrational conservatism she once resisted in her father, Margaret escapes to Belfast as a young adult. Her grandfather's wrath follows her there, however, as her name comes to betray a case of mistaken identity in the city's violence-crazed sectarian divide.

> RUTH: ...and they asked her name so they did...and she told them...so she did...and they were malign entities so they were...demons, so they were...and when my...when my Margaret went to the toilet...when my Margaret...went to the toilet...they looked in her bag, and it said "O'Neil" on her Civil Service card...she was working in the Civil Service...and another one stole a "Sex Pistols" tape on her...and when she came back...they started to beat her...for being a Catholic...but she wasn't a Catholic...she was reared a Presbyterian...they beat her because of her second name "O'Neil"...they beat her with bars...steel bars...then they went onto' kitchen knives...stabbed her a hundred and thirty four times, and then one of them cut her throat...to her spine...and then they put her in a wheelie bin...my child...and drove her to some old waste ground...and shot her six times...six times...(Elliot 1998, 12)

Delivered in the soft repetitions of her mother's "North Antrim accent," Elliot reveals Margaret's fate as inextricably connected to the language and power of Northern Irish patriarchy. While her name seals her fate in a war savaged city, Elliot's portrayal of this mother and daughter suggests that he does not believe Ireland's contemporary society has sufficiently abandoned the legacies of "Protestant and Catholic iconography" associated with the region's conservatism that would enable women to safely negotiate and express their autonomy and individuality in private and public spheres alike. Unlike Reid's Belle, who serves as a figure symbolizing a guarded optimism for Northern Ireland's emergence from cultural and political conservatism, Elliot's Margaret comes to pay for her society's ills. In her death the Calderwood line ends. And Ruth, relegated to the isolation of a domestic sphere without a husband, child or parents, is rendered all but obsolete in contemporary Ireland. Her rage and pain, delivered in the hybrid language systems of her generation, are all she has to contribute to Elliot's bleak interpretation of Irish femininity. Offering a haunting mixture of tradition and innovation in his late nineteen-nineties plays, McDonagh's "The Beauty Queen of Leenane" also suggests that Irish culture remains intolerant of female negotiation and expression of autonomy not in keeping with traditions of Protestant and Catholic iconography. Although Mag and Maureen are isolated from the violence of "The Troubles" depicted in Elliot's rendition of contemporary Northern Ireland, they are no less susceptible to the region's legacies of conservatism and violence in the rural west of Connemara. While the mother and daughter's dysfunctional and sometimes violent interactions initially appear savagely funny, McDonagh launches a critique of late twentieth-century Irish culture through the eventual matricide that leads to Mag's demise. Relegated to the domestic realm after suffering a mental breakdown as an immigrant in England, Maureen's homestead comes to serve as a prison rather than a refuge for the forty-year-old virgin. Unlike her sisters who have married and given birth to children in compliance with Ireland's traditional notions of female societal responsibility, Maureen's charge in the private sphere becomes that of caretaker for her mother. Single and childless in a conservative Irish societal structure, Maureen, like Vi, is relegated to a caretaker role regardless of her efforts to resist such an "imposition." Solely responsible for the ailing and aging Mag, Maureen resents her responsibility and eventually murders her mother, only to find her imprisonment continues in the Leenane domestic interior.

Although McDonagh claims to have never read Synge before writing his Connemara plays, the language he employs for his characters' dialogue is reminiscent of Synge's representations of the language of "the country people of Ireland." Though somewhat clumsily rendered, presumably due to McDonagh's lack of familiarity with Irish, his characters nonetheless offer an affect in the rhythm of their language patterns to symbolize "those who are thinking Gaelic" though speaking in English (Mikhail 1977, 58). Gregory's romantic notions of the role that language played in cultural and political realms at the turn of the twentieth century registers in her suggestion that the populations of Ireland's west "have a beautiful dialect, and they have an extraordinary ear," but McDonagh's portrayal suggests the dialect signifies cultural, political and social stagnancy, ignorance and isolation. Like his visions of Ireland's mothers and daughters in Mag and Maureen, McDonagh's Irish-English marks provincialism that threatens Ireland's political, economic and cultural development. Unlike Synge and Gregory, whose depictions of their perceived Irish cultural integrity in the speech patterns and supposed cultural purity preserved in the West depicted in the plays of the Celtic Twilight, McDonagh's work suggests such preservation will inevitably lead to the region's doom.

While Gregory contended that Irish drama would thrive in the twentieth century due to the region's predisposition for conversation and writers like Synge's ability to capture this perceived cultural particularity on the nation's fledgling stages, McDonagh's late twentieth-century treatment of the region's language patterns and tropes of Irish femininity suggest that his work destabilizes the myths so carefully crafted by his Celtic Twilight predecessors. Like Reid and Elliot, McDonagh's depictions of contemporary Ireland's speech patterns and Irish women challenge the seemingly stable links between language, culture and societal responsibility that fueled a century of nationalist imperatives. According to Heath A. Diehl:

> If Irish identity can in part be located in the various and varied forms of cultural representation produced by/for/about a given group of people, then Synge's assiduous desire "to restore and preserve the folk-cultural texts of the Gaelic-Irish peasantry" (Castle 265) necessarily locates his work within a nationalist endeavor. Moreover, Synge's commitment to articulating a stable Irish identity can be found in his careful record of "peasant speech," a dialect which he mirrors in his plays... If we accept that Irish identity is inflected through language, that *how* the Irish are discursively represented is as important as what the discourse reveals about them (a point that is dramatized in Brian Friel's "Translations"), then the care and precision which Synge evidences in recording peasant dialect clearly demonstrate that, as many critics have opined, "the nature of the nation was Synge's fundamental concern" (Cairns and Richards 78). Specifically, Synge creates an "authentic" Irish identity, a true self, grounded in the fold history of the Irish-Catholic peasantry. That closure in *Playboy* is achieved precisely through the expurgation of the duplicitous figure, then demonstrates the ways in which the parameters of a "true (Irish) self" are guarded against forces which threaten its stability and coherence, guarded against inauthenticity. (2001, 106)

Diehl's gratuitous reading of Synge's endeavors at the turn of the twentieth century suggests that his work was in fact in alignment with nationalist endeavors of his contemporary moment, an issue that I address in more detail in earlier chapters. McDonagh's attention to such cultural precedence (even if he truly had not read Synge before producing the Connemara plays) however, suggest a perception of supposedly stable correlations between language and identity, gender and social responsibility. McDonagh seems to assume that such relationships fueled nationalist myths throughout the twentieth century, actually leading to the limited negotiation of individual autonomy and the expression of identity in Ireland throughout the twentieth century.

In "The Beauty Queen of Leenane" McDonagh's rendition of Irish-English is a literal grafting of Irish grammar onto English that is much in keeping with Synge's "heightened" presentation of the language of specific populations inhabiting the west coast of Ireland (Mikhail 1977, 58). Standardized English speech patterns are entirely absent from the play due to its almost claustrophobic portrayal of a small rural community but distinctions in language and the political questions associated with such use arise early in the play in a discussion between Mag and Maureen.

> MAG: Is the radio a biteen loud there, Maureen?
> MAUREEN: A biteen loud, is it?
> *Maureen swipes angrily at the radio again, turning it off. Pause.*
> MAG: Nothing on it, anyways. An oul fella singing nonsense.
> MAUREEN: Isn't it you wanted it set for that oul station?
> MAG: Only for Ceilidh Time and for whatyoucall.
> MAUREEN: It's too late to go complaining now.
> MAG: Not for nonsense did I want it set.
> MAUREEN: It isn't nonsense anyways. Isn't it Irish?
> MAG: It sounds like nonsense to me. Why can't they just speak English like everybody?
> MAUREEN: Why should they speak English?
> MAG: To know what they're saying.
> MAUREEN: What country are you living in?
> MAG: Eh?
> MAUREEN: What country are you living in?
> MAG: Galway.
> MAUREEN: Not what county!
> MAG: Oh-h...
> MAUREEN: Ireland you're living in!
> MAG: *Ireland.*
> MAUREEN: So why should you be speaking English in Ireland?
> MAG: I don't know why.
> MAUREEN: It's Irish you should be speaking in Ireland.

MAG: It is.
MAUREEN: Eh?
MAG: Eh?
MAUREEN: "Speaking English in Ireland."
MAG (*pause*): Except where would Irish get you going for a job in England? Nowhere.
MAUREEN: Well, isn't that the crux of the matter?
MAG: Is it, Maureen?
MAUREEN: If it wasn't for the English stealing our language, and our land, and our God-knows-what, wouldn't it be we wouldn't need to go over there begging for jobs and for handouts?...
MAG: If it was to America you had to go begging for handouts, it isn't Irish would be any good to you. It would be English!
MAUREEN: Isn't that the same crux of the same matter?
MAG: I don't know if it is or it isn't.
MAUREEN: Bringing up kids to think all they'll ever be good for is begging handouts from the English and the Yanks. That's the selfsame crux.
MAG: I suppose.
MAUREEN: Of course you suppose, because it's true.
MAG (*pause*): If I had to go begging for handouts anywhere, I'd rather beg for them in America than in England, because in America it does be more sunny anyways. (*Pause.*) Or is that just something they say, that the weather is more sunny, Maureen? Or is that a lie, now?
Maureen slops the porridge out and hands it to Mag, speaking as she does so.
MAUREEN: You're ould and you're stupid and you don't know what you're talking about. Now shut up and eat your oul porridge.
Maureen goes back to wash the pan in the sink. Mag glances at the porridge, then turns back to her.
MAG: Me mug of tea you forgot!
Maureen clutches the edges of the sink and lowers her head, exasperated, then quietly, with visible self-control, fills the kettle to make her mother's tea. Pause. Mag speaks while slowly eating. (McDonagh 1998, 7–10)

Opening the passage with vocabulary that explicitly marks the hybridity of Irish-English, Mag asks Maureen if the radio is not "a biteen loud." In "biteen" McDonagh marks the conjunction of the English word "bit" with the ending of a phonetically rendered "een" in Irish, to indicate small in size. Engaging the politically charged question of Ireland's contested language systems, Mag and Maureen's conversation in an exaggerated Irish-English suggests that Crowley's "common ground upon which both agreement and disagreement are possible" has become the status quo for contemporary Ireland. McDonagh's staging of this historic question between Mag and Maureen, however, not only destabilizes nationalist myths associated with an Irish speaking Ireland but also challenges connections between Irish femininity, motherhood and the region's mother tongue.

Connecting Mag and Maureen's exchange on Ireland's contested language systems to Hyde's Gaelic Revival movement at the turn of the twentieth century, McDonagh suggests a generational repetition that has imprisoned Ireland. The "crux of the matter" to which their conversation continually returns, mirrored in the repetitive cycles of the question and answer pattern of Mag and Maureen's conversation, suggests a connection between the rhythms of Irish-English and the contradiction and misconception of Ireland ever returning to its precolonial language or culture. Just as the language patterns in which Mag and Maureen converse are neither Standardized English nor Irish, Ireland cannot shed its centuries of historical interaction with Britain or even the United States. As McDonagh stages an exaggerated version of Hiberno-English to connote the specific locale of rural western Ireland, his grafting of English vocabulary on to Irish grammatical structures seems to suggest the ridiculous rather than the historical significance of Ireland's perpetual return to questions of sovereignty, language and culture, and its impact on the region's political integrity. While the basic sentiment behind syntactical structures like Mag's "Not for nonsense did I want it set" and "Me mug of tea you forgot!" is to demonstrate foregrounding, which is evident in Irish-English as it is often spoken in Gaeltacht regions, McDonagh's presentation seems to border on the comic (Todd 1989, 41). The absurdity of Mag's ignorance in the late nineteen-eighties, when the play is set, considering her exposure to American, Australian and British media in the form of television and radio suggests that McDonagh's play's presentation of language moves to undermine the iconic relationship between language and nationalism in twentieth-century Ireland.

Seeming to cast Mag and Maureen as contemporary instantiations of dated tropes like Cathleen ni Houlihan and the Shan Van Vocht, McDonagh's mother and daughter's discussion on Ireland's linguistic past and future suggests a stinging criticism of Irish nationalism. Unlike Reid's varied challenges to Protestant and Catholic Irish iconography, McDonagh's aggressive portrayal of the potential damage associated with women breaking from conformity is mirrored in the apparent absurdity associated with public efforts to questions of sovereignty, cultural particularity and gendered societal responsibility amidst the region's introduction to the revolution of economic and cultural globalization.

Maureen's abrupt ending to the conversation with Mag, "You're oul and you're stupid and you don't know what you're talking about. Now shut up and eat your ould porridge" not only truncates any further discussion of the region's linguistic past and future but also offers a glimpse of a potential flair for violence in their relationship. Tried for patience, Maureen repeatedly lashes out at Mag in flashes of anger, blaming Mag for her limited social and political mobility. But the sinister elements of Ireland's history of cultural conservatism and violence emerges in Maureen's comments in the final passages of the first scene:

> MAG: ...The fella up and murdered the poor oul woman in Dublin and he didn't even know her. The news that story was on, did you hear of it? (*Pause.*) Strangled, and didn't even know her. That's a fella it would be better not to talk to. That's a fella it would be better to avoid outright.
>
> *Maureen brings Mag her tea, then sits at the table.*
>
> MAUREEN: Sure, that sounds exactly the type of fella I would *like* to meet, and then bring him home to meet you, if he likes murdering oul women.
>
> MAG: That's not a nice thing to say, Maureen.
>
> MAUREEN: Is it not, now?
>
> MAG: Sure why would he be coming all this way out from Dublin? He'd just be going out of his way.
>
> MAUREEN: For the pleasure of me company he'd come. Killing you, it'd just be a bonus for him.
>
> MAG: Killing *you* I bet he first would be.
>
> MAUREEN: I could live with that so long as I was sure he'd be clobbering you soon after. If he clobbered you with a big axe or something and took your oul head off and spat in your neck, I wouldn't mind at all, going first. Oh no, I'd enjoy it, I would. No more oul Complan to get, and no more oul porridge to get, and no more...

Escalating from seemingly benign verbal insults to abruptly ended conversations to a violent fantasy that may serve as a viable means of escape from her domestic prison, Maureen's dream of a man rescuing her from Leenane through murdering her mother is only the more chilling in her decision to share the vision with Mag. Seeing Mag's death as her only escape from "oul Complan to get, and no more oul porridge to get," McDonagh's depiction indicates Maureen's desperation to assert some level of autonomy from her imposition in the domestic sphere. Unlike the Shan Van Vocht or Cathleen ni Houlihan of early twentieth-century Irish iconography, neither Mag nor Maureen will be freed from their imprisonment through the spilling of Irish male blood. Instead, Maureen's fantasy suggests their only escape from the purgatory of Ireland's societal expectations for the region's women is compliance and imposition in domestic roles or death. Although Maureen's suggestion that she "could live with that so long as I was sure he'd be clobbering you [Mag] soon after" bears some of the humor and resistance reminiscent of Dolly Horner's reference to Jack's face as a "Lurgan spade," Mag's eventual murder at Maureen's hand undermines the integrity of the joke.

McDonagh's suggestion that Maureen and Mag will not escape their dysfunctional relationship without the release valve of impending violence and death is much in keeping with the pessimism Elliot offers in his depiction of Ruth in "A Mother's Heart." In the final scene where Ray angrily shouts, "I was going to pull the fecking door after me!" McDonagh all but slams Maureen's jailer's gate to close the play. As Maureen "gently rocks" in her mother's chair "until about the middle of the fourth verse, when she quietly gets up, picks up the dusty suitcase, caresses it slightly, moves slowly to the hall door and looks back at the empty rocking-chair awhile," we learn even her mother's death cannot free Maureen from a purgatorial existence (McDonagh 1998, 84). Rendered obsolete in public and private spheres, single, childless and without parents like Elliot's Ruth, Maureen haunts her Leenane homestead. Although she attempts to trade one domestic situation for another in the prospects offered by a marriage to Pato, McDonagh suggests that even immigration could not have erased the ills of Ireland's cultural and social influence on contemporary Irish femininity. Unable to escape her sentence even after her violent fantasy becomes a reality, McDonagh's Maureen suggests that Irish women are imprisoned not by the individuals who seem to limit their expression of autonomy and individuality, as is evident in the eradication of Mag, but the region's cultural and societal expectations that will continue to hamper the development and sophistication of Ireland's contemporary politic.

It remains to be seen if the work of contemporary Irish playwrights like Reid, Elliot and McDonagh will "merely... express Irish life" or if their work will come "to establish a new school of writing" as Ireland moves into the twenty-first century (Mikhail 1977, 58). While recent years have certainly demonstrated a virtual flood in Irish letters, only the remove of time can enable critics to determine the value and influence of this work in coming decades. It is clear, however, that Lady Gregory's assessment of an Irish compulsion towards drama due to the region's predisposition towards conversation has certainly yielded a considerable opus of exploratory theater throughout the twentieth century. While visions of femininity in Irish letters have certainly challenged the precedents offered in the early twentieth-century fledgling national theater movement in recent decades, Reid's, Elliot's and McDonagh's work suggest that aesthetic representation will only do so much to contribute to cultural and societal change in the region. As contemporary writers continue to offer Irish and international audiences "a public realm where a people perform themselves to themselves, a part of the region's cultural and national self-presentation," one can only hope that its delivery in language systems that should *sound* familiar to an indigenous ear will ensure that the messages are clearly received. As Ireland continues to teeter on the brink of ever-sophisticating democratic processes, what role will the region's historical and contemporary literary figures continue to play in such development?

Notes

1 A "Habitable Grief"?: The Legacy of Cultural and Political Strife in Ireland's Contentious Language Systems

1. "In Belfast, a set of social procedures based on the concept of the individual's social network was applied in order to gain access to as wide a range as possible of everyday speech styles of nonstandard speakers. Note that the term social network refers quite simply to the informal social relationships contracted by an individual. Since all speakers everywhere contract informal social relationships, the network concept is in principle capable of universal application and so is less ethnocentric than, for example, notions of class or caste... since the network concept, unlike that of socio-economic class, is not limited by intercultural differences in economic or status systems, it is a valuable tool of sociolinguistic analysis also." Lesley Milroy, *Language and Social Networks*. Baltimore: University Park Press, 1980.
2. W.B. Yeats, *"Easter, 1916,"*
3. Edward Said, *Orientalism*.
4. Gayatri Chakravorty Spivak, "Can the Subaltern Speak?"
5. John Millington Synge, "The Playboy of the Western World" and "Riders to the Sea."
6. Loreto Todd, *The Language of Irish Literature*.

2 A Republic of One: Individuality, Autonomy and the Question of Irish Collectivity in Seamus Deane's *Reading in the Dark* and Dermot Healy's *A Goat's Song*

1. Walter Benjamin, *Illuminations*.
2. See Chapter 1 reference to Lesley Milroy, *Language and Social Networks*.
3. "It's a frequently used phrase, certainly in the Derry region. If someone has a great trouble in their life, it was standard to say they had a sore heart. I don't know any specific Gaelic origin," email from Seamus Deane in response to inquiry on the use of "a sore heart" on page 41 of *Reading in the Dark*.
4. Markku Filppula: "The difference between the rural and urban varieties could be explained in terms of the recentness of direct contact with Irish. That would imply, though, that Wicklow dialect has preserved contact features remarkably well, given that Irish ceased to be spoken in that area a couple of hundred years ago and that most of the informants from there had had the minimum or no exposure to Irish at school or elsewhere. In fact, the discussion below will show that the same trend emerges with respect to a few other features, some of which derive indisputably from the Irish substratum" (69).

3 Writing Republicanism: A Betrayal of Entrenched Tribalism in Belfast's Own Vernacular

1. "Between 1970 and August 1989, according to data collected by the Campaign for Free Speech in Ireland and the London-based research group, the Irish Information Partnership, a total of 76 TV programmes on NI – documentaries, plays and even church services – were either banned, refashioned, cut or postponed because of either internal or external pressure. That was an average of one every three months" (4). For details see Ed Maloney's "Closing Down the Airwaves: The Story of the Broadcasting Ban" collected in *The Media and Northern Ireland*. Basingstoke: Macmillan – now Palgrave Macmillan, 1991.
2. Danny Morrison, *Preface* to Patrick Magee's *Gangsters or Guerillas? Representations of Irish Republicans in 'Troubles Fiction'* (v).
3. *Guardian* (London), 2 April 1988.
4. Catholic West Belfast was dubbed a "terrorist neighborhood" by figures like the former Secretary of State Peter Brooke in the late 1980s (*Féile an Phobail: A Sunburst of Celebration:* Féile an Phobail Public Relations).
5. "Apart from my own sense of achievement, where I got the sense of satisfaction from is that people who have read the book and who come from here and who are often used to being put down or misrepresented or maligned, tell me 'that was a good story' or 'I remember something like that happening to me,' so it was very modest in terms of who it was aimed at" (Jackson 2).
6. Bill Rolston's "Dealing With the Past: Pro-State Paramilitaries, Truth and Transition in Northern Ireland" collected in *Human Rights Quarterly* 28, 2006, attends to the complicated nature of such trajectories in post-conflict Northern Ireland. The subject becomes particularly contested in regard to Loyalist communities who see such calls for truth as serving "republican insurgent agendas."

4 The Misfit Chorus Line: Ireland from the Margins in Patrick McCabe's *Call Me the Breeze*

1. "On the Borderline" *New York Times*, 18 January 2004.
2. "A Refusal to Join the Ghosts," *Spectator*, 27 September 2003.
3. McCabe's work is Vician not simply in its cyclical structure, emulated in his repeated references to Eliot. It reflects such a trajectory more so in the simultaneous forms of poetic expression to which McCabe continually refers throughout the work: Canonical literature as exemplified in Joyce and Eliot references, radio, film, theater and music also serve as venues simultaneously available for Tallon's use or somehow influencing the character's forms of expression throughout the text.
4. The success of the new is by no means guaranteed, however; it, too, is prone to contamination by the traces of the past, so that in whatever way we choose to read these texts – as heralding the birth of a New Ireland, as mourning or celebrating the loss of the old, as testament to the difficulties of cultural transition – the interface between modernity and tradition is imagined by both writers as seriously pathological. This interface is a zone in which past and present contaminate each other; neither is settle or secure. Tom

Herron, "ContamiNation: Patrick McCabe and Colm Tóibin's Pathographies of the Republic" in *Contemporary Irish Fiction: Themes, Tropes, Theories*, ed. Liam Harte, Michael Parker (London: Macmillan – now Palgrave Macmillan, 2000), p. 168.

5 Casting Cathleen: Femininity and Motherhood on the Contemporary Irish Stage

1. This is demonstrated in pieces like "What is 'Popular Poetry'" (1902), "The Symbolism of Poetry" (1900), "Ireland and the Arts" (1901) and "The Reform of the Theatre" (1903) amongst others. Ed. Richard J. Finneran. *The Yeats Reader*. New York: Scribner Poetry, 2002.
2. Carla J. McDonagh. "'I've Never Been Just Me': Rethinking Women's Positions in the Plays of Christina Reid." Collected in *A Century of Irish Drama: Widening the Stage*. Ed. Stephen Watt, Eileen Morgan and Shakir Mustafa. Bloomington: Indiana University Press, 2000.
3. *Christina Reid Plays: 1*. Introduction by Maria M. Delgado. London: Methuen Drama, 1997.
4. Mária Kurdi. "Interview With Christina Reid" *Abei Journal*. Volume 6, June 2004.

Works Cited

Adams, Gerry. *The Street and Other Stories*. Dingle: Brandon, 1992.
Anderson, Benedict. *Imagined Communities*. New York: Verso, 2003.
Austin, James. "Patrick McCabe." *British Writers: Supplement IX*. New York: Scribners, 2004.
Bakhtin, Mikhail. *The Dialogic Imagination*. Austin: University of Texas Press, 1981.
Benjamin, Walter. *Illuminations*. New York: Harcourt, Brace & World, Inc., 1968.
Boland, Eavan. *Object Lessons*. New York: Norton, 1995.
Boland, Eavan. *The Lost Land*. New York: Norton, 1998.
Bourke, Richard. "'Imperialism' and 'Democracy' in Modern Ireland, 1898–2002." *Boundary 2*, Spring 2004, 94–118.
Cale, J.J. "Call Me the Breeze." Mercury / Universal, 1971.
Conroy, John. *Belfast Diary: War as a Way of Life*. Boston: Beacon Press, 1987.
Crane, David. "A Refusal to Join the Ghosts". *The Spectator*, 27 September 2003.
Crowley, Tony. *The Politics of Language in Ireland: 1366–1922*. New York: Routledge, 2000.
Curtis Jr., L. Perry. *Apes and Angels: The Irishman in Victorian Caricature*. Washington DC: Smithsonian Books, 1996.
Deane, Seamus. *Celtic Revivals*. London: Faber and Faber, 1985.
Deane, Seamus. *Reading in the Dark*. New York: Knopf, 1997.
Deane, Seamus. *Strange Country*. New York: Oxford, 1997.
Diehl, Heath A. "Classic Realism, Irish Nationalism and a Breed of Angry Young Man in Martin McDonagh's 'The Beauty Queen of Leenane'." *Journal of the Midwest Modern Language Association*, Vol. 34, No. 2, Spring 2001.
Eliot, T.S. *Four Quartets*. New York: Harcourt, 1943.
Elliott, Pearse. "A Mother's Heart." Unpublished. Produced by Dubbeljoint Theatre Co., Belfast, Northern Ireland, 1998.
Fanon, Frantz. *The Wretched of the Earth*. New York: Grove Press, 1963.
Filppula, Markku. *The Grammar of Irish English: Language in the Hibernian Style*. New York: Routledge, 1999.
FitzSimon, Christopher. "St. Macartan, Minnie the Minx and Mondo Movies: Elliptical Peregrinations Through the Subconscious of a Monaghan Writer Trauma." *Irish University Review*, Volume 28, Issue 1, 1998.
Gutman, Les. "Binlids": A Curtain Up Review. 12 October 1998, http://www.curtainup.com/binlids.html
Hamilton, Hugo. *The Speckled Children*. New York: HarperCollins, 2003.
Healy, Dermot. *A Goat's Song*. Toronto: Little, Brown, 1994.
Hearst, David. "Jobs Boost for Belfast." *Guardian* (London) 2 April 1988.
Henry, Alison. *Belfast English and Standard English*. New York: Oxford, 1995.
Herr, Cheryl. "The Erotics of Irishness." *Critical Inquiry*, Vol. 17, No. 1 (Autumn, 1990), 1–34.
Herron, Tom. "ContamiNation: Patrick McCabe and Colm Tóibín's Pathographies of the Republic." Collected in *Contemporary Irish Fiction: Tropes, Theories*. Edited

by Liam Harte and Michael Parker. New York: MacMillan – now Palgrave Macmillan, 2000.

Jackson, Andra. "Street Credibility". *Sunday Age* (Melbourne, Australia), 27 June 1993.

Joyce, James. *A Portrait of the Artist as a Young Man*. New York: Penguin, 1977.

Joyce, James. *Ulysses*. New York: Vintage, 1990.

Kiberd, Declan. *Inventing Ireland*. New York: Vintage, 1996.

Knapp, James F. "History Against Myth: Lady Gregory and Cultural Discourse" *Eire-Ireland*, Fall 1987.

Kurdi, Mária. "Interview With Christina Reid". *Abei Journal*. Volume 6, June 2004.

MacCabe, Colin. *T.S. Eliot*. Devon: Northcote House Publishers Ltd., 2004

MacCabe, Colin. *Ireland Into Film: The Butcher Boy*. Cork: Cork University Press, 2007.

MacSiacáis, Jake, Danny Morrisson, Brenda Murphy and Christina Poland. "Binlids." Unpublished. Produced by Dubbeljoint Theatre Co., Belfast.

Magee, Patrick. *Gangsters or Guerillas?* Belfast: Beyond the Pale, 2002.

Maloney, Ed. "Closing Down the Airwaves: The Story of the Broadcasting Ban." Collected in *The Media and Northern Ireland*. Edited by Bill Rolston. Basingstoke: Macmillan – now Palgrave Macmillan, 1991.

McCabe, Patrick. *The Butcher Boy*. New York: Delta, 1992.

McCabe, Patrick. *Call Me the Breeze*. New York: HarperCollins, 2003.

McCabe, Patrick. *Winterwood*. New York: Bloomsbury, 2006.

McCarthy, Conor. "Seamus Deane: Between Burke and Adorno." *Yearbook of English Studies*, (35) 2005, 232–48.

McCarthy, Dermot. "Recovering Dionysus: Dermot Healy's A Goat's Song." *New Hibernia Review*, Volume 4, Issue 4, Winter 2000, 134–49.

McDonagh, Martin. *The Beauty Queen of Leenane and Other Plays*. New York: Vintage, 1998.

Mikhail, E.H. *Lady Gregory: Interviews and Recollections*. New York: Macmillan – now Palgrave Macmillan, 1977.

Milroy, Lesley. *Language and Social Networks*. Baltimore: University Park Press, 1980.

Morrison, Danny. *West Belfast*. Boulder: Rinehart, 1989.

Morrison, Danny. *The Wrong Man*. Niwot, CO: Rinehart, 1997.

Murphy, Brenda. "A Curse." Collected in *Territories of the Voice*. Edited by Louise De Salvo, Kathleen Walsh D'Arcy and Katherine Hogan. Boston: Beacon Press, 1989.

Plato. *Republic*. New York: Barnes and Noble Classics, 2004.

Reid, Christina. *Christina Reid Plays: 1*. Introduction by Maria M. Delgado. London: Methuen Drama, 1997.

Rolston, Bill. "Dealing With the Past: Pro-State Paramilitaries, Truth and Transition in Northern Ireland." *Human Rights Quarterly* 28, 2006.

Said, Edward. *Orientalism*. New York: Vintage Books, 1979.

Said, Edward. *Culture and Imperialism*. New York: Vintage Books, 1994.

Said, Edward. *The World, The Text and The Critic*. Cambridge, MA: Harvard University Press, 1999.

Schrank, Bernice and William W. Demastes (eds.). *Irish Playwrights 1880–1995*. Westport, CT: Greenwood, 1997.

Skurnick, Lizzy. "On the Borderline." *New York Times*. 18 January 2004.

Spivak, Gayatri Chakravorty. "Can the Subaltern Speak?" *Marxism and Interpretation of Culture*. Illinois: University of Illinois Press, 1988.

Synge, John Millington. "The Playboy of the Western World" and "Riders to the Sea" collected in *The Complete Plays: J.M. Synge*. New York: Vintage, 1960.

Todd, Loreto. *The Language of Irish Literature*. New York: St. Martin's Press – now Palgrave Macmillan, 1989.

Vico, Giambattista. *The New Science*. Ithaca: Cornell University Press, 1984.

Watt, Stephen, Eileen Morgan and Shakir Msutafa (eds.). *A Century of Irish Drama: Widening the Stage*. Bloomington: Indiana University Press, 2000.

Wordsworth, William and Samuel Taylor Coleridge. *Lyrical Ballads*. New York: Routledge, 2002.

Yeats, W.B. *The Yeats Reader*. Edited by Richard J. Finneran. New York: Scribner Poetry, 2002.

Bibliography

Adams, Gerry. *Falls Memories*. Niwot, CO: Rinehart, 1982.
Adams, Gerry. *The Street and Other Stories*. Dingle: Brandon, 1992.
Adams, Gerry. *Cage Eleven*. Niwot, CO: Rinehart, 1997.
Ahlqvist, Anders. *Paper From the Fifth International Conference on Historical Linguistics*. Amsterdam: John Benjamins, 1982.
Anderson, Benedict. *Imagined Communities*. New York: Verso, 2003.
Anderson, Linda. *To Stay Alive*. London: Futura, 1984.
Aretxaga, Begona. "Dirty Protest: Symbolic Overdetermination and Gender in Northern Ireland Ethnic Violence." *Ethos*, Vol. 23, No. 2, 1995.
Austin, James. "Patrick McCabe." *British Writers: Supplement IX*. New York: Scribners, 2004.
Bakhtin, Mikhail. *The Dialogic Imagination*. Austin: University of Texas Press, 1981.
Benjamin, Walter. *Illuminations*. New York: Harcourt, Brace & World, Inc., 1968.
Beresford, David. *Ten Men Dead*. New York: Atlantic Monthly Press, 1997.
Bild, Àída Díaz. "*Reading in the Dark:* The Transcendence of Political Reality Through Art." *International Journal of English Studies*, Volume 2, 2002.
Boland, Eavan. *Object Lessons*. New York: Norton, 1995.
Boland, Eavan. *The Lost Land*. New York: Norton, 1998.
Boles, William C. "Violence at the Royal Court: McDonagh's *The Beauty Queen of Leenane* and Mark Ravenhill's *Shopping and Fucking.*" *Theatre and Violence*, Vol. 7, 1999.
Bolland, O. Nigel. "Creolisation and Creole Societies: A Cultural Nationalist View of Caribbean Social History." *Intellectuals in the Twentieth-Century Caribbean*, Vol. 4, 1992.
Bourke, Richard. "'Imperialism' and 'Democracy' in Modern Ireland, 1898–2002." *Boundary 2*, Spring 2004, 94–118.
Boyle, Patricia. *My Self, My Muse: Irish Women Poets Reflect on Life and Art*. Syracuse: Syracuse University Press, 2001.
Bray, Alison. "Radio Adverts For Adams Book Pulled." *Irish Independent*, 1 December 2003.
Brown, James. "Things Not Meant to Heal: Irish 'National Allegory' in Doyle, McCabe and McCann." *Nua: Studies in Contemporary Irish Writing*, Autumn 1997.
Brown, Malcolm. *The Politics of Irish Literature*. Seattle: University of Washington Press, 1972.
Cale, J.J. "Call Me the Breeze." Mercury / Universal, 1971.
Cairns, David and Shaun Richards. *Writing Ireland: Colonialism, Nationalism and Culture*. Manchester: Manchester University Press, 1988.
Castle, Gregory (ed.). *Postcolonial Discourses: An Anthology*. Malden, MA: Blackwell, 2001.
Chafe, Wallace. *Discourse, Consciousness and Time*. Chicago: University of Chicago Press, 1994.

Colleran, Jeane and Jenny S. Specer (eds). *Staging Resistance: Essays on Political Theatre*. Ann Arbor: University of Michigan Press, 2001.
Conroy, John. *Belfast Diary: War as a Way of Life*. Boston: Beacon Press, 1987.
Crane, David. "A Refusal to Join the Ghosts" *Spectator*, 27, September 2003.
Crowley, Tony. *The Politics of Discourse*. London: Macmillan – now Palgrave Macmillan, 1989.
Crowley, Tony. *The Politics of Language in Ireland: 1366–1922*. New York: Routledge, 2000.
Cullingford, Elizabeth Butler. *Ireland's Others: Gender and Ethnicity in Irish Literature and Popular Culture*. Indiana: University of Notre Dame Press, 2001.
Curtis Jr., L. Perry. *Apes and Angels: The Irishman in Victorian Caricature*. Washington DC: Smithsonian Books, 1996.
D'Arcy, Margaretta. *Tell Them Everything: A Sojourn in the Prison of Her Majesty Queen Elizabeth II at Ard Marcha*. London: Pluto Press, 1982.
D'Arcy, Margaretta and Arden/ *D'Arcy and Arden Plays: 1*. London: Methuen, 1991.
Deane, Seamus. "Why Bogside?" *The Honest Ulsterman*, Vol. 27, 1971.
Deane, Seamus. *Celtic Revivals*. London: Faber and Faber, 1985.
Deane, Seamus. *Reading in the Dark*. New York: Knopf, 1997.
Deane, Seamus. *Strange Country*. New York: Oxford, 1997.
Deane, Seamus. "Derry: City Besieged Within the Siege." *Fortnight*, 1983.
Devlin, Anne. *Plays*. London: Faber, 1986.
Devlin, Polly. *All of Us There*. London: Weidenfield and Nicolson, 1983.
Diehl, Heath A. "Classic Realism, Irish Nationalism and a Breed of Angry Young Man in Martin McDonagh's 'The Beauty Queen of Leenane'." *Journal of the Midwest Modern Language Association*, Vol. 34, No. 2, Spring 2001.
Eagleton, Terry. *Heathcliff and the Great Hunger*. New York: Verso, 1995.
Eliot, T.S. *Four Quartets*. New York: Harcourt, 1943.
Elliott, Pearse. "A Mother's Heart." Unpublished. Produced by Dubbeljoint Theatre Co., Belfast, Northern Ireland, 1998.
Fallon, Brian. *An Age of Innocence: Irish Culture 1930–1960*. New York: St. Martin's Press – now Palgrave Macmillan, 1998.
Fanon, Frantz. *The Wretched of the Earth*. New York: Grove Press, 1963.
Fennell, Desmond. *State of the Nation: Ireland Since the Sixties*. Dublin: Ward River Press, 1984.
Filppula, Markku. *The Grammar of Irish English: Language in the Hibernian Style*. New York: Routledge, 1999.
Fitzpatrick, Lisa. "Disrupting Metanarratives: Anne Devlin, Christina Reid, Marina Carr, and the Irish Dramatic Repertory." *Irish University Press*, Vol. 35, Issue 2, 2005.
FitzSimon, Christopher. "St. Macartan, Minnie the Minx and Mondo Movies: Elliptical Peregrinations Through the Subconscious of a Monaghan Writer Trauma." *Irish University Review*, Volume 28, Issue 1, 1998.
Friel, Brian. *Translations*. London: Faber, 1981.
Gauthier, Tim. "Identity, Self-Loathing and the Neocolonial Condition in Patrick McCabe's *The Butcher Boy*." *Critique*, Vol. 44, Issue 2, Winter 2003.
Gellner, Ernest. *Nations and Nationalism*. Ithaca, NY: Cornell University Press, 1983.

Gibbons, Luke. *Transformations in Irish Culture*. Indiana: University of Notre Dame Press, 1996.
Glissant, Edouard. *Caribbean Discourse: Selected Essays*. Charlottesville, VA: University Press of Virginia, 1989.
Gonzalez, Alexander. *Contemporary Irish Women Poets: Some Male Perspectives*. Westport, CT: Greenwood Press, 1992.
Graham, Brian. *In Search of Ireland: A Cultural Geography*. New York: Routledge, 1997.
Graham, Colin and Glen Hopper. *Irish and Postcolonial Writing*. New York: Palgrave Macmillan, 2002.
Gutman, Les. "Binlids": A Curtain Up Review. 12 October 1998, http://www.curtainup.com/binlids.html
Hamilton, Hugo. *The Speckled Children*. New York: HarperCollins, 2003.
Harrington, John P. and Elizabeth J. Mitchell. *Politics and Performance in Northern Ireland*. Amherst: University of Massachusetts Press, 1999.
Harris, John. *Phonological Variation and Change: Studies in Hiberno English*. New York: Cambridge University Press, 1985.
Harris, Peter James. "Sex and Violence: The Shift from Synge to McDonagh." *Hungarian Journal of English and American Studies*, Vol. 10, Issue 1–2, 2004.
Harte, Liam. "History Lessons: Postcolonialism and Seamus Deane's *Reading in the Dark*." *Irish University Review*, Vol. 30, Spring /Summer 2000.
Harte, Liam and Michael Parker. *Contemporary Irish Fiction: Themes, Tropes, Theories*. New York: St. Martin's Press – now Palgrave Macmillan, 2000.
Heaney, Seamus. *Opened Ground: Poems 1966–1996*. London: Faber, 1998.
Healy, Dermot. *A Goat's Song*. Toronto: Little, Brown, 1994.
Hearst, David. "Jobs Boost for Belfast." *Guardian* (London) 2 April 1988.
Henry, Alison. *Belfast English and Standard English*. New York: Oxford, 1995.
Herr, Cheryl. "The Erotics of Irishness." *Critical Inquiry*, Vol. 17, No. 1 (Autumn, 1990), 1–34.
Herron, Tom. "ContamiNation: Patrick McCabe and Colm Tóibín's Pathographies of the Republic." Collected in *Contemporary Irish Fiction: Tropes, Theories*. Edited by Liam Harte and Michael Parker. New York: Macmillan – now Palgrave Macmillan, 2000.
Herron, Tom. "Derry is Donegal: Thresholds, Vectors, Limits in Seamus Deane's *Reading in the Dark*." *Etudes Irlandaises*, Vol. 29, Issue 2, Fall 2004.
Holland, Jack. *Hope Against History: The Course of Conflict in Northern Ireland*. New York: Holt, 1999.
Hooley, Ruth. *The Female Line*. Belfast: Northern Ireland Women's Rights Movement, 1985.
Innes, Catherine Lynette. *Woman and Nation in Irish Literature and Society, 1880–1935*. Athens: University of Georgia Press, 1993.
International Phonetic Association. *The International Phonetic Alphabet*. http://www.arts.gla.ac.uk/ipa/ipa.html, 2005.
Jackson, Andra. "Street Credibility." *Sunday Age* (Melbourne, Australia), 27 June 1993.
Johnson, Daniel. "Adams Brought to Book." *The Times*, 16 September 1994.
Johnston, Jennifer. *Shadows On Our Skin*. London: Hamilton, 1977.
Jones, Marie. *The Crack in the Emerald: New Irish Plays*. London: Nick Hern Books, 1994.

Jones, Marie. *Stones in His Pockets and A Night in November*. London: Nick Hern Books, 2000.
Joyce, James. *A Portrait of the Artist as a Young Man*. New York: Penguin, 1977.
Joyce, James. *Ulysses*. New York: Vintage, 1990.
Kearney, Richard. *Postnationalist Ireland: Politics, Culture, Philosophy*. New York: Routledge, 1997.
Kiberd, Declan. *Inventing Ireland*. New York: Vintage, 1996.
Knapp, James F. "History Against Myth: Lady Gregory and Cultural Discourse" *Eire-Ireland*, Fall 1987.
Krystek, Izabela. "Looking for the Self: Dermot Healy's *A Goat's Song* as an Irish Tragedy of Indecision." *Ironies of Art / Tragedies of Life: Essays on Irish Literature*. Frankfurt: Peter Lang, 2005, 177–94.
Kryzaniak, Dagmara. "A Disrupted Family in a Troubled Country. A Sociolinguistic Insight into the Domestic / National Crises in the Works of Two Irish Playwrights: Sean O'Casey and Martin McDonagh." *Ironies of Art / Tragedies of Life: Essays on Irish Literature*. Frankfurt: Peter Long, 2005, 195–212.
Kurdi, Mária. "Interview With Christina Reid." *Abei Journal*, Volume 6, June 2004.
Lacey, Colin. "Patrick McCabe: A Comedy of Horrors." *Publishers Weekly*, 16, November 1998.
Lee, Joe J. *Ireland 1912–1985: Politics and Society*. New York: Cambridge University Press, 1990.
Lentin, Ronit. *Gender and Catastrophe*. London: Zed Books, 1997.
Lloyd, David. *Anomalous States: Irish Writing and the Post-Colonial Movement*. Durham, NC: Duke University Press, 1993.
Lojek, Helen Heusner. *Contexts for Frank McGuinness's Drama*. Washington, DC: The Catholic University of America Press, 2004.
Longley, Edna. *The Living Stream*. Newcastle: Bloodaxe Books, 1994.
Loughran, Christina. "Armagh and Feminist Strategy: Campaigns Around Republican Women Prisoners in Armagh Jail." *Feminist Review*, No. 23, Summer 1986.
Luft, Joanna. "Brechtian Gestus and the Politics of Tea in Christina Reid's 'Tea in a China Cup'." *Modern Drama*, Vol. 42, Issue 2, Summer 1999.
Luftig, Victor. "Review of *Stories by Contemporary Irish Women* by Daniel J. Casey; Linda M. Casey and *Territories of Voice: Contemporary Stories by Irish Women Writers* by Louise DeSalvo; Kathleen Walsh D'Arcy; Katherine Hogan." *Tulsa Studies in Women's Literature*, Vol. 10, No. 1, Spring 1991.
Lundy, Patricia and Mark McGovern. "The Ethics of Silence: Action Research, Community 'Truth-Telling' and Post-Conflict Transition in the North of Ireland." *Action Research*, Vol. 4, No. 1, 2006, 49–64.
MacCabe, Colin. *Revolution of the Word*. New York: Palgrave Macmillan, 2003.
MacCabe, Colin. *T.S. Eliot*. Devon: Northcote House Publishers Ltd., 2004.
MacCabe, Colin. *Ireland Into Film: The Butcher Boy*. Cork: Cork University Press, 2007.
MacSiacáis, Jake, Danny Morrisson, Brenda Murphy and Christina Poland. "Binlids." Unpublished. Produced by Dubbeljoint Theatre Co., Belfast.
Magee, Patrick. *Gangsters or Guerillas?* Belfast: Beyond the Pale, 2002.
Maloney, Ed. "Closing Down the Airwaves: The Story of the Broadcasting Ban." Collected in *The Media and Northern Ireland*. Edited by Bill Rolston. Basingstoke: Macmillan – now Palgrave Macmillan, 1991.

Bibliography

Mastors, Elena. "Gerry Adams and the Northern Ireland Peace Process: A Research Note." *Political Psychology*, Vol. 21, No. 4, 2000.
Maynes, Mary Jo. *Gender, Kinship, Power: An Interdisciplinary and Comparative History*. New York: Routledge, 1996.
McCabe, Patrick. *The Butcher Boy*. New York: Delta, 1992.
McCabe, Patrick. *Call Me the Breeze*. New York: HarperCollins, 2003.
McCabe, Patrick. *Winterwood*. New York: Bloomsbury, 2006.
McCarthy, Conor. "Seamus Deane: Between Burke and Adorno." *Yearbook of English Studies*, (35) 2005, 232–48.
McCarthy, Dermot. "Recovering Dionysus: Dermot Healy's A Goat's Song." *New Hibernia Review*, Volume 4, Issue 4, Winter 2000, 134–49.
McCready, Sam. "Coole Lady: The Extraordinary Story of Lady Gregory." Belfast: Lagan Press, 2005.
McDonagh, Martin. *The Beauty Queen of Leenane and Other Plays*. New York: Vintage, 1998.
McGuinness, Frank. *Someone Who'll Watch Over Me*. Boston: Faber, 1992.
McGuinness, Frank. *Frank McGuinness: Plays*. Boston: Faber, 1996.
McGuinness, Frank. *The Stone Jug*. Oldcastle: Gallery, 2003.
Mikhail, E.H. *Lady Gregory: Interviews and Recollections*. New York: Macmillan – now Palgrave Macmillan, 1977.
Milroy, James. *Linguistic Variation and Change*. Cambridge, MA: Blackwell, 1992.
Milroy, James and Lesley Milroy. *Authority in Language* (third edn). New York: Routledge, 1999.
Milroy, Lesley. *Language and Social Networks*. Baltimore: University Park Press, 1980.
Morrison, Danny. *West Belfast*. Boulder: Rinehart, 1989.
Morrison, Danny. *The Wrong Man*. Niwot, CO: Rinehart, 1997.
Murphy, Brenda. "A Curse." Collected in *Territories of the Voice*. Edited by Louise De Salvo, Kathleen Walsh D'Arcy and Katherine Hogan. Boston: Beacon Press, 1989.
Murphy, Brenda. "Forced Upon Us." Unpublished. Produced by Dubbeljoint Theatre Co., 1997.
Nolan, Emer. *James Joyce and Nationalism*. New York: Routledge, 1995.
Ochshorn, Kathleen. "Shaky Peace Offers Reason for Optimism in Ireland." *Tampa Tribune*, 23 November 2003.
O'Dwyer, Ella. *The Rising of the Moon*. Sterling, Virginia: Pluto Press, 2003.
Paisley, Rhonda. "Feminism, Unionism and 'the Brotherhood.'" *Irish Reporter*, Vol. 8, No. 4, 1992.
Pelan, Rebecca. *Two Irelands: Literary Feminisms North and South*. Syracuse: Syracuse University Press, 2005.
Plato. *Republic*. New York: Barnes and Noble Classics, 2004.
Potts, Donna. "From Tír na nÓg to Tír na Muck: Patrick McCabe's *The Butcher Boy*." *New Hibernia Review*, Vol. 3, Issue 3, 1999.
Reid, Christina. *Christina Reid Plays: 1*. Introduction by Maria M. Delgado. London: Methuen Drama, 1997.
Robinson, Lennox (ed.). *Lady Gregory's Journals 1918–1930*. New York: Macmillan, 1947.
Rolston, Bill. "Dealing With the Past: Pro-State Paramilitaries, Truth and Transition in Northern Ireland." *Human Rights Quarterly* (28), 2006.

Rose, Gillian and Alison Blunt. *Writing Women and Space: Colonial and Postcolonial Geographies*. New York: Guilford Press, 1994.
Ross, Andrew. "Irish Lies: Interview with Seamus Deane." www.salon.com, 11 April 1997.
Said, Edward. *Orientalism*. New York: Vintage Books, 1979.
Said, Edward. *Culture and Imperialism*. New York: Vintage Books, 1994.
Said, Edward. *The World, The Text and The Critic*. Cambridge, MA: Harvard University Press, 1999.
San Diego Bakhtin Circle. *Bakhtin and the Nation*. Toronto: Bucknell University Press, 2000.
Sands, Bobby. *Writings From Prison*. Cork: Mercier Press, 2001.
Scaggs, John. "Who is Francie Pig? Self-Identity and Narrative Reliability in *The Butcher Boy*." *Irish University Review*, Vol. 30, Issue 1, 2000.
Schrank, Bernice and William W. Demastes (eds). *Irish Playwrights 1880–1995*. Westport, CT: Greenwood Press, 1997.
Schwall, Hedwig. "Ruse, Rite and Riot: A Psychoanalytic Approach to Seamus Deane's *Reading in the Dark*." In *Interpreting Minority: A Comparative Approach*. Edited by Geert Lernout and Marc Maufort. Antwerp: Vlaamse Vereniging voor Algemegne en Vergelijkende Literatuurwetenschap, 1995.
Skurnick, Lizzy. "On the Borderline." *New York Times*, 18 January 2004.
Sloan, Barry. *Writers and Protestantism in Northern Ireland: Heirs to Damnation?* Ballsbridge: Irish Academic Press, 2000.
Smith, James M. "Remembering Ireland's Architecture of Containment: 'Telling' Stories in *The Butcher Boy* and *States of Fear*." *Eire-Ireland*, Vol. 36, No. 3/4, Fall/Winter 2001.
Spivak, Gayatri Chakravorty. "Can the Subaltern Speak?" *Marxism and Interpretation of Culture*. Illinois: University of Illinois Press, 1988.
Stevenson, Jonathan. "Northern Ireland: Treating Terrorists as Statesmen." *Foreign Policy*, No. 105, Winter 1996–1997.
Synge, John Millington. "The Playboy of the Western World" and "Riders to the Sea" collected in *The Complete Plays: J.M. Synge*. New York: Vintage, 1960.
Synge, J.M. *The Aran Islands*. New York: Penguin, 1992.
Taylor, Peter. *Behind the Mask: The IRA and Sinn Fein*. New York: TV Books, 1999.
Todd, Loreto. *The Language of Irish Literature*. New York: St. Martin's Press – now Palgrave Macmillan, 1989.
Tylee, Clare. " 'Name Upon Name': Myth, Ritual and the Past in Recent Irish Plays Referring to the Great War." *Dressing Up For War: Transformations of Gender and Genre in the Discourse and Literature of War*. Edited by Aránzazu Usandizaga and Andrew Monnickendam. Amsterdam: Rodopi, 2001.
Vico, Giambattista. *The New Science*. Ithaca: Cornell University Press, 1984.
Watt, Stephen, Eileen Morgan and Shakir Mustafa (eds.). *A Century of Irish Drama: Widening the Stage*. Bloomington: Indiana University Press, 2000.
Weekes, Ann Owens. *Irish Women Writers: An Uncharted Tradition*. Lexington, KY: Kentucky University Press, 1990.
Welch, Robert. *Changing States: Transformations in Modern Irish Writing*. New York: Routledge, 1993.
Whalen, Lachlan. " 'Our Barbed Wire Ivory Tower' The Prison Writings of Gerry Adams." *New Hibernia Review*, Summer 2006.

Wills, Clair. *Improprieties: Politics and Sexuality in Northern Irish Poetry.* Newcastle: Bloodaxe Books, 1998.
Wilson, Robert MacLiam. *Eureka Street.* New York: Arcade, 1997.
Wilson, Robert MacLiam. *Ripley Boogle.* New York: Arcade, 1998.
Wordsworth, William and Samuel Taylor Coleridge. *Lyrical Ballads.* New York: Routledge, 2002.
Yeats, W.B. *The Yeats Reader.* Edited by Richard J. Finneran. New York: Scribner Poetry, 2002.

Index

Abbey Theater Co. 137, 141, 158
Act of Union, 1, 2
Adams, Gerry, 59–68, 70, 71–88, 89, 151
AE (George William Russell), 142
Anderson, Benedict, 42
Anglicization, 18, 21
Anglo-Irish Treaty, 25, 87
Anglo Saxon, 2, 5
Anti-Colonialism, 7, 9, 10, 11, 14, 17, 22, 25, 27, 137, 141
Arnold, Matthew, 12

Bakhtin, Mikhail, 13, 14, 15, 16, 96–7, 102, 106
BBC, 69
Belfast, 18, 24, 45, 51, 54, 59, 60, 63, 64, 65, 71, 72, 142, 144, 145, 148, 150, 151, 153, 155, 157, 158, 162, 167
Belfast English, 64, 71, 73, 74, 78, 79, 81, 82, 86, 87, 91, 96, 98, 149
Benjamin, Walter, 26
Boland, Eavan, 3–5, 8–9
Bourke, Richard, 58
Brighton, Pam, 88, 90
British Imperialism, 9, 11, 12, 13, 17, 19, 21, 25, 28, 39, 42

Capitalism, 9
Catholic, 7, 13, 28, 30, 31, 33, 41, 45, 47–50, 56, 60, 62, 64, 66, 67, 71, 72, 80–4, 86, 87, 90, 92, 94, 96, 98, 113, 119, 123, 125, 126, 143, 145, 151, 154, 161, 162, 163, 165, 167, 168, 172
Celtic, 2, 3, 5
Celtic Literary Revival, 22
Celtic Twilight, 11, 130, 140, 141, 169
Censorship, 68, 69, 70, 71, 90, 113
Crowley, Tony, 2

Deane, Seamus, 7, 24, 25–43, 50, 51, 55, 57, 63
Democracy (Democratization), 11, 42, 58, 66, 67, 81, 87, 89, 99, 106
Derry, 24, 25, 26, 28, 31, 33, 37, 38, 41, 42, 44, 70

Donegal, 33
Dublin, 16–22, 24

Edgeworth, Maria, 27
Eliot, T.S., 101, 106, 109, 110–12, 120, 134
Elliott, Pearse, 141, 160–9, 174, 175
Enlightenment English, 1, 2, 3, 9, 13, 14, 15, 18, 22, 26, 27, 34, 42, 43, 106

Fanon, Franz, 8
Fermanagh, 49, 56
Filppula, Markku, 1, 13, 14, 27, 30–1, 32

Gaelic, 19, 25, 26, 27, 35, 38, 39, 40, 42, 43, 74, 87, 101, 106, 107, 125, 139, 151, 168, 169
Gaelic League, 15, 19, 138, 139
Gaeltacht, 13, 14, 19, 33, 55, 56, 74, 172
Galway, 170
Good Friday Peace Agreement, 6, 58, 162
Gregory, Lady Augusta, 2, 3, 7, 27, 63, 137–42, 144, 158, 160, 168, 169, 175
Griffin, Arthur, 7

Healy, Dermot, 24, 25, 44–57, 63, 151
Heaney, Seamus, 25
Henry, Allison, 64, 65, 71–4, 83, 92, 96, 151
Herr, Cheryl, 121, 122, 126
Heteroglossia, 13, 15, 16, 18, 21, 64, 106
Hiberno English, 27, 29, 32, 73, 74, 86, 151, 161
Hume, John, 67
Hyde, Douglas, 137, 138, 142, 172

Industrialization, 11, 15
Irish (Language), 6, 9, 13, 14, 15, 18, 21, 32, 49, 50, 51, 52, 54, 55, 56, 64, 65, 74, 79, 86, 87, 103, 132, 137, 151, 153, 168, 170–2
Irish Constitution, 5–6, 39
Irish-English, 2, 3, 5, 9, 10, 13–16, 18–23, 25–8, 30–1, 32, 34, 35, 37, 38, 42, 43, 65, 103, 117, 119, 125, 132, 135, 141, 153, 171, 172
Irish Literary Renaissance, 7, 9, 15, 18, 20

190 *Index*

Irish Nationalism, 8, 9, 12, 14, 16, 19, 20, 23–8, 31, 36, 37, 38, 43, 46, 47, 56, 57, 59, 62, 86, 87, 95, 111, 113, 120, 121, 122, 126, 129, 169, 172
Irish Question, 6
Irish Republican Army (IRA), 24, 25, 41, 49, 58, 60, 63, 80, 81, 92, 98, 117

John Bull, 11
Joyce, James, 2, 3, 7, 16–22, 25, 27, 35, 63, 101, 105, 134, 136

Kiberd, Declan, 12–13, 16
Knapp, James F., 9, 14, 28

MacSiacais, Jake, 88
Magee, Patrick, 61, 72, 81, 84, 87, 91
Martin, Edward, 140, 142
McCabe, Patrick, 7, 101–35
McCarthy, Conor, 25, 37
McCarthy, Dermot, 46, 51
McDonagh, Martin, 141, 160–2, 168–75
McGuinness, 99
Milroy, Lesley, 5, 18
Milroys, 74
Moore, George, 140, 142
Morrison, Danny, 61, 63, 88
Mother Ireland, 61, 120, 121, 124, 126, 127, 128, 130, 131, 142, 143, 144, 161
Mullet, 44, 47, 49, 50, 51, 55, 56
Murphy, Brenda, 7, 63, 88

Nation, 2, 7, 10, 27

O'Connell, Daniel ("The Emancipator"), 10
Oral Tradition, 9, 10, 27, 78, 115, 150
Orange Order, 65

Paisley, Ian, 45, 99
Parnell, Charles Stewart, 137–41
Partition (Ireland's), 22, 27, 37, 66, 103
Peace Process, 6, 25
Peacelines, 64, 68
Pearse, Padraic, 2, 7, 21
Plantation, 65
Poland, Christine, 88
Power Sharing, 58
Presbyterianism, 152, 162, 163, 165, 166, 167

Protestant, 7, 25, 41, 45, 47–50, 58, 60, 64, 66, 67, 68, 71, 80–4, 86, 87, 90, 97, 98, 142–58, 159–60, 161, 162, 165, 167, 169, 172, 174

Reid, Christina, 7, 142–58, 159–60, 161, 162, 165, 167, 169, 172, 174
Renan, Ernest, 12
Republican, 16, 20, 22, 38, 45, 59–64, 65, 67, 71, 81, 87, 88, 91, 95, 96, 97, 117
RTE, 68, 71
Rural Ireland, 9, 23

Said, Edward, 7, 112
Shan Van Vocht, 35, 36, 37, 121, 172, 175
Social Networks, 5, 17, 18, 19, 20, 29, 34, 35, 150
Standard English (Standardized), 26, 27, 30–1, 34, 35, 41, 53, 64, 66, 71, 73, 74, 78, 79, 83, 87, 95, 96, 98, 103, 116, 119, 122, 125, 143, 148, 149, 151, 153, 164, 165, 166, 170, 172
Statutes of Kilkenny, 1
Synge, John Millington, 2, 3, 7, 9–16, 18, 19, 20, 21, 27, 59, 136, 137–42, 144, 145, 160, 161, 168, 169, 170

Thackeray, William Makepeace, 11
The Troubles, 6, 24, 28, 48, 59, 60, 66, 79, 81, 89, 90, 91, 95, 108, 109, 111, 115, 131, 144, 162, 168
Todd, Loreto, 74, 103, 104, 151, 153, 172

Ulster English, 54
Ulster Scots, 54, 64, 74
Unionism or Unionist (British), 26, 27, 43, 45–9, 56, 57, 61, 68, 84, 86, 87, 94, 142, 145, 148, 151, 153, 155, 156, 162
Urban, 18, 23, 145

Victorian Era, 12, 61, 126

Wilde, Oscar, 136
Wordsworth, William, 11–12, 16, 20

Yeats, William Butler, 2, 3, 7, 21, 27, 120, 136–41, 160